To Show Heart

George Pierre Castile

To Show *H*eart

Native American Self-Determination and

Federal Indian Policy, 1960–1975

The University of Arizona Press   Tucson

The University of Arizona Press
© 1998 The Arizona Board of Regents
First printing
03 02 01 00 99 98   6 5 4 3 2 1

Library of Congress Cataloging-in-Publication Data
Castile, George Pierre
To show heart : Native American self-determination and federal Indian
policy, 1960–1975 / George Pierre Castile.
p. cm.
Includes bibliographical references and index.
ISBN 0-8165-1837-8 (cloth : alk. paper). — ISBN 0-8165-1838-6 (pbk. : alk.
paper)
1. Indians of North America—Government policy. 2. Indians of North
America—Government relations. 3. Indians of North America—Politics
and government. 4. Self-determination, National—United States. I.
Title.
E93.C37 1998
323.1'197073'09046—dc21   97-33775

British Library Cataloguing-in-Publication Data
A catalogue record for this book is available from the British Library.

Publication of this book is made possible in part by the proceeds of a
permanent endowment created with the assistance of a Challenge Grant
from the National Endowment for the Humanities, a federal agency.

To **James Officer** and **Philleo Nash**,

anthropologists "in the arena"

Contents

Preface

*T*his book began back in 1965, though I did not know it at the time. In 1965 the Office of Economic Opportunity, flagship agency of Lyndon Baines Johnson's War on Poverty, was newly created and hastily enlisting troops for its first battle, Project Head Start. In need of a job, I signed on as a foot soldier in "grant review" to approve the applications of local groups to run their own versions of that program. The agency was making itself up as it went along, and in that freewheeling atmosphere I came to be something of an impromptu "expert" in the programs being started in various Native American reservation communities, as I had an undergraduate major in anthropology.

It was a remarkable experience, not at all like the phrase "working for the government" might conjure up. Operating in ever-shifting working groups and housed in a condemned hotel, it was not an exercise in normal bureaucracy. More than anything, the job of the grant reviewers seemed to be to help the applicants tell us the right things in the right way so that we could approve their requests. The very process of granting funds directly to local community groups (Community Action agencies) to run their own programs—bypassing the usual chain of welfare distributors—was something of a revolution in federal and local government relations. Being new to government, I didn't realize at the time how much of a change it was.

The OEO Community Action Program's battle cry was "maximum feasible participation of the poor," which ended up meaning a lot of things to a lot of people, but to most of us it implied some variant of empowering the powerless. To some it sounded dangerously similar to a radical slogan of the time—"power to the people." In many ways, the CAP was indeed a federally sponsored "poor people's" movement, often acting as an incitement to rebellion against the established charity—welfare bureaucracy—and, as such, politically doomed. It doesn't take a Marxist dialectician to see the contradictions here, and the politicians saw them soon enough.

While we often weren't sure what we were doing, we were quite sure that whatever the welfare establishment was doing had to be wrong. In the Native American case, the Bureau of Indian Affairs, BIA, was obviously the established wrong-doer and we brashly dismissed its many years of effort. I hope, now, that the many dedicated BIA people whose corns we crunched will have forgiven our youthful arrogance. The OEO's saving grace was that we really did have a better idea, and it was one that the Bureau itself came to embrace. That's what this book is about.

After my Head Start baptism in the new art of community grantsmanship, I moved over to the Program Development and Evaluation office of the Community Action Program, an even more freewheeling lot. The OEO set out to aid the "poorest of the poor," but my own work was often with the programmatic oddest of the odd. The research and demonstration offices set out to deliberately fund the new and innovative, a sort of weapons development facility for the War on Poverty. These necessarily covered a lot of unconventional ground, in token of which one of the people I worked for bore the nickname of Dr. Strangegrant (the film *Dr. Strangelove* was popular at the time).

Indian "expert" that I was, I found myself willy nilly involved in "demonstrations" in Sioux housing, Navajo education, and what seemed at the time to be a simple self-help housing project for a Tucson Mexican barrio, but which turned out to be the beginning of the creation of the Yaqui "tribe." Many of these projects had unforeseen long-range impact. Collectively these demonstrations and the mainstream Community Action programs ended up changing the direction of the relationship between the federal government and the Indians.

I learned a great deal from this experience, but most of all I came to understand that I did not know much. I met some remarkable people, like Sandy Kravitz and Vine Deloria. Working with the Yaqui, I met the anthropologist Edward H. Spicer, who seemed to understand more than most the nature of "peoples." I resolved to go back to school, so as to return to the poverty wars better armed. While I was retooling, President Nixon declared a victory in that war (as in the other) and largely withdrew federal forces from the field, leaving me on the beach, in academia.

Since my introduction in 1965, federal Indian policy has changed a great deal, and that change is my focus in this book—not a personal recherché, which I will confine to this preface. I bring up my intellectually barefoot boyhood with a cheeky agency only because it set me on a path that thirty years later has led to this attempt to sort out what we did in the War on Poverty in relation to Indian affairs. Our ideas about empowerment mostly failed, but the Indian people themselves fastened on the new opportunities that the OEO grant process represented, and the result was a new federal Indian policy.

Acknowledgments

*T*he shifts in Indian policy during the era in question are largely reflected in changes in presidential policy, and much of my work has involved examining the Indian-related White House papers administered by the National Archives in the presidential libraries of John Fitzgerald Kennedy, Lyndon Baines Johnson, and Gerald R. Ford. The papers of Richard M. Nixon's administration were examined in the Nixon Project of the National Archives, where they still largely reside, rather than in the Richard Nixon Library and Birthplace, the only private presidential library. The Stewart Udall papers at the University of Arizona, the Henry Jackson papers at the University of Washington, and the papers of Philleo Nash at the Harry S. Truman Library were also very useful. My thanks go to the staff of all of these libraries.

Thanks also to the Gerald R. Ford and Lyndon Baines Johnson foundations, which provided grants for research travel, as did the Whitman College Aid to Faculty Scholarship fund. Some of the work in the Udall papers was done while attending an NEH-sponsored seminar in Indian history offered by Roger Nichols of the University of Arizona. I am most of all indebted to James Officer for access to his personal papers, and for generous amounts of his time and advice before his untimely death.

Introduction

[President Nixon] feels very strongly that we need to show more
heart, and that we care about people, and thinks the Indian problem
is a good area for us to work in.
—H. R. Haldeman to James Keogh, January 13, 1969

The two hundred years of federal policy guiding the relationship
between the United States government and the Native Americans is, overall,
remarkably uniform. A former commissioner of Indian affairs observed,
"From the beginning of its history until 1934, the federal government's Indian policy was based on the understanding that sooner or later all Indians
would be assimilated into the American melting pot. . . . The fluctuations of
the Indian policy during the nineteenth and early twentieth centuries were
manifestations of the differing means" (Butler 1978:51). Only twice has federal policy turned from this seamless pattern toward acknowledgment of the
permanency of the Indian communities and encouragement of their self-
governance.

The first federal turning away from the goal of assimilation occurred
between 1934 and 1946 under the Indian "New Deal," expressed in the landmark Indian Reorganization Act of 1934 (Prucha 1990:222). After 1946 this
policy was largely abandoned and assimilationist goals were again put in place,
this time under the label termination, as expressed by Congress in House
Concurrent Resolution 108 in 1953 (233). This book is about the turning away
from that second, relabeled form of assimilation, termination, which took
place from 1960 to 1975 and which led to the Indian Self-Determination Act
of 1975 (274).

This introduction is intended to set the scene for the later chapters—
which discuss the emergence of self-determination—by sketching in the policy
of termination, to which the new policy was a counterpoint. Termination

was itself something of a reaction to the Indian New Deal, and so some short commentary on that policy era is necessary as well (Koppes 1977; Philp 1983). Those well versed in these earlier episodes in the history of Indian affairs might want to pass over this reprise and begin with Chapter 1. For those new to the topic of Indian policy, let me recommend some general surveys as background.

An essential source is S. Lyman Tyler's *History of Indian Policy* (1973). The best overall historical survey is Francis Paul Prucha's *The Great Father: The United States Government and the American Indians* (1984). Prucha has also compiled invaluable bibliographies to the literature of Indian-white relations covering a wide range of topics (1982, 1977), and a history of the treaty-making process, *American Indian Treaties* (1994). For the text of many major documents of Indian policy there is the four-volume collection *The American Indian and the United States: A Documentary History*, by Wilcomb Washburn (1973). Washburn is also editor of a wide-ranging collection of useful essays, *History of Indian-White Relations* (1988). More recent documents are accessible in Prucha's *Documents of United States Indian Policy* (1990).

Much of Indian policy hinges on federal law and its interpretation through the federal courts. Felix Cohen's *Handbook of Federal Indian Law* is a classic (1942, 1982). A modern examination of case law is *Cases and Materials on Federal Indian Law* (Getches et al. 1993). A short, readable treatment is the ACLU handbook *The Rights of Indians and Tribes* (Pevar 1992). Good discussions of the issues, albeit leaning toward advocacy, are in Charles Wilkinson, *American Indians, Time and the Law* (1987) and Vine Deloria and Clifford Lytle, *American Indians, American Justice* (1983).

Indian Deorganization

The primary focus of Indian policy up until the 1870s was not so much on Indians as on their land. Russel Lawrence Barsh observed, "A strong case can be made that Indian policy has been marked by a diversity of forms, but a continuity of effect, at least as far as land and resources are concerned" (1991:1). Having at first freed much of the land of the eastern United States of Indians piecemeal by means of individual treaties, the government later resorted to

wholesale methods in the Indian Removal Act of 1830, sweeping the remnants across the Mississippi (Prucha 1962; Satz 1975).

The lands west of the Mississippi were then similarly freed for settlement by the creation of the "reservations" and the opening up of the non-
reserved lands by the middle of the nineteenth century (Trennert 1975; Utley
1984). While their land was being taken in this process, the Indian peoples
remained largely self-governing up until the 1870s through whatever traditional organization they managed to retain and adapt, but with the reservation system in the late 1800s, the federal government undertook to directly
administer the surviving Indian communities, with "agents" to direct their
affairs and with the planned end of assimilation.

Assimilation entered its most energetic phase in the 1880s with the passage of the Dawes Act, which sought through individual land allotment and
education to cause the complete disappearance of the remaining Indian en-
claves (Hoxie 1989; McDonnell 1991). Called an "Assault on Tribalism" by one
historian, this policy, pursued into the 1920s, set out to deliberately eliminate
all Indian communal land ownership and all distinctive Indian customary
practices—including religion and community organization—in the name
of civilization (Washburn 1975; Prucha 1976).

The Dawes Act was successful in further reducing the Indian land base
and in disrupting Indian traditional organization, reducing most tribes to
economically impoverished communities administered by the Bureau of Indian Affairs through its agents (Castile 1974). Had assimilation been pursued
much longer in this fashion it might well have led to the final dispersal of the
physical communities of the Indian nations, reducing them to landless rural
ethnic groups without any special federal relationship. Many groups did suffer exactly that fate (Porter 1992).

Indian Reorganization

In the 1920s a political reaction began among various "friends of the Indian,"
stirred by the Bursum Bill, a particularly outrageous bit of land legislation
aimed at the Pueblos of the Southwest (Kelly 1983:213). The political lobbying undertaken on behalf of the Pueblos by their friends—organized as the
American Indian Defense Association—was successful in halting the land

grab. Despite this momentum, it is unlikely that the reformers would have had much further success in altering the basic policy of Indian assimilation if larger political events having nothing to do with Indian affairs had not intervened. The Great Depression of 1929 devastated the nation and brought to office in 1932 the New Deal administration of Franklin Delano Roosevelt (FDR) with a mandate for radical domestic social change (Clarke 1996). The New Deal set out to alter many of the relationships between the government and its citizens, and Indian relations were swept along in this larger turn in the tide of change and reform.

FDR brought in a committed social activist as secretary of the interior, Harold Ickes, who had been among those involved in the 1920s Pueblo upheavals, and he in turn brought in one of the leaders of that struggle, John Collier, as commissioner of Indian affairs (Clarke 1996:42). With a Democratic Congress prepared to support much of the New Deal social experimentation, Ickes and Collier were able to push through their own vision of a "new deal" for the Indians amidst the flood of general society legislation, in the form of the Indian Reorganization Act of 1934 (IRA). Their original proposal was much watered down by the objections of those in Congress still wedded to the long-standing assimilationist goals in Indian affairs, but the resulting bill was still a fundamental change in federal policy (Taylor 1980; Philp 1977).

In his attempts to work with a Congress still leaning toward assimilation, one source noted "Collier's position on assimilation was deliberately enigmatic," leading some to conclude that his reorganization effort was just another variant on that theme (Taylor 1980:23; Barsh 1991). Whatever the ambiguity of Collier's public rhetoric, as William Kelly noted, the bill was "in effect, a reversal of the Dawes Act," the centerpiece of assimilation (1954:ii). After half a century of attempting to atomize and disperse the Indians, what Collier and the IRA proposed to do was put them back together again as viable communities. The act stopped further land allotment, thus preserving the Indians' physical communities, and created potential mechanisms for tribal self-government—to build, not to disrupt community, to restore what Collier called "the *grouphood* of Indians" (1954:7).

His approach, as we will see, presaged the self-determination policy. "Collier's ideal was indirect administration: the BIA would outline broad policies, grant power and funds to the local community and then allow each group to devise indigenous means of implementation" (Koppes 1977:553). Critics have pointed out the IRA provided only a potential mechanism for restructuring; the new governments were not a success everywhere. Initially, the model IRA constitutions prepared by Felix Cohen were ill-suited to some of the diverse tribes, some tribes refused to adopt the constitutions at all, and many governments, once created, tended to continue to be simply administrative instruments of the Bureau (Haycox 1994; Kelly 1975). There have been several useful studies examining how the New Deal actually played out on particular reservations, where it often created as much factionalism as community (Biolsi 1992; Hauptman 1981; Parman 1976).

Wilcomb Washburn has reviewed the many critical examinations of the IRA reorganization but nonetheless concluded that in the end "Collier succeeded in preserving Indian identity from complete absorption in the 'melting pot' by creating a system of autonomous tribal entities *within* the political and economic superstructures of American society as a whole" (1984:287). Philp similarly observed, "The Indian Reorganization Act was a flawed product that failed to meet the needs of a diversified population, but it did stop land allotment and set up mechanisms for self government, as well as providing needed credit facilities and allowing the Indians time to define their role in American society" (Philp 1977:244). Time and breathing space for the tribes to pursue their own visions of reorganization were undeniable benefits of the IRA.

Whatever their initial problems, in the long run, as we shall see, the Indian peoples seized upon the proffered political mechanism and put it to their own uses—actual self-government. D'Arcy McNickle commented, "Indians were not held back by Collier's efforts to build upon the tribal past. Instead, they have plunged affirmatively into the twentieth century, asserting their identity, and acquiring the skills that will enable them to survive as Indians and members of an Indian community" (1980:118).

For all its flaws, without the IRA there would have been no federally acknowledged Indian governments in place to resist the resurgence of assimilation that shortly followed. Later, when the War on Poverty came with its new ideas of community action, these governments were available and able to grasp the new opportunities and to inspire new policy by their success in administering OEO programs. Peter Iverson quoted McNickle: "To appreciate Collier," McNickle said, "what one had to do was consider what had happened before him and what happened after him" (Iverson 1994:150).

Indian Voices

Although I intend to argue that the impact of Indian voices in the self-determination era is critical, an argument can be made that all *prior* policies were made with virtually no regard for the opinion of Native Americans. The policies of land confiscation prevailing until the 1920s, whose end result for the Native peoples was economically dependent reservations, were relatively blatant resource grabs only thinly veiled with talk of an exchange for "civilization." If there were Indian voices being heard, they were not persuasive since these outcomes are not credible as "Indians' policy."

Had things changed in 1934? D'Arcy McNickle observed of Collier and the IRA, "It was the first piece of major legislation dealing with Indian affairs ever taken into Indian country and discussed in open meetings" (1980:109). But even Collier did not always listen to the opinions he was the first to bother to solicit, most notably in the case of the Navajo (Parman 1976). There was arguably little or no effective Indian political activism prior to 1960—if one means by that organized national-level attempts directed by Native Americans to influence overall federal Indian policy.

Native Americans were never passive and did, of course, struggle to mold their own destinies. As Hoxie has shown for the Crow or Fowler for the Arapahoe, there was always plenty of active Indian leadership on the *individual* reservations powerfully influencing tribal responses and adaptations to federal policy efforts—but little in the way of pan-Indian policy movements (Fowler 1982; Hoxie 1992, 1995). To the extent that there were any effective national movements for Indian rights they were non-Indian organizations such as the Indian Rights Association and Collier's American Indian Defense Association (Hecht 1991; Hertzberg 1971, 1988; Mardock 1988, 1971).

There were occasionally a few recognized national-level Indian spokespersons such as Carlos Moctezuma or "Bright Eyes" (Susette La Flesche), but they played out their influence in the context of the movements controlled by the non-Indian friends, whose policy themes they echoed rather than created (Iverson 1982; Clark and Webb 1989). Their voices were heard only because they spoke words the friends, who provided the national forum, wanted to hear, and they were little if at all representative of reservation community sentiment.

The first steps toward an effective Indian-dominated national organization emerged during the Collier years when he encouraged BIA employees, led by D'Arcy McNickle, to form what became in 1944 the National Congress of American Indians (Bernstein 1991:112; Johnson 1992:106). The NCAI did not emerge as a pan-tribal voice or truly effective legislative lobby until the '60s, but the '50s saw it start toward Indian political influence (Cowger 1996; Hertzberg 1988:312; Philp 1977). While the newly organizing Indian voices could not prevent the turn to termination in the 1950s, the policy created a crisis of sheer existence for the tribes that was an important background and stimulus for still more activism and organization, leading to what Cornell called "the return of the native" (1988).

After their creation by the IRA, individual Indian governments slowly gained in real power and independence and, through the NCAI, began to wield some collective political influence on federal policy. Yet a permanent barrier to their becoming true sovereign governments remained—economic and political dependency. They had few remaining resources after years of land confiscation and had to rely on federal funding for virtually all civic funding. The federal monies were directly administered by the Bureau on each reservation, and Bureau staff were directed from Washington, not Window Rock or Sells. The tribal "governments" governed very little of the daily life on the individual reservations and had even less control over the overall policy processes that guided those operations.

The Terminators

If the Great Depression had made possible the New Deal and its social reforms, including those in Indian affairs, World War II drew attention away from all such social programs. The BIA budget declined, various relief agencies that had benefited Indians were curtailed and, symbolic of its loss of status, the Bureau itself was exiled to Chicago in 1942 to make room for more important war-related matters (Bernstein 1991:89). The assimilationist voices in Congress resurged and increased their attacks on the IRA in these years, in the name of the war. They cited the contributions of Native Americans to the war effort and the success of their integration into the armed services as proof that the BIA was no longer needed (100). John Collier, increasingly ineffective and frustrated in his relations with an assimilationist-minded Congress, resigned as the war was ending in 1945 (109; Philp 1977:211).

The end of the war and the presidency of Harry S. Truman ushered in yet another sea change in Indian affairs, the move toward "termination." Two trends emerged in the Truman years that were to have an impact on social programs in general and Indian affairs in particular. Truman envisioned continuing some of the social policies of the New Deal in his Fair Deal, but his administration reflected a general post-war trend toward government cost cutting and retrenchment (Ferrell 1994:285). Cost cutting after the war was a bipartisan affair. President Truman created the Hoover Commission, headed by the Republican ex-president, to recommend reorganization of government with an eye to saving money. Among its recommendations was the elimination of the BIA and the incorporation of its functions in a Department of Natural Resources (Ferrell 1994:194; Fixico 1986:49).

In this atmosphere of cutbacks on social programs and federal spending, it was inevitable that those who had long sought to "get out of the Indian business," to terminate the federal special relationship, would gain a fresh audience.

The second trend to emerge and influence Indian policy was the withdrawal of federal sanctioning of formal racial segregation. Of Truman and civil rights one historian observed, "it is possible to say that during his presidency the black revolution, the attainment of rights long denied, really began" (Ferrell 1994:285). Although Congress was not supportive with legislation, Truman was, among other things, to begin to end segregation in the armed forces by executive order (298).

However, some, including Truman, thought the reservations represented segregation as much as did Jim Crow. Unlike the later phases of the civil rights movement, which, as we shall see, strengthened Indian claims to self-determination, here in its initial stage it ironically seems to have weakened them and promoted the turn toward termination. Truman's language in signing the 1946 Indian claims commission legislation strongly suggested his own view that integration—assimilation—was the proper course for Indian affairs.

Truman noted that the bill "removes a lingering discrimination against our first Americans and gives them the same opportunities that our laws extend to all other American citizens. . . . I hope this bill will mark the beginning of a new era for our Indian citizens. . . . With the final settlement of all outstanding claims which this measure ensures, Indians can take their place without special handicap or special advantage in the economic life of our nation and share fully in its progress."[1]

Fixico noted that "Truman's Fair Deal ideals aimed at fitting everyone to a middle-class America, including Indians" (Fixico 1986:184). Philleo Nash, later commissioner of Indian affairs under Presidents Kennedy and Johnson, worked for Truman in the civil rights area (Ferrell 1994:296). He noted of Truman and Indian affairs: "This was a problem that Mr. Truman never cottoned to. I worked with him on every kind of minority problem, but his view of Indian affairs, to the very end of his administration, remained that the problem of the Indians was the Indian Bureau; the quicker we got rid of it the better. I knew this was both untrue and unfair and highly impractical, but I never convinced him of it."[2]

The assimilationist aims of Truman matched those of Congress. Rep. Henry Jackson, head of the House subcommittee on Indian affairs, sponsored the claims legislation Truman signed. In 1946 Jackson wrote to a constituent concerned about adding land to the Colville reservation: "I have always been a strong advocate of the release of Indians from their present wardship status just as fast as it can be carried out by the government."[3] Senator Arthur Watkins noted, "A basic purpose of Congress in setting up the Indians Claims Commission was to clear the way toward complete freedom of the Indians by assuring a final settlement of all obligations—real or purported—of the federal government to the Indian tribes and other groups" (1957:50). The claims act was even supported by the new National Congress of American Indians, since it did at least offer Indians a chance to press their claims to gain compensation for past unjust loss of lands (Bernstein 1994:123).

There was no other significant termination legislation beyond the claims act under Truman, but things were shifting still further in that direction throughout his presidency. After Collier, leadership at the BIA was in some disarray until 1950 when Truman appointed Dillon S. Meyer, the former director of the War Relocation Authority; he had been responsible for the Japanese internment program (Officer 1984:78). Meyer has come to occupy a place as arch villain in many accounts of termination: note, for example, Drinnon's book title, *Keeper of Concentration Camps: Dillon S. Meyer and American Racism* (1987). Philp treated him more evenhandedly and noted, "He was honestly, if perhaps mistakenly, convinced that the time had come when it was in the best interests of Indians to abrogate their treaties and special relationship with the federal government" (1988:59).

No one disagreed that Truman's choice as his Indian commissioner was very much opposed to the IRA policies of Collier and strongly convinced that terminating the special Indian relationship was the preferable path. He was not the first to move in this direction, but he was arguably the most effective in shifting policy. Officer noted, "He was a devout believer in termination and established a program unit within the Bureau to prepare proposals for withdrawal of federal services. Under his stimulus Congress began looking at a variety of termination related bills. . . . Meyer organized a cadre of BIA staff members who shared his views regarding termination, and the administrative machinery for a national withdrawal program was largely in place when Meyer departed early in 1953" (1984:78). It was Meyer who first formalized the program of "relocation" to encourage Indians to move entirely away from their homelands into jobs in the cities. "Relocation took its place beside termination as the second goal of federal policy in the 1950's" (Fixico 1986:135).

Meyer, who facilitated the move toward termination, was also responsible for the rapidity of the Indian reaction against it. Philp pointed out that after their experiences in World War II many young Native Americans were interested in something new in Indian affairs and initially shared some of Meyer's interest in "greater freedom" and "self determination" (1988:45). But as the rhetoric of freedom turned into bureaucratic reality, it was clear to Native American groups such as the NCAI that the freedom being peddled was not the same as the Indians envisioned. Where Meyer's vision sought a complete end to the federal relationship, "The NCAI's did not advocate an end to all federal supervision . . . it emphasized that Federal trusteeship, tax free land, and Indian self government were vested legal rights" (45–46).

Meyer used up his good will with Native Americans through a series of highhanded paternalistic gestures. He denied tribes even simple elements of self-governance, like the right to hire their own attorneys, which had been granted under the IRA. Meyer insisted on Bureau approval of the attorneys and refused it when it seemed "unnecessary." He also resisted tribal councils' use of their own trust funds to finance lobbying visits to Washington (Drinnon 1987:189). The result was "Indians and their defenders raised a chorus of protest against Meyer's policies. Ickes and Collier again assumed the role of anguished critic" (Koppes 1977:563).

Philp has suggested that "in 1944 Collier himself seemed to be edging toward termination." If so, he quickly gained a second wind under the stimulus of Meyer and was prominent among those attacking the termination policies by 1952 (1983:182). In a 1954 retrospective on the IRA, he was unrepentant and declared "the philosophy of the IRA stands un-repudiated, even uncontested, being a philosophy consonant with American realities and American values and ideals" (Collier 1954:2).

The new Republican president, Dwight David Eisenhower, like Truman, "was convinced that Americans did not want another pulse of domestic reform. He therefore sought to reduce the size and intrusive nature of the administrative state" (Galambos 1993:ix). His few statements on things Indian reflected a general agreement with the emerging philosophy of termination. Signing the 1954 bill terminating the Menominee he said: "In a real sense they have opened up a new era in Indian affairs—an era of growing self reliance which is the logical culmination and fulfillment of more than a hundred years activity by the Federal Government among the Indian people."[4] He did express some doubts about PL 280, which would allow states in future to unilaterally impose their jurisdiction on reservations, suggesting it be amended with a "requirement of full consultation," but agreed "its basic purpose represents still another step in granting complete political equality to all Indians in our nation."[5]

In the Eisenhower administration, with its new Republican majority, the policy of termination hit its legislative high point in the 83d Congress. "What really happened in 1953 and 1954 is that an incubation process underway for at least a decade finally hatched some chicks" (Officer 1986:124). When Glen Emmons became the new Republican-appointed commissioner in July 1953, Officer noted, "just four days later Congress approved House Concurrent Resolution 83–108 endorsing termination. . . . Two weeks afterward, Congress enacted Public Law 83–280, directing the transfer of legal jurisdiction over certain Indian reservations to several states and authorizing others to assume such jurisdiction when they chose" (1984:79). The new Republican administration adopted Meyer's termination policy as its own and turned it into legislative reality.

Many of the nineteenth-century proponents of assimilation, like Senator Henry Dawes of Massachusetts, had been Easterners, but the new wave of congressional support for termination was coming from Westerners. Richard White noted a political power shift to the Western states during and after the war in which "New Deal Democrats . . . and conservatives could make common cause in advocating sectional interests" (1991:514). Indian affairs were such a sectional interest. Burt noted "federal expenditures in the West vastly increased during the war and resulted in a tremendous economic boom in the region. . . . This naturally put pressure on the remaining Indian holdings. . . . Out of this situation emerged a bloc of conservative congressmen known as terminationists" (1982:4–5). One of the results of termination, as in the earlier assimilationist era, was of course "freeing" of considerable Indian land in the West (Fixico 1986:185).

Senator Arthur Watkins, prominent among the terminationists, recalled, "I was chairman of the Indian subcommittee of the Interior Committee of the Senate. For a number of years, at least while the Republicans were in power, I put over a lot of projects for the Indians along with my western associates" (in Fixico 1986:193). In 1946 House and Senate committees on Indian affairs had been merged with those on public lands and insular affairs. "These changes made the welfare of Indians an even more remote consideration in the formation of policy affecting them, since committees under the influence of various western economic interests replaced those that had been exclusively concerned with Native Americans" (Burt 1982:5).

Senator Arthur Watkins of Utah and Rep. E. Y. Berry of South Dakota, the Republican heads of the Indian subcommittees, were the principal spokesmen for termination in Congress. Schulte noted, "Western politicians such as Berry and Watkins have usually chosen to satisfy the demands of white constituents in issues involving Indians and non-Indians" (Burt 1984:49). Another Westerner, Wyoming Rep. William Henry Harrison, introduced HCR 108—the termination resolution—which passed both houses unanimously and virtually without discussion (Burt 1982:22).

The resolution listed a number of specific tribes presumed suitable for termination and stated, "it is the policy of Congress, as rapidly as possible, to make the Indians within the territorial limits of the United States subject to the same laws and entitled to the same privileges and responsibilities as are applicable to other citizens of the United States, to end their status as wards of the United States, and to grant them all of the rights and prerogatives pertaining to American Citizenship" (Prucha 1990:233).

With little opposition or interest, Watkins and Berry held joint hearings on the termination of specific tribes in 1954. "By August . . . several dozen tribes . . . had been stripped of federal services and protection. Terminated tribes included the Klamath of Oregon, the Menominees of Wisconsin, the Ottawa, Wyandot and Peoria tribes of Oklahoma, and the Paiute tribe of Utah" (Schulte 1984:57). Efforts were also made to dismantle the Bureau and reduce its service functions for those Indian communities not entirely terminated. For example, in 1954 the Indian Health Service was successfully transferred out of the BIA to the Public Health Service in HEW (Burt 1982:55).

By the end of the '50s there was some softening of this drive toward totally ending the special relationship. There was a slight shift of emphasis toward "voluntary" or consensual termination. Secretary of the Interior Fred Seaton made a speech in 1958 suggesting that no tribe would be terminated without "consultation and consent" (Officer 1984:81). But this was an isolated speech that, absent any policy shift, created as much confusion as clarification for the Bureau (Burt 1982:127). It was also in 1958 that Senator Watkins said, "Following in the footsteps of the Emancipation Proclamation of ninety-four years ago, I see the following words emblazoned in letters of fire above the heads of the Indians—THESE PEOPLE SHALL BE FREE!" (Watkins 1957:55).

This is the scene as our story begins. In 1960 termination was still the avowed policy of the U.S. Congress, and the BIA continued to act under that mandate. No significant political figure had renounced the policy and no laws were being considered to revoke HCR 108 or halt the ongoing termination of several tribes, including the Menominee and Klamath. "In truth from 1946 until enactment of the amendments to Public Law 83–280 in 1968, Congress took no formal action that we can clearly interpret as a retreat from the withdrawal policy articulated in House Concurrent Resolution 108" (Officer 1986:119). Assimilation of the Native Americans was, as it had almost always been, the law of the land.

To Show Heart

The New Frontier and the New Trail

With a good conscience our only sure reward.

—John F. Kennedy, Inaugural Address, January 20, 1961

*P*resident John Fitzgerald Kennedy has been the subject of many biographies and commentaries on his policies, but one searches in vain for discussion of his views on Indian policy in these works (Claflin 1991; Giglio 1991; Goodwin 1988; Salinger 1966; Schlesinger 1965; Sorenson 1965; Wofford 1993).

Prior to becoming president, Kennedy had no apparent contact with Indian affairs except as an eastern Democrat with the Tammany "Indians." However, in the 1960 campaign the presidential candidates promised solutions to the concerns of a wide range of constituencies, including Native Americans. A Kennedy staffer asserted that in the transition after the election they toted up eighty-one such promises made (Goodwin 1988:133).

During the campaign, both the Kennedy staff and the staff of his opponent, Eisenhower's vice president, Richard M. Nixon, were solicited for statements on their positions on Indian affairs by Oliver La Farge of the Association on Indian Affairs (AIA), and by the National Congress of American Indians (NCAI). Both campaigns provided statements, but it would appear that Richard Schifter with the AIA provided the Kennedy staff with a draft of answers to the questionnaire.[1] Even without such help, Nixon's task was the more difficult, since he could not disassociate himself from prior Eisenhower administration policy, a policy—termination—that was already unpopular among Native Americans.

Nixon tried to put a good face on it, and without specifics he declared, "Since 1953 we have had more progress toward a better way of life for the American Indian than in any comparable period in our national history." He did allow that more needed to be done, specifically in education and "consolidating land holdings." He also suggested more would have been done but for the interference of foot dragging by congressional Democrats. Nixon attempted to finesse the delicate topic of termination by shifting from acting as administration spokesman to offering his own opinion: "I personally believe that it would be wholly unwise and unjustifiable for the Federal government to terminate its special relationships with any tribal group unless such a plan is fully understood and accepted by the group that would be affected." But in the end, all he could promise for the future was more of the same: "The constructive Indian programs of the past eight years will be continued, expanded and intensified."[2]

What Nixon defended, Kennedy of course attacked, listing nine areas in which he claimed the Republicans had failed and he would deliver. His proposals were, in general, simply a promise to do "more and better" in health, education, and economic development. He also promised to include the Native Americans in new programs to be proposed by his administration—the Area Redevelopment Program and the Youth Conservation Corps, for example. He was able to denounce the termination policy as a product of a Republican president and Congress, ignoring Truman's role in instigating terminationist policies. Kennedy claimed, inaccurately, that termination "slowed down when the Democratic party regained control of Congress in 1955. Since then, the Congress has been a protective shield against bureaucratic attacks."[3] His only new direction for the future was inclusion. "Indians would benefit not only from our specific programs in the field of Indian affairs, but also from our programs for help to underprivileged groups generally. . . . My administration, as you can see, would make a sharp break with the policies of the Republican party."[4]

There was, in fact, little practical difference in the positions of the two candidates. Both claimed credit for a slowdown and adherence to "consent," but neither specifically renounced termination per se. While acknowledging problems with current policy, neither offered any specific new themes or innovative programs. There was little in this campaign rhetoric from either party to offer hope that any real turn away from termination as a policy was imminent; nor was there any sign of a new direction.

In the end, Kennedy's administration did have some impact by the promised act of "inclusion," as Indians were written into various bills. Nixon's views were not put to the test until 1968, by which time they had become very different than the defensive vagueness of his 1960 campaign message.

Stewart Udall

After winning the election, JFK's most significant act for the future of Indian affairs was his selection of Stewart Udall as secretary of the interior. Kennedy and his White House staff did not subsequently take an active role in the promotion of new Indian policy initiatives, and Congress would continue to lean toward termination, so it was to be up to the secretary of the interior and his staff at the Bureau of Indian Affairs (BIA) to provide new directions if any were to emerge.

Udall was not chosen on the strength of his views on Indians but for his standing as a conservationist and to increase western representation. Udall published a book while in office, *The Quiet Crisis,* which set out his views on the environment. It touched upon Indians in a section entitled "The Land Wisdom of the Indians" but only to use them as a contrast to postcontact times (Udall 1963:3). Increasingly in the 1960s Indian imagery would come to be used in this way by the environmental movement (Castile 1996).

Udall, like all interior secretaries, devoted the bulk of his time to questions of land and resources rather than Native Americans. However, while he spent most of his time on land, dams, and parks, he did spend more than most on Indian matters. Unlike most prior interior secretaries, Udall had a genuine interest in Indian affairs. Udall, while an Arizona congressman, had established familiarity with the many tribes of that state, and had served on the House Interior and Insular Affairs Committee's Subcommittee on Indian Affairs. He jokingly declared, "I might be my own Indian commissioner."[5]

Before the election, Udall sought new ideas about Indian affairs from some of his Arizona friends and advisors. Probably the most influential were William King of the Indian Health Service, who became superintendent of the Salt River Agency under Udall, and University of Arizona anthropologist James Officer, who became associate commissioner of the BIA. Officer was the author of an influential study, *Indians in School* (1956). Politically active as a supporter in Udall's congressional campaigns, he had long acted as an informal advisor to him on Indian matters during Udall's House years. Both

King and Officer continued to be important sounding boards for Udall throughout his administration, and the three of them began the shift to a new policy.[6]

Udall asked King and Officer to write up their ideas for him as to "what a sound Indian policy might be, what changes we thought needed to be made."[7] Their report foreshadowed many of the themes that were to emerge in the Udall administration, but Officer himself later characterized the report as "naive in a lot of respects."[8] They began: "Indians must take their place along-side other Americans, must accept the same responsibilities, must have the same (but no more) privileges. . . . To achieve it as quickly as possible with minimum trauma is the goal for which those responsible for policy in Indian administration must strive." This was not very different from existing policy, but King and Officer did not believe that "immediate termination of special federal services for Indians," or the "trustee responsibility" was desirable. They accepted that termination of the federal "subsidy" and administration of Indian communities must eventually occur—but not soon.[9]

They suggested that "administrative responsibilities for Indian special services must be transferred wherever possible to state and local agencies." This devolution of administration from federal to state hands was consistent with prevailing terminationist thinking, as seen, for example, in PL 280. King and Officer, however, stressed not a simple absorption of Indian groups but a turn to Indian self-government and self-reliance. They suggested that "no consistent planning or programming has taken place to implement Indian 'self reliance,'" and, for the future, "preparing Indians to become 'self reliant' is a major task of Indian Administration." This arguably foreshadowed the coming policy of Indian self-administration, to be know as self-determination.[10]

King and Officer stressed the need to restructure and reallocate the federal BIA system in two directions. As noted above, they suggested shifting services to state hands, with some interim federal subsidy. To promote the transfer of Indian administration to the hands of Indians themselves, they suggested that Indian problems were primarily local and recommended "turning over to local superintendents the maximum responsibility for planning and executing programs." In effect, they proposed local self-determination (first placed in the hands of the superintendent, from where it could then be more easily transferred to the tribal governments themselves), and decentralization as a way station to self-administration.[11]

Philleo Nash

Udall thought well enough of these ideas to ask both Officer and King to join his administration. Retaining Deputy Commissioner John O. Crow as acting commissioner, Udall also began a search for a new commissioner of Indian affairs. It was his intention to appoint a Native American, who he knew would be the first Indian to serve as Indian commissioner since Grant's choice of the Seneca Ely Parker. Udall's longtime Arizona Republican colleague Senator Barry Goldwater was writing to JFK to urge the same thing, indicating that as early as 1953 he had urged that a Navajo, Tom Dodge, be made commissioner. "I feel that the interest of the United States and of the Indian people," he said, "would best be served by the appointment of a qualified Indian to this office."[12]

All of the candidates seem to have been of Cherokee ancestry, including John O. Crow. In addition to Crow, Udall also sounded out his friend Will Rogers Jr. and approached William Keeler, who was Cherokee paramount chief as well as an executive of Phillips Petroleum. Both Rogers and Keeler declined, and while Crow wanted the job, he was judged unsuitable by some key staff.[13] Meanwhile, the Kennedy presidential transition staff headhunters, led by Robert Kennedy, were making still other recommendations to Udall, among them the eventual choice, Philleo Nash (Szasz 1979).

Philleo Nash was not a Native American but a fascinating mixture of old-time Wisconsin Democratic Party pol, applied anthropologist, and cranberry farmer. He had served Harry Truman as a special assistant on civil rights and had also served as lieutenant governor of Wisconsin. An early Hubert Humphrey supporter, he had finally supported Kennedy in the race, and came to Washington actively looking for the reward of a job in the administration. When Udall found it hard to locate what he felt was a suitable Native American candidate, Nash eventually became the choice (Nash 1986:196).[14]

Udall temporarily postponed the selection of a commissioner but decided to form a secretarial Task Force on Indian Affairs to consider policy directions. He appointed William Keeler as chairman and William Zimmerman, a former assistant commissioner who had been much involved in the preceding termination policy. William Keeler was already a member of another ongoing but non-governmental investigation of Indian affairs, the Commission on the Rights, Liberties, and Responsibilities of the American Indian, established by the Fund for the Republic in 1957. This group issued a preliminary report in January 1961, but it was not generally available until published in 1966 as *The Indian, America's Unfinished Business* (Brophy and Aberle 1966). This study was not cited by the task force, nor does it seem to have had any other policy impact at the time. When published it became only one more voice in a growing chorus calling for change. Also appointed to the Task Force on Indian Affairs were Philleo Nash and James Officer. John A. Carver, Udall's assistant secretary for public lands, though not a formal member, was very active in the subsequent policy deliberations, as was Crow.

Nash's candidacy as commissioner was put on trial during the task force deliberations. Udall said, "I felt that with Jim Officer, who I was very close to, and with Keeler, that they would test him. . . . Well they felt he came through very well." In the same task force process, Officer concluded that Crow had lost out as a candidate in part by losing the support of Keeler. When finally appointed, Nash immediately made Crow his deputy commissioner and asked Officer to become associate commissioner, a role that turned out to be largely one of troubleshooter.[15]

The Task Force Report

While the task force's deliberations tested and produced a commissioner, its report (delivered to the secretary on July 10, 1961) was not very innovative and still did not point out clear new policies or programs (Keeler et al. 1961). The process was primarily valuable in building a sense of participation and inclusion of Native Americans. During its deliberations, the task force met with a great many tribal representatives and solicited their input. Nash observed, "we traveled and held hearings and invited the elected leaders, of all tribes, 98 percent of the population was represented by the elected leaders that appeared before us and offered programs."[16] He put this consultation first in his list of their overall aims, which were "Indian voice, confidence, workability, and then a general absence of phoniness."[17]

The term "workability" referred to the notion that the policy goals were meant to be modest and attainable within a reasonable amount of time, and the bulk of the seventy-eight-page report was concerned with such straightforward and "workable" themes as economic development and more efficient delivery of services on the reservations. Change in the structure of Indian self-government was limited to a brief section suggesting the need for BIA help in improving day-to-day tribal administrative structures (Keeler et al. 1961:69). It was, overall, simply another modest call for the better carrying out of existing policy through existing BIA structures.

What it most definitely did not do was to renounce termination explicitly. Some historians, including Francis Prucha, have suggested that "The Task Force rejected the current objectives of government Indian policy, which included termination" (Prucha 1984:1090). Anthropologist Fred Eggan similarly observed that Nash "set about implementing the recommendations of the Task Force, including the reversal of termination" (Eggan 1989:9). I suspect they have mistaken Nash's own personal agenda and hopes for actual policy.

Philleo Nash himself was clearly opposed to termination and had been since his service with Harry Truman. Nash had also actively opposed Menominee termination when he was lieutenant governor of Wisconsin.[18] In his retrospective of his term of office as commissioner, he said, "I came up the political ladder fighting Termination and I went out the same way" (Nash 1986:198). Nash fought, yes, but not the task force.

What the report itself did suggest was that *too much* emphasis had been placed on termination: "Placing greater emphasis on termination than on development impairs Indian morale and produces a hostile or apathetic response which limits the effectiveness of the Federal Indian program. The Task Force believes it is wiser to assist the Indians to advance socially, economically and politically to the point where special services to this group of Americans are no longer justified. *Then, termination can be achieved with maximum benefit for all concerned*" (Keeler et al. 1961:6; emphasis mine).

What they were renouncing was not termination but talking about termination or overtly keying programs specifically to its achievement, reminiscent of the recent "don't ask, don't tell" policy of the military. They were suggesting a slowdown, although termination remained the ultimate outcome. It was even at hand, for some "eligibility for special Federal services should be withdrawn from Indians with substantial incomes and superior education experience, who are as competent as most non-Indians to look after their own affairs. Furthermore Indians should not receive federally administered services which duplicate State and local benefits" (Keeler et al. 1961:7).

Nash, in retrospect, suggested that the task force was trying to avoid a confrontation with Congress by not explicitly denouncing termination, while to the Indian country audience it was "trying to get back into communication by not talking about termination" (Nash 1986:196). Udall was not at all sure that they *could* retreat from termination: "One of the questions Carver and I wrestled with at great length was whether the '54 Termination Act [sic] was a permanent set up in law—a permanent policy we had to repeal."[19] But, he said, "the Indians, I think we quieted their fears. I think they recognized that we were going to hold the line against any termination efforts. But we weren't able to do anything very dramatic. We weren't able to get any big new programs going."[20]

Termination Proceeds

In the background during this rethinking process, the Bureau was still following its termination mandate, and was moving too slowly for some. A review of the process by the comptroller general in March 1961, for example, reported to Congress that "We believe that the Department's policies will not result in any significant progress in fulfilling the goal of the Congress of terminating Federal supervision over Indian affairs."[21] However slowly, they were in fact still trying, as witness the case of the Menominee, who had been among the first to be slated for termination in 1954. John O. Crow, as acting commissioner, forwarded to Assistant Secretary Carver (and concurred in) a memo prepared by Martin Magnan, senior program officer: "The Menominee delegation is glooming and dooming about their prospects, and have sponsored the drafting of bills which would provide an eight year extension of the trust termination date." But, he optimistically affirmed, "If Menominee Enterprises, Inc. and Menominee County are launched on May 1, 1961 as now required by law, they will probably be the only such entities of such magnitude in the United States which are unencumbered by any indebtedness." As to termination, "it is doubtful if there will ever be a more propitious time for it. An extension of the trust period for eight more years might well be a great disservice to the Menominee people."[22] The Menominee were terminated by the Kennedy administration.

The Democrat-led Congress was still very much committed to termination despite Kennedy's campaign claims to the contrary. Philleo Nash was only confirmed as commissioner in September 1961 after contentious Senate hearings in which he thought "the members wanted me to feel the weight of their views on Termination, individualization of tribal property, and cultural assimilation" (Nash 1986:197).[23] His relationship with the Indian Affairs committees was initially rocky and stayed that way until "five years later it was the Chairmen of these two Committees who successfully demanded my resignation" (Nash 1986:197). Nash began as commissioner with a very modest mandate for change, the need to tread very delicately with Congress, and a Native American population fearful of the termination that Congress still demanded.

Termination proceeded, though at as reduced a pace as Nash could manage. The administration did not extend the deadlines in 1961 of the final phases of the termination already in motion of both the Klamath and Menominee tribes, or the Catawba in 1962. Pressure remained strong to terminate some others, notably the Colville, and Nash found himself in hot water with Senator Henry Jackson of Washington for airing contrary views on Colville termination (Officer 1989:15). Jackson wrote to Assistant Secretary Carver complaining that Nash had said, "termination of the Colville confederation would be highly undesirable and would create a 'pocket of poverty.' I have told several inquirers about this matter that it is hardly credible that the Commissioner of Indian Affairs would make remarks for public notice that attacked the bipartisan policy of his own authorizing committee and its chairman."[24] Jackson was still pushing for Colville termination as late as the 1970s, long after Nash had gone and two presidents had spoken out against the general policy (Dahl 1994).

Congress and the Commissioner

Native American leaders have often justifiably complained of a lack of government consultation, but about Nash that complaint could not be made. He spent a great deal of his time out in Indian country soliciting input and giving talks explaining federal programs. He also held a great many meetings with BIA field staff and created an ongoing operating committee of his top staff to maintain an internal dialogue. Some came to feel that he spent too much time on these efforts at diplomacy and communication. Officer, for example, while approving of most of his efforts to reach the Indian people, said, "I sometimes found the two hour operating committee sessions an annoyance" (1989:12). Udall, especially, came to feel that Nash was spending too much time on the hustings. He observed:

> Nash seemed to want to settle in, and spent a great deal of time the way all the Indian commissioners do, you know traveling around, meeting with the Indians. He'd take his guitar with him and play music. They liked him as a person. He was very popular. This was almost a disease they all fell into. Bennett [Robert L. Bennett] was the same way. As though if the Indian commissioner was popular, this made the Indian program a success. . . . He concentrated on wooing the Indians so much that he neglected to establish very good relations on the hill. . . . To make dramatic or rapid progress with Indian affairs the obstacle has always been the Congress.[25]

There was a good deal of evidence to support Udall's conviction that Congress was the key barrier to any change. A relatively minor piece of legislation designed to address the problem of fractionization of Indian landholdings, so-called "heirship," was a typical case (Officer 1984:82).[26] This had been addressed by the task force and a corrective bill introduced in Congress in 1961, but it never emerged from committee. Udall observed, "Some of them, including some of the Democratic liberals, had surprisingly illiberal ideas on Indian affairs, and some of them were quietly and privately down on Indians in general. . . . So we didn't have the congressional support ever for a new policy because, after all, these were some of the same congressmen that had passed the termination bill."[27]

Udall also felt Nash and John Carver both failed to seek change. "I also think he [Nash] fell into the feeling that all we could hope for was gradualism," Udall said. As a result, "We didn't shake the bureaucracy." As an example, he said of Indian education: "we inherited this nice old lady who'd been teaching in Indian schools and knew all the things. And again, her idea was, well, if you did a little better this year than last year with Indian education, why, that was good enough."[28] This is a rather unkind reference to Hildegard Thompson, who served as director of the Education Branch from 1952 to 1965 (Szasz 1974:123).

The New Trail

The administration flew the battle flag of the New Frontier, but that slogan would obviously not be very appealing to Native Americans, who had bad memories of the old frontier. The phrase "New Trail" appeared in the task force report, and that became the substitute buzzword in Commissioner Nash's public rhetoric (Keeler 1961:77). Although a trained academic (an anthropologist with a strong interest in the applied aspects of that field), Nash actually published very little formal analysis about his years as commissioner either before or after his time in office. What he did do was give speeches about his New Trail.[29]

When not struggling with Congress, what public face did Nash attempt to create in his speeches for the administration? A sampling shows a considerable consistency from 1961 to 1963. Above all, nowhere was heard that discouraging word *termination* despite its status as congressional policy. The word that was most often heard and stressed was *development,* to whatever audience: to the National Congress of American Indians (NCAI), "This is a development report"; to a group of superintendents, "The Task Force report was a developmental report."[30] The next most common theme was inclusion: to the NCAI, "the ideas in this report are yours"; to the superintendents, the report had had "the benefit of comment from all the men and women in this room today."[31]

Nash's pace and aim seemed to have taken clear shape by 1963. "The New Trail along which we are moving with the Indian people is the sound path of economic development. . . . It is not an easy path, nor can we expect progress along it to be rapid. The main thing is that we have made a beginning."[32] There were no suggestions of radical change in the federal relationship itself nor even in the structure of the BIA. Nash's view of the pace of change was reflected in an anecdote he attributed to the president about the urgency of planting a tree that will not bloom for a hundred years: " 'In that case plant it this afternoon.' I think the President's story speaks for itself."[33]

Nash was committed to long-term incremental change, evolutionary development rather than revolution.[34] Perhaps his most radical contribution was his insistence on the inclusion of an Indian voice, always seeking to make the BIA more responsive to the Native American peoples. Officer observed, "Philleo sought to do two things: to capture the support of the Indians for himself personally and the things that he stood for, and at the same time to gain the support of the Indian Bureau personnel." Udall thought he had captured the Indians, and Officer felt he had succeeded with the Bureau: "Philleo gained the support of the BIA people as no other commissioner ever had. More so than John Collier by far."[35]

JFK and the Indians

In his speeches Nash periodically made reference to the president's personal interest in Indian affairs, but he was unable to repeat more than the general promises made in the campaign. The fact is that JFK and his core staff were not very concerned with the Native Americans and said little for Nash to cite. President Kennedy did put his name to an introduction to the *American Heritage Book of Indians* (Kennedy 1961:7). This had been solicited through Pierre Salinger by Alvin Josephy and was drafted by someone on Udall's staff. Salinger wrote Udall, "I would think this should be a mood piece on the role of American Indians in American history and culture. Above all it has to be a high class job."[36] The result was a one-page review of Indian history remarkable only in observing that "the League of the Iroquois, inspired Benjamin Franklin to copy it in planning the federation of states" (Kennedy 1961:7). This is a story, like President Millard Fillmore's installation of the first White House bathtub, that has gained authority by repetition (Johansen 1996; Tooker 1990; Mencken 1991:617).

Barring occasional passing mentions of Indians, there were few presidential statements of substance on Indian affairs. The JFK library reveals no more than the published presidential record, no informal notes or letters by JFK himself or statements by others in his name stating his views or interest in things Native American. The only incident reflecting a decision made by the president himself concerned the Kinzua Dam project, which was not a very proud moment.

In a campaign statement to La Farge, Kennedy had promised that "There would be no change in treaty or contractual relationships without the consent of the tribes. . . . There would be protection of the Indian land base. . . . Indians have heard fine words and promises long enough. They are right in asking for deeds."[37] But when he took office there was a long-standing dispute between the Seneca and the Corps of Engineers over Seneca lands that would be lost to the Kinzua Dam. Kennedy was asked at a news conference, "Have you any inclination at all to halt that project?" He replied, "Well I'm not—I have no plans to interfere with that action."[38] Seneca president Basil Williams personally appealed to Kennedy, who replied, "I have now had an opportunity to review the subject and have concluded that it is not possible to halt construction of Kinzua Dam currently under way."[39]

John Carver indicates there was at least some debate in the White House about this since it was "one case where the President was directly involved . . . because he was embarrassed by the equivocation really involved, in terms of his campaign statement." According to Carver the issue was, "Do the tribes have such a relationship to the Americas as to be immune from the eminent domain power? . . . [W]e resolved that hard question by going for fair compensation, but as a result the Federal government became extraordinarily generous, to the point of having a lot of trouble in the Congress."[40]

Cash compensation, however "generous," did nothing to quell disappointment in Indian country, particularly when compensation was coupled with legislative language requiring Interior to submit a termination plan for the Seneca (Josephy 1984:143). This one and only Kennedy presidential decision on Indian affairs even found itself shortly celebrated in a popular novel in which fictional Indians remarked, "If even a nice fellow like that there Kennedy would screw us—what the hell's the use?" (Huffaker 1967:89).

Only twice did Kennedy address representative Native American groups at the White House. Both turned out to be purely ritual visits, not involving the discussion of issues, the signing of legislation, or the announcement of policy initiatives. In one meeting in 1962, Kennedy received representatives of the American Indian Chicago Conference and suggested the visit was "more than ceremonial . . . a very useful reminder that there is still a good deal of unfinished business."[41] In the other, in 1963, he met briefly with leaders of the National Congress of American Indians and declared that visit, too, "a useful reminder to us all of our responsibilities to some of our most distinguished and in a very real sense first citizens."[42] The meetings did not remind anyone of any clear path of action.

RFK and the Indians

Robert Kennedy, attorney general in his brother's administration, would later—as a senator and presidential candidate—became actively involved in Indian education. But while attorney general he demonstrated a profound lack of knowledge and sensitivity to Indian affairs. *Life* magazine published an article under his byline, "Buying It Back from the Indians," illustrated with cartoons of ludicrous Indian caricatures holding signs inscribed with statements such as, "Pay for Vermont Now, and Get Massachusetts Free." In this article he wrote, "I had thought contentedly, along with most Americans, that at least the real estate within the United States had been bought, conquered or otherwise acquired so long ago by our ancestors, that the matter is beyond dispute" (R. Kennedy 1962:17).

The article was basically a compendium of anecdotes of far-fetched Indian claims being overturned by clever government attorneys. It was disturbingly similar in tone to "Must We Buy America from the Indians All Over Again?" a diatribe by terminationist congressman Blake Clarke, urging the repeal of the Indian claims legislation (Clarke 1958). "Until this is done," he wrote, "the Indians and their lawyers will continue to collect big wampum from the American Taxpayers" (49).

This view of Indian affairs by the attorney general, the man responsible for the claims procedures, complete with cigar store Indian images and a tone of ridicule, touched off a response in Indian country. A memo titled "Uprising: Indians" was sent to him by an aide, arranging a meeting with

Robert Burnette (executive director of the NCAI) to discuss "How you might improve your Indian image, dimmed a bit by the March article, which has been called smug by Cong. Berry and Sen. Bennett."[43] Senator George McGovern wrote to arrange a meeting with Indian leaders, saying, "the Indians feel that the article makes them objects of ridicule."[44] RFK backtracked rapidly in a letter to Walter Wetzel (president of NCAI). He explained, "The purpose of the article was not to minimize or make light of these Indian claims cases. My purpose in writing the article was to acquaint the American public with the existence and complexity of the Indian claims program. . . . With respect to the cartoons, I was not aware of them until I saw them in the magazine."[45] A sympathetic biographer suggests that RFK was, in fact, genuinely concerned with fair settlement of the claims and took considerable interest in them (Schlesinger 1978:408–9). Publicly, however, he had done little more than his brother to build confidence in the good intentions of the administration among Native Americans.

Dangerous Primitives

The White House staff left little trace of time spent on Indian affairs. Lee White, assistant special counsel to the president, said, "Dick Goodwin and myself concerned ourselves with the formulation and implementation of policy and legislative programs as it related to the domestic side of affairs," but the only Native American theme he recalled was the Kinzua Dam crisis.[46] Jim Officer observed, "I can't think of a single person in Kennedy's office who, in my opinion, was very much involved or interested in becoming involved in Indian affairs. . . . Bobby Kennedy couldn't have cared less about Indians."[47]

One White House document seemed to reflect a "let sleeping policy dogs lie" approach to Native American affairs. In an "Inter Cabinet Briefing Book," there was a short statement on things Indian. It is worth quoting at length:

> *Indians*—The greatest emotional impact of any of our programs is in Indian administration. Almost every public official, elective or appointive, who has had any contact with tribal organizations or other Indian groups fancies himself an expert. The implications of a government program devoted to the welfare of Indians are frightening. In no other field

of American law is a Government program seemingly based upon ethnic origin.... If it should ever be conceded that the Federal Government has the responsibility for educating Indians simply because they are Indians, we are in deep trouble. The States will deny Indians admittance to schools just as they deny them admittance to their hospitals.[48]

In a preceding section of this document on the trust territories, the peoples there were declared to be "extremely primitive socially and culturally."[49] With this sort of staff input, it is no wonder that the Kennedy White House was hesitant to venture among the dangerous and the primitive. In an attached compilation of Indian affairs legislation to be proposed to the 88th Congress, there was a section entitled, "President's Program Proposals," which bore the notation "None."[50]

Indian Voices

Native American political activism was not great during the Kennedy years, though there were stirrings. The American Indian Chicago Conference in June 1961 was conceived and orchestrated by anthropologist Sol Tax, and it can be described as at best a stimulus to future Indian activism, not an instance of it. Nash tried and failed to get some presidential participation or recognition of this congress, though he did arrange a presidential reception for some selected delegates and acceptance by the president of a copy of their "Declaration of Indian Purpose."[51]

Remarks by Indian spokesmen Robert Burnette and Dennis Bushyhead on that occasion were decidedly not a foretaste of coming militancy. They declared, "we are steadfast as are all other Americans in our absolute faith in the wisdom and justice of the American form of government." *De rigueur* in the Kennedy Cold War era, they loyally denounced "efforts of the promoters of any alien form of government to plant upon our shores . . . the ideology or way of life which inflicts slavery."[52] Was this an oblique echo of the various accusations of socialism that were leveled against John Collier and the Indian Reorganization Act (IRA)?

The declaration they presented was not a very radical document, though it did call for the renunciation of termination. Recounting the history of Native American subjugation, they forgivingly suggested that "Their life ways survived subject to the will of a dominant sovereign power. This is not said in a spirit of complaint." Their concluding statement was a less than ringing demand: "In short, the Indians ask for assistance, technical and financial, for the time needed, however long that may be" (quoted in Prucha 1990:245–46). The legislative proposals were modest, with an emphasis not on claiming self-determination but on decentralizing BIA authority by shifting it to superintendents, much as suggested in the King-Officer proposals. Nash observed: "with a few exceptions the Declaration of Purpose did not differ from the report of the Task Force on Indian Affairs."[53]

The National Congress of American Indians (mostly Native American) and the Association on Indian Affairs (mostly friends), were still the principal lobbying organizations at the time. Udall observed, "you didn't have a very good Indian lobby, and the Indians themselves went with hat in hand to see these congressmen, senators, you know, and they were always very passive."[54] But he thought they did have a more general sympathy clout. "No. They didn't have a great deal of clout. They had a lot of moral clout as, you know, any friends of the Indian had moral clout—but they weren't influential on the hill."[55] Udall aide Oren Beatty observed, "I think the Indians have a constituency outside their immediate states. They've got more support in New York city [sic] or Chicago than they do in Albuquerque or Phoenix. And so I think there was good political mileage in it as well as just the desire to do something good for them."[56] But he also noted about the lobbies, "Indians were pretty docile."[57]

We Have Moved Quite a Distance?

While the Kennedy White House could and did largely ignore the seemingly (to them) docile Native Americans, there were other constituencies that increasingly demanded more active social reform. By 1961 the civil rights movement was entering its militant phase. Sit-ins, voter registration drives, and marches were publicly testing the limits of segregation and the willingness of the administration to support them. The Kennedy administration slowly, and apparently reluctantly, responded to the pressures. "The new President considered civil rights an admirable goal but one that should not occasion undue passion or Federal provocation" (Weisbrot 1990:54). Toward the end of the Kennedy era, protest hit a symbolic high point with the March on Washington and Martin Luther King's "I have a dream" speech, but this produced no legislative breakthroughs (Weisbrot 1990:82). "At the end of his term the poor were still poor, the voiceless still voiceless, and, if anything the gap between rich and poor had widened" (Cronin 1988:1).

The immediate aims of the civil rights movement—desegregation and voting rights—had little direct relevance for the problems of Native Americans. However, the limited Kennedy administration concern with those disadvantaged by segregation began to join with a concern for the more general problem of poverty. Once the administration began to consider the special needs of the "Other America" and consider programs to alleviate poverty, Indians were affected as they had been under Franklin Delano Roosevelt (Harrington 1964). Anyone concerned with poverty sooner or later had to notice that as a group the Native Americans were as poor as anyone in the United States.

As the Kennedy administration tinkered with policies to help the disadvantaged—none of which were designed with Indians as a focus—Udall and Nash worked to be sure that the Native Americans were included. The Kennedy poverty programs were experimental and relatively small in scale, nothing like Johnson's coordinated War on Poverty. Some glimmerings of what were to become "Community Action" programs focused on "empowering the poor to take over their own neighborhoods" and were embedded in experimental juvenile delinquency programs (Matusow 1984:117). This concept was later to be critical to the emergence of new efforts at self-determination on the reservations, but at this point it was entirely urban in focus, and no one planned to include Indians in such empowerment.

Despite the lack of new programs designed specifically for Indians, a little more money was available on the reservations as a result of the new directions. Kennedy claimed credit for this new social spending in a letter to Oliver La Farge in 1963, recollecting his campaign statements and saying, "We have moved quite a distance on the road we set out to travel."[58] The only programs designed for Indians per se were the construction of some new schools and the Bureau's relocation program. The Manpower Development and Training Act of 1962 provided a few more dollars for vocational training programs but was not applied on the reservations until 1963. The Area Redevelopment Administration provided some funds for feasibility studies to be managed by the BIA's new Division of Economic Development, created in 1962. But studies had been done before, and there was no significant increase in actual development investment. At $12 million, the Accelerated Public Works Program was probably the single largest dollar increase, but that was concentrated in a few locations.[59] The road the Kennedy administration had traveled had not led very far.

In the end, whether because of congressional inertia or the lack of presidential initiatives, not much had changed by the close of the Kennedy years. Alfonso Ortiz observed, "There was no policy as such that can be associated with the Kennedy Presidency" (Ortiz 1986b:16). Calling Kennedy a "Hollow Icon," M. Annette Jaimes came to much the same conclusion (Jaimes 1990). Termination remained official policy, however little talked about or slowly pursued, and Commissioner Nash dared not repudiate it too publicly for fear of congressional wrath.

Without presidential or congressional support, there was little Udall and Nash could do. There was a little more money for housing, education, and job training, but fundamental structures and aims were not altered, and the increased funds were administered, as always, by non-Indians. There was no clear notion as to what direction change might take, and no real alternatives were offered to the status quo. Alvin Josephy wrote unprophetically to Udall in 1964, "The goals and proposals of the Task Force are still valid, though new ideas are needed. What is required is vigorous, determined administration rather than alteration in any policies."[60]

2

The Great Society
Tribes and Warriors

Give *everybody* eat. —Major ___ de Coverley
—Joseph Heller, *Catch 22*

*W*ith JFK's death in office, Vice President Lyndon Baines
Johnson assumed the presidency and the problems of Indian affairs. The literature analyzing Johnson, his rise in politics, and his term as president has
little to say about his Indian policies (Caro 1982; Conkin 1986; Dallek 1991;
Divine 1987; Dugger 1982; Roell 1988). Johnson himself had nothing to say
about Native Americans in his own account of his presidency, *Vantage Point*
(1971). During his long congressional career there were no federally recognized Indian groups in Texas which would have attracted LBJ's wide-ranging
populist political attentions.[1] The "Big Daddy from the Pedernales," as one
writer titled his Johnson biography, would surely have concerned himself
with the welfare of a Native American constituency (Conkin 1986).

There is a considerable argument in the Johnson literature about whether
LBJ simply carried on Kennedy's social policy or pursued his own (Bernstein
1991; Heath 1975; Henggeler 1991; Stern 1992), but a key difference between
Johnson and Kennedy was in legislative results. A dramatic contrast can be
seen in the reluctant, step-by-step approach of Kennedy to civil rights and
the sweeping changes introduced by LBJ almost immediately upon taking
office (Stern 1992:160). Perhaps the liberal words were often the same, but
where Kennedy made rhetorical promises, Johnson delivered with legislation. On the front flyleaf of *The Vantage Point*, Johnson listed 207 "Landmark
Laws" instigated by his administration (1971).

As to whether the social ideas being turned into legislation were Johnson's
own, Joseph Califano, one of his closest advisors on domestic policy, said of

LBJ, "His commitment to racial justice and eliminating poverty was genuine and consuming. It stemmed in part from a Texas youth in which he witnessed the effects of poverty and bigotry and in part from his southern populist's gut" (Califano 1991:11). Johnson's personal model for legislative social activism was not Kennedy but rather his old mentor FDR, whose New Deal programs were Johnson's introduction to public affairs (Heclo 1986:319). Aide James Gaither noted that underlying his social programs was "a very deep conviction that everybody in this country should be given a full and complete chance to make his own way."[2]

Whatever the debates about the source of Johnson's policy initiatives, the innovative Indian policies that soon appeared were clearly not Kennedy legacies. Even JFK's most partisan admirers cannot argue that LBJ adopted the legislative directions of the Kennedy program for Native Americans, since there were no such pre-existing initiatives. Under JFK, Udall and his staff, especially King and Officer, had new ideas which had lain dormant. Under Johnson, new ideas were the order of the day, and when Johnson retained Udall as secretary of the interior the stage was set for the emergence of new thinking in Indian affairs.

Two large-scale domestic policy tides crested during the Johnson years; neither had to do with Indians directly, but both were critical for what was to become of Indian affairs. The first was the general shift in the politics of things ethnic in America. In the civil rights struggle African Americans had created a new political force to which the Johnson administration and Congress responded with major legislation (Stern 1992:171). That favorable political background—in which sensitivity to any ethnic group's situation was the better part of political valor—created an increasingly positive new context for Indian affairs.

Philleo Nash, whom Udall kept on as commissioner, observed of Indian affairs in this era, "It is not the most important practical issue or the most important economic or program issue before the President, but it's one of those ways in which the liberal establishment, those people who are for women's rights, and for peace, and for education, and for welfare and who are largely urban and are very apt to be eastern, this is one of the ways in which they test a president to find out whether he's on the right side of things."[3] Felix Cohen similarly observed, "Like the Miner's canary the Indian marks the shifts from fresh air to poison gas in our political atmosphere; and our treatment of Indians, even more than our treatment of other minorities, reflects the rise and fall of our democratic faith" (Cohen 1953:390). More and more, Native Americans were to serve as a kind of political litmus test in ethnic policy.

The second domestic policy tide rising during the Johnson years was the emergence of Johnson's plan to build the Great Society. "What Lyndon Johnson was about during his presidency was social and economic revolution, nothing less" (Califano 1991:12). Of LBJ's wide-ranging social activism as president one biographer noted, "The breadth of expressed concerns, the sheer number of bills, and new programs made even comprehension let alone evaluation, almost impossible. Johnson talked about a perfect America. He seemed to want to solve all its problems susceptible to political correction and do it all quickly" (Conkin 1986:209). Presidential aide Joseph Califano observed, "As we went over a hundred ideas that afternoon, I kept thinking: There will never be enough for this man; he adopts programs the way a child eats rich chocolate chip cookies" (Califano 1991:180).

Indian affairs were inexorably swept along in the tsunami of legislation that the Johnson presidency unleashed. As in the Kennedy programs, Native Americans were very often an afterthought in the new policies, most of which were directed at the larger ethnic constituencies of Hispanics, blacks, and "the poor" in general. Still, in one area in particular these sweeping Johnson programs designed for others produced fundamental changes in federal Indian administration in ways not planned for or expected by anyone. The Office of Economic Opportunity, central to the War on Poverty, turned out to be the key to the emergence of self-determination as a new direction in Indian affairs.

The Warriors

Many attempts have been made to sort out the political origins of the War on Poverty, the Office of Economic Opportunity—the war's flagship agency—and the Community Action Program—the war's Marines (Heclo 1986; Lemann 1989; Levine 1970; J. Patterson 1994; Matusow 1984; Moynihan 1969; Sundquist 1969). Johnson flatly announced in his State of the Union address on January 8, 1964, that "This administration, here and now, declares unconditional war on poverty in America," but there is a considerable debate about what was the social Pearl Harbor that provoked this declaration of war.[4]

Late in his administration JFK had asked Walter Heller, chair of his Council of Economic Advisors, to look into poverty and to prepare legislative ideas to help solve the problem (Matusow 1984:120). Heller, who had only begun to gather information, came to Johnson on his first full day in office (November 23, 1963). He said, as Johnson recalled, that "Kennedy had approved his going ahead with plans for a program but had given no guidance as to the specific content. . . . Did I want the Council of Economic Advisors to develop a program to attack poverty?" (Johnson 1971:69). Harkening back to his populist past Johnson remembered, "I had first run for public office in 1937 under the slogan 'He gets things done.' . . . The poverty program Heller described was my kind of undertaking." Johnson told Heller, "Go ahead. Give it the highest priority" (Johnson 1971:71).

Some observers have suggested that JFK was bearish on fighting poverty and at best had planned only limited experiments of the sort already being carried out by David Hacket and Richard Boone through the President's Committee on Juvenile Delinquency (Evans and Novack 1966:428; Bauer 1982:113). The Hacket programs, modest in scale, were potentially revolutionary in concept. Based on the work of sociologists Lloyd Ohlin and Richard Cloward, the programs suggested that the cure to social problems was "restoring to slum dwellers a sense of social competence" (Matusow 1984:109). This competence was to be achieved by community restructuring and organization of the poor to actively participate in solving their own problems, not to passively receive largess.

Whatever Kennedy's views, Johnson was definitely bullish on the concept of doing something about poverty. His model was almost certainly the New Deal and its emphasis on job creation, not social experiments like community organization. He said to Heller, "I am a Roosevelt New Dealer. As a matter of fact to tell the truth John F. Kennedy was a little too conservative for my taste" (Bauer 1982:114).

What he meant by "too conservative" was perhaps more a matter of scale than direction. When Heller sold the poverty war concept to him he responded by suggesting the program had to be "big and bold and hit the nation with real impact," proposing to "launch the campaign at the $1 billion dollar level" (74). He enlisted Peace Corps director Sargent Shriver to take charge of the task force planning the legislation and to direct the agency that would administer it. The result was the Economic Opportunity Act, sent to Congress on March 16, 1964, and signed by Johnson on August 20, 1964 (Matusow 1984:125).

The centerpiece of the new Office of Economic Opportunity (oeo), created by the act and headed by Shriver, was the Community Action Program (cap). Native Americans were simply one among the many groups of the poor to be included in its efforts, not a primary focus of the political debate creating the act, but they were on the minds of some of the task force members who created the act. Among those involved in the early Hacket planning efforts was Sanford Kravitz, who became part of the poverty task force and later head of research and demonstration for the oeo. He said of the plans for cap:

> Our model of how the community-action program would work went something like this: A community would study its poverty problem, locate the most severe pockets of need and identify them as target areas slated for intensive effort. It would plan a program for those areas that would effect all relevant institutions, that is, the schools, social services, job opportunities. It would enhance its ability to implement its program objectives by inclusion of political leadership. It would remain "honest" to its purposes by inclusion of voices representing the poor, residents of the target neighborhoods. (Kravitz 1969:60)

Recognizing the "essentially urban" origins of the model, he observed, "The model fitted the Indian situation, since a reservation could be the locus for a program and the Indians themselves would run the program. This was seen as an added plus, since there was a general lack of sympathy among the program planners for the Bureau of Indian Affairs" (62). The Bureau was not alone in this lack of sympathetic consideration. The Community Action Program was the handiwork of a group of relatively radical social activists. "Experience had taught these men to despise local schools, police, welfare departments, and private charity institutions for dispensing demeaning fragmented services to the poor" (Matusow 1984:244). What they proposed instead was "maximum feasible participation" of the poor (a term apparently invented and written into the legislation by task force member Richard Boone), in which "community action would seek to reform institutions by empowering the poor" (Matusow 245).

The program of empowerment writ large was doomed from the beginning. In many ways it amounted to a federally funded and sponsored revolutionary movement against local and state governments. Piven and Cloward noted, "the hallmark of the Great Society programs was the direct relationship between the national government and the ghettos, a relationship in which both state and local governments were undercut" (1971:261). Opposition was soon encountered from those undercut in the cities and states, but on the reservations there already existed a direct federal relationship, and the only government undercut was another federal agency, the BIA.

Many of the trials and tribulations of the Community Action programs were chronicled by Patrick Moynihan in his revealingly titled *Maximum Feasible Misunderstanding* (1969). An early source of political furor was a program in Syracuse, New York, to train community organizers in radical tactics of political confrontation as taught by Saul Alinsky (Alinsky 1971). The result was predictable: "Soon the fledgling organizers were forming tenant unions in public housing projects, spending public money to bail out protesting welfare mothers, and conducting a voter-registration drive whose purpose could only be to defeat Republican Mayor William Walsh" (Matusow 1984:248).

Protests by afflicted mayors and governors all over the country resulted within a year in the soft pedaling of the social radicalism of the CAP, although some local CAPS continued to outrage the establishment. Johnson soothed the offended, but "he was willing to weather the political flak, because he knew the poor had to organize to be heard" (Califano 1991:78). He did, however, come to refer to the CAP warriors as "kooks and sociologists" (Matusow 1984:270).[5]

There were OEO successes praised by all. Project Head Start—providing preschool education—and Legal Services—providing the poor access to legal aid—were two programs that did well by any standard. The more troublesome Community Action programs were largely taken over by local political structures. Rather than having created institutional change through com-

munity mobilization, a Brandeis University study of twenty-two of the programs indicated that most had "employed strategies to co-opt the poor rather
than to empower them" (Matusow 1984:268).

Poverty was not eliminated by the War on Poverty, and indeed some
have argued that the social programs put in place by Johnson aggravated
rather than improved the plight of the poor (Murray 1984). By 1969, with the
coming of the administration of Richard Nixon, the OEO programs were politically reined in at all levels and dispersed to other agencies. The OEO itself
was converted to a truncated Community Services Administration, a return
to service, not action, made clear in the name change (Hoff 1994:60–65;
Matusow 1984:270). Whether or not one agrees with Murray's argument that
the OEO's efforts made things worse for the poor in general, I think there is no
question that by the time of its passing it had made an irrevocably positive
impact on Indian affairs.

The Warriors and the Tribes

The experience of the Native Americans in the lost cause of the War on Poverty was unique. The results of the OEO programs on the reservations were
far closer to what the early guerrilla planners had in mind but were unable to
achieve with the targeted urban constituencies in terms of empowering the
poor.

The special problems of operating in Indian country were recognized at
the OEO from the start, and reservation programs were handled through an
Indian "desk" rather than being processed with general programs which were
eventually funneled through regional area offices. As with any startup federal
agency, there was a lot of raiding of employees from existing programs, and
the Indian desk at first relied on borrowed BIA personnel. These old Indian
hands brought with them their experience from that agency, for good or ill. I
recall one of them invariably chomping on a cigar butt and just as invariably
pronouncing a "It's been tried, it can't be done" judgment on the admittedly
often naive plans of the OEO.

Dr. James J. Wilson, a more optimistic Sioux educator and once a BIA
teacher who had worked in the Indian education program at Arizona State
University, manned the desk in its heyday.[6] Sandy Kravitz, heading up the

research office, was responsible for and receptive to proposals for innovative experimental programs to be tried on the reservations.

As it had in other new federal offerings, the Bureau worked from the beginning to include Native Americans in these programs. At the American Indian Capitol Conference on Poverty, on May 12, 1964, Commissioner Philleo Nash (after plugging what the Bureau was already doing in "programs of tested effectiveness") declared that, "President Johnson's declaration of unconditional war on poverty was welcomed as enthusiastically by the Bureau of Indian affairs as it was by the Indian people . . . we will fight this war side by side."[7] In June, Secretary Udall said at a superintendents' conference, "we are here to plan how to integrate our Indian programs and Indian problems and Indian opportunities into the war on poverty." Udall was also keeping LBJ informed of the effort through weekly memos.[8] All this happened before the Community Action programs had hit the ground.

There might have been considerably more tension between the OEO and the BIA were it not for the efforts of Commissioner Philleo Nash. Recognizing the intention of the OEO to work directly with the tribes and not through the Bureau, he nonetheless early on indicated a willingness to cooperate. A report of a meeting with top staff in November 1964 indicated that "he intends the entire Bureau to take full advantage of the community action concept in developing Bureau programs and to support the OEO fully. He stated that our relationship with the OEO should be one of cooperative support, that it is a resource to be drawn upon and that we should not be too concerned at this time whether our views prevail. . . . he did not want the Indian Bureau to have full approval or disapproval power with respect to programs originated by Indian tribes in the form of proposals to the OEO."[9] More publicly, in a speech titled "The American Indian and the Great Society," given at the National Conference on Poverty in the Southwest, he struck a strong note of such cooperation.[10]

Recently, Burt has suggested that "In the original plan for implementation, the BIA was to administer Indian Community Action Agencies," and that only after protest by the Navajo and others "the OEO allowed tribal councils to designate themselves as CAA's" (1992:482). This was remarkably inconsistent with the statements of Kravitz, Nash and Udall, and was not reflected in the hearings on the EOA (Equal Opportunity Act) bill. Burt himself cited an interchange between Shriver and Senator McGovern during the hearings on the legislation in which McGovern accepted Shriver's assurance that the draft legislation would allow programs to "be made available directly to the Indian people without the necessity of some intermediate bureau or level of government."[11]

The relationship between the War on Poverty newcomers and the Bureau was not always a happy one, though in the end they managed to cooperate. Many in the OEO (including myself) tended to assume that all that had gone before was in error—not a view to win the hearts and minds (to borrow a Johnson phrase) of the BIA staff. Even OEO director Sargent Shriver was unable to resist using the Bureau as a straw man. In an address to the NCAI he bashed the Bureau and indicated a considerable misunderstanding of the federal trust relationship. He said that an Indian must "lie to the government official" to withdraw "his own money from his own bank account." As a counterpoint to himself and the OEO, he cast the Bureau as nay-saying "experts who told us . . . the Indian wasn't ready for a program based on local initiative."[12]

Associate Commissioner James Officer drew Udall's attention to the Shriver speech, pointing out its errors and commenting, "We have been getting along very well with the OEO at the reservation level and have only a minimum of differences with them here in Washington. Nevertheless, it would certainly be helpful if someone at your level could get across to Mr. Shriver what we have been trying to do in the past few years in BIA."[13] Undersecretary John Carver reported to Udall: "There is mounting evidence that top-level orientation of the poverty people is not only anti-Indian Bureau but also anti-government agency generally."[14] This was an accurate observation.

Officer reported Nash had foreseen the problem. "They're gonna drive you crazy, but at the same time it would be very nice if we could work out a rapport with them and maybe help them to see things a little differently while at the same time they're helping us to see things a little differently." Despite many problems with the OEO's arrogant staff, Officer suggested that "it was the structure of the OEO that I think did make an important contribution and did oblige the Bureau, maybe even against its will to move in the direction of more participation. It might have come without that but it would have come more slowly."[15] Nash himself later observed of the turnover of programs to the tribes that "the diffusion out of BIA had to take place and was significantly advanced by the OEO and its successors" (Nash 1988:273).

With or without Bureau encouragement, the Community Action Program turned out to be widely and rapidly accepted in the reservation communities. "Within three years after the agency was established it supported 67 Indian community action agencies on 170 reservations" (Levitan and Hetrick 1971:91). There were several reasons for this popularity, but one was the fact that the OEO dealt directly with the local community and its leaders rather than working through the BIA. The BIA was only one of the many established programs bypassed deliberately—OEO framers were very much predisposed to circumvent all elements of welfare establishment (Matusow 1984:244)—but here it set a positive precedent not reversed by local pols. Later, other federal agencies created Indian desks to deal directly with tribal governments, similarly bypassing the Bureau.

Much of the job of the CAP Indian desk was acquainting the reservation people with the possibilities of OEO and then making them believe in the organization. The OEO prepared an elaborate guide to assist those wishing to form Community Action agencies and, almost uniquely among federal agencies, rather than acting as a filter, much OEO staff time was spent helping the people to find a way to qualify for funds (CAA 1965). They also went outside the agency for "explainers." Pueblo anthropologist Alfonso Ortiz was among the many enlisted to the cause and recalled, "The Santa Ana council could not believe that they could apply directly to Washington for funds. We offered to help them with the forms, and they finally agreed to start the application process. This was repeated in Pueblo after Pueblo. They were astounded that they could bypass the Indian agency and the area office and go directly to Washington" (Ortiz 1986a:220).

More than once in the research offices of OEO, staff were sent out to help prepare applications submitted by communities with ideas that looked interesting but that were not properly attuned to the magic words needed for approval. For example, I was sent to Tucson to help the Pascua Yaqui Improvement Association rewrite a grant application for a demonstration in self-help housing. To overcome the problem of Native American unfamiliarity with the arcane art of grantsmanship, the OEO finally funded a consortium of three universities (later increased to six) to provide training and technical assistance (University of Utah et al. 1966).

The amounts of funding at the disposal of the various reservation Community Action programs was never very great; the BIA and PHS continued to spend the lion's share of federal funding for the reservations (Levitan and Hetrick 1971:92; Sorkin 1971). The impact of OEO funding, however, was out of proportion to the dollar amounts involved because these funds were being spent by the Indians themselves. Prior to the entry of the Community Action programs, virtually all funds on reservations were directly administered by the federal agencies that allocated them.

The OEO did directly administer some programs—for example, the Job Corps camps. The Community Action Program, however, was not such an administrative entity. The agency set wide-ranging guidelines as to what was fundable and then made direct grants to local communities which had the full responsibility of actual administration, including hiring and firing. Although no one knew it at first, here was a new model for a government-to-government relationship between tribes and the federal government, one that broke sharply from the long-standing system of federal administration of virtually every aspect of reservation life.

On the reservations, the Community Action programs solved few problems; certainly they never succeeded in eliminating poverty. However, I want to argue that the content and economic impact of CAP programs was almost beside the point. The underlying aim of the OEO planners, harkening back to Lloyd Ohlin, was the creation of social "competence," the creation of new structures of self-administration for the disorganized poor. Operating through grants rather than direct external administration was not in itself more programmatically efficient—many of the newly organized poor wasted funds as freely as any Chicago alderman, or stressed maximization of employment over the achievement of planned outcomes as in the Soviet Union (Fowler 1982; Bee 1981; Iverson 1981). The Indian people made many mistakes, but they made them on their own, which was a new experience for them.

In many cases on the reservations, local administration did not even create much difference in program content. There was nothing especially "Indian" about Indian-run CAA's strong preference for a program like Head Start, which was a big favorite everywhere. The Indian CAA's had much the same problems and took much the same approaches as other rural poverty populations. The major difference was in the pre-existing political structure of tribal governments created by the Indian Reorganization Act, which facilitated the easy entry of the OEO programs and which was in turn much strengthened by its control of them, particularly by the new patronage of awarding jobs.

On the reservations there was no problem of forming governing councils that were representative of the poor, as CAA "maximum feasible" guidelines called for, nor avoiding pre-emption by the welfare establishment. Here the communities of the poor and their governments were more or less coincident. Jim Wilson of the OEO Indian desk observed, "Conditions of poverty cut across all lines on the reservations. . . . So that representation of the poor among the tribes we deal with is really one hundred percent of the people" (Steiner 1968:208). The OEO accepted tribal governments as the representatives of the poor and, as one federal agency to another, easily avoided control by the Bureau. As a result, Indian CAAs became not only branches of the existing Indian self-government structure but also inspirations to the independence of the rest of the Indian government.

Of course, the OEO's impact on the reservation was not entirely planned. Robert Bee noted, "The Federal anti-poverty programs of the mid 1960s livened things up considerably. The [tribal] council became a pivotal planning and overseeing body as ever more programs were added. In the Quechan public view, the council was there 'to get something for the people'" (1990:57).

Given the emphasis on child-centered programs such as Head Start, a disproportionate number of the new employment positions tended to go to women, thus in many cases strengthening the role of women in emerging tribal governments (Hoikkala 1995). Like any new resource to be distributed, control of the programs tended to fan the fires of existing factionalism, and some Indian leaders viewed the new freedom with alarm. Robert Burnette, for example, observed, "[LBJ's] so called self determination policy unleashed a tidal wave of embezzlement, graft and corruption" (Burnette and Koster 1974:162).

The Legal Services program tended to create controversy. The attempt to provide legal representation to the poor often found tribal members becoming increasingly litigious in dealing with their own tribal officials. On the Navajo reservation, for example, a strong and effective legal services program created a classic political struggle for its control (Iverson 1981:91–100). In the long run, however, the new legal resources became increasingly integrated into the emerging new structure of tribal self-administration (Deloria and Lytle 1983:151–55). A direct spin-off of the OEO-funded California Indian Legal Services was the Native American Rights Fund (NARF), established in 1970 and now among the most active national legal advocacy groups for Native American issues (NARF 1996:2).

These internal battles were a reflection of the fact that there was now something in Native American hands worth struggling for. Despite the disputes, OEO-funded programs strengthened tribal government because they tended to attract a new class of more highly trained Indian professional administrators, many of whom had previously had to seek employment off the reservations. Even out of the seemingly divisive example of the Navajo struggles over OEO administration, Ortiz noted, "two successive Navaho tribal chairman came directly out of the OEO programs. Peter McDonald, who served as chairman for twelve years, was enticed out of a comfortable middle class existence in Southern California where he worked as an engineer. McDonald went back to Window Rock to run the new Office of Navaho Economic opportunity. . . . Peterson Zah, the tribal chairman who succeeded him in 1982, started out in the OEO legal services program" (Ortiz 1986:221).

Some of the CAAS were intertribal, and one of these—Oklahomans for Indian Opportunity—later grew into a very influential national lobbying organization headed by LaDonna Harris, Americans for Indian Opportunity (Hertzberg 1971:317). Of the OEO experience she later said, "I will stand up and defend the OEO as long as I live. Indian leadership developed out of that program. . . . OEO taught us to use our imagination and to look at the future as an exciting adventure. It taught us there are other ways of doing things" (Harris 1985:223). An opinion survey of Indian policy participants in the '70s quoted an anonymous informant: "Had there been no War on Poverty there would have been no opportunity for educated and experienced Indian people to come home to find an outlet for their abilities" (Gross 1989:55).

Demonstrations

The Research and Demonstration programs were even more innovative and freewheeling (if that is possible) than the mainstream CAP programs. This is where I came in. Of those I personally dealt with, two stand out in retrospect as having far-reaching and to some extent unguessed consequences: the Pascua Yaqui village self-help housing project and the Navajo Demonstration School at Rough Rock.

The Yaqui Tribe

The Yaqui project has best been described by anthropologist Edward H. Spicer, who was the principal non-Yaqui directly involved (Spicer 1970, 1980). William Willard, the project director responsible for the training of community workers, has also written on the general project (1990, 1994). It is therefore one of the few well-documented illustrations of the many OEO demonstration programs. The OEO engaged in a number of similar self-help housing efforts for Native Americans, the largest of which was the Rosebud Sioux project, but few have been well examined.[16]

The Yaqui project, like all the other self-help housing projects, placed its greatest emphasis on skill training and community mobilization rather than on actual construction. As a federal agency, the OEO had no brief to provide actual housing; "bricks and mortar" per se were a forbidden activity. But houses could be built if they were a by-product of training/organization efforts. Local people would be trained and organized to build their own houses and purchase them with sweat equity. The project took place on a 200-acre tract of federal land which the Yaqui had gotten in 1963 through the efforts of the Pascua Yaqui Association and Arizona congressman Morris Udall. Over the three-year span of the OEO grant, from 1966 to 1969, only about twenty houses were built, but they formed the nucleus of a new community on the federal land grant.[17]

All this may seem straightforward, but a complex sequence of events had been set in motion with this simple effort to organize people for housing improvement. With the OEO housing grant at stake, long-standing Yaqui factions maneuvered to manipulate access to the housing and jobs. Local non-Yaquis, "patrons of the poor," struggled to maintain their own influence over the Yaqui as they shifted to the new location (Spicer 1970). The result was that, by the time the adobe dust settled, there were not one but two Pascua Yaqui villages: the original "Old Pascua" and, at the new site, "New Pascua." They are both still there today.

Old Pascua remained an urban "Mexican" barrio, albeit with greater organization and a distinctive Indian profile. New Pascua went on to develop a
highly effective leadership which used its OEO-honed skills to seek out other
federal grants and assistance. It eventually grew to a community of nearly
two thousand, the largest Yaqui settlement in the Southwest. The Pascua Yaqui
Association successfully petitioned in 1978 to become a federally recognized
tribe; the association then became a tribal government (Willard 1994).

A self-help housing project by the OEO thus turned out to be the spark
for a process of ethnogenesis. Where there had been a barrio of poor "Mexi-
cans," there was now an Indian tribe with their lands taken into trust status
as a reservation (Spicer 1980:253–58). During the administration of President
George Bush, one of these Arizona Yaqui, Eddie Brown, would even become
the assistant secretary for Indian affairs. As elsewhere in Indian communities, the OEO here helped ignite a great deal of community action at a level
beyond its highest expectations.

Rough Rock

Sometimes the demonstrations actually demonstrated what they were designed to demonstrate. The Navajo Rough Rock school was perhaps the best
documented and most publicly remembered of the various Indian educational efforts of the OEO. It was also the one with the most direct legislative
impact (Szasz 1974:169–75). Rough Rock has, perhaps, had a rosier press than
it might otherwise have had, due to the skill at advertisement and promotion
of its first director, Robert Roessel (Roessel 1977, 1979). An evaluation team
contracted by the OEO to examine the project commented, "the primary focus of administrators seemed to be on public relations" (Erickson et al.
1969:9.4). There were other innovative Indian education programs run by
the Bureau—for example, Rocky Point (also on the Navajo reservation)—
but they tended to be lost in the glare of Rough Rock publicity and controversy (Fuchs and Havighurst 1972).[18]

Much of the Indian educational literature describing Rough Rock has
discussed it in terms of the effectiveness of its many bicultural and bilingual
curricular innovations (Coombs 1972; McCarty 1987, 1989; Wax 1970). I want
to suggest that in the long run, the success or failure of these pedagogical

efforts was as irrelevant as the specific content of CAA programs in general, and that what was important about Rough Rock was the same thing that was important about all CAA programs on reservations: the innovation of self-administration. Ultimately Rough Rock was successful because its use of a local school board and tribal control, rather than direct Bureau administration, became a model for federal Indian education policy.

The Rough Rock school was not created by any sort of Navajo grassroots demand, as its propaganda often claimed, but was the brainchild of a non-Indian educator, Robert Roessel, who personally "sold" it to the OEO—specifically to Sanford Kravitz of the Research and Demonstration Office (Castile 1968). For years Roessel had been promoting his ideas about "both/and" (bicultural) education from the Indian education program at Arizona State University. He had had some earlier mixed success attempting innovations at the Navajo school at Low Mountain (Roessel 1960; Szasz 1974:170). His approach was, of course, not de novo; other studies examining Indian education on the Sioux and Apache reservations had made similar suggestions stressing the need for involvement of the Indian community in the educational process (Parmee 1968; Wax 1968).

The initial version of the project funded by the OEO was a failure. It was established in July 1965 at a BIA school at Lukachukai, where it dismally failed to attract community support or achieve anything but an adversarial relationship with the BIA school personnel (Castile 1968; Levitan and Hetrick 1971:55). The OEO Research Office, after a visit by this author, was at the point of ending the school's funding and closing it down as a failed experiment.[19] The Navajo area director, Graham Holmes, accurately reported to the commissioner that "The OEO experimental school at Lukachukai School appears to be in serious trouble," but Commissioner Bennett reported to Udall that "Holmes is attempting to do all that he can to cause a workable program to be provided and intends to cooperate in every way possible to see that it succeeds so that it will be of some benefit to the Navaho people."[20]

The result of this last-ditch cooperation between the OEO and the BIA, largely through the efforts of Holmes, was an offer by the Bureau to make available a new but as yet unstaffed boarding school facility at Rough Rock. Here it could be run entirely by demonstration personnel selected specifically for the project, without the complications involved in imposing the school as an overlay on an existing BIA staff and structure.[21] There may have been some challenging "put up or shut up" element in the BIA's offer, since Roessel was regarded as something of a gadfly by many in the Bureau. Whatever the motivation, both the OEO and the BIA quickly agreed to fund this new and larger-scale phase of the project. With their combined contributions, the school began operating with about twice the usual funding of a Bureau school of similar size.

The new school found no Navajo tribal entity ready to accept the responsibility for its sponsorship, and in the process of negotiating the turnover the tribal council went out of session without acting. So DINE (Development in Navajo Education; in the Navajo language, *diné* is the term Navajos use for themselves), a private nonprofit corporation, was hastily formed by default to provide a suitable recipient for the grant. Yazzie Begay of the tribal education committee was DINE's chair, with Roessel serving as director of the school (Castile 1968:25–26).

After this rather ad hoc beginning, the program was largely run by its director and the professional teaching staff, not by the Navajo parents and community. Local ideas were largely represented by the director to the outside world, and they were almost always universally found by him to be consistent with his a priori reading of what such a community would want. However, from the very beginning Roessel insisted that the "community," in the form of its school board, was in direct control of all aspects of the school (Roessel 1979:205–9). Many in the Bureau were still unconvinced: "the general attitude of the Bureau was this was the greatest patronizer of Indians who ever lived . . . out there manipulating the Indians, directing them wherever he wanted them to go."[22]

In addition to the Bureau's jaundiced view of Roessel, two outside studies independently noted that the actual academic participation of the local people was minimal (Castile 1968; Erickson et al. 1969). Both suggested that the local community had little interest or competence in linguistic models of bilingualism or other educational arcana which made up most of the instructional innovation. Examination of the minutes of the school board meetings shows clearly that what did interest the community was economic development, which is to say jobs. There they did indeed take an active role in decision-making, with a focus on distributing jobs widely and fairly in the local community (Castile 1968:109; Erickson et al. 1969:3, 15–17).

The pattern that developed with the Rough Rock school board and its focus on jobs was not unique in this period of emerging tribal self-administration. Wherever Native Americans were given a degree of community control over federally funded programs, a similar pattern emerged, stressing maximizing the distribution of jobs as widely as possible in the community (Fowler 1982:236; Bee 1981:128). The people of Rough Rock pursued an existing community concern—the lack of jobs—using the device of the new board. They did not become instant experts on bicultural education, hooked on phonics, or otherwise enthusiasts of just exactly the brand of pedagogy promoted by the outsiders.

The tribal government eventually took over much of the Navajo educational system, so thoroughly, in fact, that they dispensed with the services of many of the non-Navajo educators, including Roessel, who was replaced by Dillon Platero (Iverson 1981:122). However, it was Navajo professional educators who were replacing outside professionals, not a seizure of power by local grassroots parental rebellions. The Rough Rock experiment in local school governance was a long-range success, but in much the same way as the governments created by the Indian Reorganization Act of 1934. It took a while for the reality to match the rhetoric in both cases.

At Rough Rock, as with the IRA, a new structure of governance was introduced from outside rather than demanded internally. Both early IRA tribal councils and the Rough Rock school board were initially and necessarily instruments of their "expert" introducers. The IRA governments, an alien device, were eventually truly seized upon by the local people as their own, but only after considerable time and experimentation (Washburn 1984). The Community Action programs, the school boards, and the tribal governments were not overnight successes, but they all succeeded in the long run because they provided what Dobyns called the "therapeutic experience of responsible democracy" (1965).

The true significance of Rough Rock was ultimately as a demonstration of self-administration in an area easily shifted to tribal control. But all of the CAA programs offered much the same lesson in the joys of running one's own affairs. The demonstration projects of the OEO like Rough Rock deliberately sought to pursue the model builder's craft, demonstrating the feasibility of new approaches in the hopes that others would emulate them. What was demonstrated in all cases by the entire Community Action approach on the reservations was the feasibility of self-administration of federally funded programs by Indian tribes.

By 1969 this move toward self-administration was not an unplanned end of the OEO programs. The OEO's Indian Division director, James Wilson, said, "The basic philosophy of the Indian division has been defined thus: a) To direct fund Indian tribes to develop the program sophistication necessary for all levels of government to develop in their relationship to the Federal government and b) to develop through a process of conditioning, the social responsibility of the tribal governing body to the reservation residents . . . expected of local governments in non reservation communities" (Wilson 1969:372). To build self-government and self-administration—as much as to fight poverty—emerged as a positive and deliberate goal.

The tribes learned their new lesson in handling their own affairs long before overall federal Indian policy changed. Observers noted of the Mississippi Choctaw, for example, that "funding of the Choctaw Community Action Agency . . . allowed the Choctaw government to begin experiencing self-government. Continued assistance from the Office of Economic Opportunity helped the Choctaw to establish its own philosophy of self determination" (McKee 1987:178). Another observer said that, "From this beginning, in less than twenty years the Choctaw Tribe was directly administering over $10 million in federal grants and contracts" (Peterson 1992:144).

The Indian people gladly embraced their first taste of self-government since the creation of the reservation system. Vine Deloria, then director of the National Congress of American Indians, commented in a letter to Sol Tax that "The Poverty program is extremely popular and for the first time tribes can plan and run their own programs for their people without someone in the BIA dictating to them."[23] D'Arcy McNickle, himself long with the Bureau, noted of the OEO that the "transferral of authority and responsibility for decision making to the local community was an administrative feat which the Bureau of Indian Affairs, after more than one hundred years of stewardship, had never managed to carry out" (1973:119).

Many in the Bureau began to take note of this Indian reaction to the OEO. Graham Holmes, himself a highly innovative BIA area superintendent, observed, "Indians under my jurisdiction really enjoyed the short but happy life of the Office of Navaho Economic Opportunity" (Philp 1986:219). The NCAI editorialized, "The War on Poverty, which we believe to be this generation's 'New Deal,' places major emphasis on the participation of the poor. . . . There is a new sense of self determination for the individual in this war on poverty" (NCAI 1966a:1).

The OEO lasted only from 1965 to 1974, too short a time and with too little funding to actually change very much of the condition of poverty on the reservations. Its real impact, as we shall see in the next chapter, was not its own achievements but its influence on tribal governments, the BIA, and the federal approach to Indian administration.

A New Goal: Self-Determination

I propose a new goal for our Indian programs: A goal that ends the old debate about "termination" of Indian programs and stresses self-determination.

—LBJ, *The Forgotten Americans*

*W*hile LBJ's administration changed a great many things very rapidly in the shift from New Frontier to Great Society, things at Interior and the BIA moved relatively slowly. There was no initial change of staff at Interior. Though Udall's close advisors worried that he himself might be replaced, they were advising him to shake up the Bureau.[1] They feared inertia. Oren Beatty wrote to Udall, "the Bureau will be left with Nash and a top echelon filled with career bureaucrats dedicated to finding ways not to do what you want done."[2] But LBJ retained Udall, and initially Udall retained Nash.

Udall soon developed a close relationship with LBJ, and in the Great Society atmosphere of sweeping change, Udall's earlier hopes for reform in Indian affairs, dimmed under the Kennedys, were soon revitalized. LBJ did not personally take a very active role in things Indian but he was certainly interested in new ideas and was willing to be guided by Udall in this area. At a BIA staff meeting early in LBJ's term, Udall said, "We have the support from the White House to do something really spectacular."[3]

Nash's pragmatic and benign attitude toward change had helped smooth over the rough spots of the transition to the Great Society, but he was not to be allowed to stay around to see the outcome; Philleo Nash had lost the support of Udall. Clashing with Udall's hopes for legislative movement, Nash's karmic debt with Congress appeared to have led Udall to begin to seek his replacement. Nash himself publicly attributed his fall to the demands of Congress and said nothing for publication about his differences with Udall (Nash

1986:197). Since Nash was popular in Indian country, Udall thought that, "In order to get Nash out, because he had support, I felt the best way to do this was to pick the best Indian that I could find to be Commissioner." This, of course, had been his intention at the beginning of the Kennedy administration.[4]

Udall wrote to LBJ in February 1966 pointing out that he had already recommended Nash's replacement in November 1965 and "I now, with great urgency, renew this recommendation. Nash has the poorest Congressional relations of any bureau chief in my Department. He is disliked and distrusted by most of the key congressional leaders. Worse, I have been unable to establish an effective day-to-day working relationship with him." In Nash's place he requested Deputy Commissioner Robert Bennett take over, who, he said, "will not only provide the type of leadership that is needed—but your appointment will make him the first Indian Commissioner in nearly a century."[5]

John Macy of the White House staff handled the lengthy negotiations with Nash, who submitted his resignation on March 9, 1966. LBJ distanced himself from the decision by having the announcement made by Interior.[6] In accepting Nash's resignation, he praised him and plugged the Great Society, writing to Nash, "You led an early attack in the War on Poverty before that war was declared."[7] That Nash was indeed popular in Indian country was evident in the NCAI editorial on his leaving, which declared, "he has been one of the two outstanding Commissioners in American history" (NCAI 1966b:13). It also noted that "His work was one of unspectacular but steady progress to open the doors of our society to Indians in a manner in which they could understand and feel confident to try for themselves" (13). Nash remained active in Indian affairs and in the field of applied anthropology until his death in 1987 (Officer 1988).

Robert Bennett, an Oneida tribal member, was an innovation as an Indian commissioner, but as a lifelong BIA bureaucrat he was an unlikely choice as an innovator. He had joined the BIA in 1933 at the age of twenty-one, and except for the war years he had been with it ever since (Ellis 1979:325). In summing him up Ellis noted, "Bennett was an effective bureaucrat who worked within the system rather than a leader who announced new policies and sought to develop public support for change" (1979:330). It was an odd description of a man chosen to provide "imaginative new leadership for our

Indian programs."[8] When Udall solicited confidential comments on Bennett's first year in office from some of his staff, one said, "Frankly I think it is too much to expect a product of over 30 years in the Bureau to provide dynamic leadership. I think we have made some genuine accomplishments during the past year but would not ascribe many of them to the Commissioner's leadership."[9]

Bennett's own oral history interview reflected his less than optimistic perspective on innovation: "If we could solve the Indian problems, we could solve the problems of humanity, because theirs are the problems of humanity."[10] Looking back on the years of his participation in the War on Poverty, he seemed to dismiss its impact. "Indians had lived with poverty so long they did not know they were poor until the poverty programs came along. The War on Poverty did a lot of good things. I am not arguing that point. But I am suggesting that reservation communities will have to go back to old ways of dealing with these problems now that the federal government is dropping programs" (Bennett 1986:224–25).

During his confirmation hearings, Commissioner-nominee Bennett, like Nash before him, was treated to a strong dose of the views of those inclined toward termination. Such a beginning was not conducive to independence and innovation even if he had been so inclined.[11] Much of the needed dynamic for change in Indian affairs would be provided from above since both Udall and LBJ were very much interested in new policy directions. On the occasion of Bennett's swearing-in ceremony, LBJ said in typical style, "I want you to put on your hat and go back over there to that Bureau and begin work today on the most comprehensive program for the advancement of the Indians that the government of the United States has ever considered. I want it to be sound, realistic, progressive, venturesome and farsighted." LBJ also told him that if he met resistance, "go over there and find some of those tomahawks that are still around the Smithsonian."[12]

More pressure would also come from below since, in addition to change-oriented staff already on board, like James Officer and William King, Udall brought in what he hoped would be an innovative new team for Bennett—Theodore W. Taylor from the Smithsonian as deputy commissioner, William R. Carmack from the staff of Senator Fred Harris as assistant commissioner for social and government affairs, and Dr. Carl Louis Marburger as assistant commissioner for education. Udall commented that Marburger was "the luckiest catch of all," but he was to have a short and rather tumultuous tenure as the head of the education programs, resigning after only one year.[13]

BIA to HEW

Udall and some of his staff thought that the beginning of the new administration might be the appropriate occasion for some degree of major change in the structure of Interior itself. In April 1965 he recommended to the president "the transfer to the Office of Education (in HEW) of Interior's *education* program . . . and the transfer from HEW to Interior of the *water pollution* and *air pollution* programs. . . . The educators at HEW could give Indian education the emphasis and direction it lacks; on the other hand, Interior could provide the conservation focus and enthusiasm which the pollution programs seem to lack at HEW."[14]

Udall's motive for this scheme had more to do with his longstanding interest in conservation than it did with things Indian. In December 1965 he recommended to Joseph Califano that the president move to create a "Department of Natural Resources" out of the existing Department of the Interior through a gradual sorting out of existing programs. He suggested "the transfer to Interior of water pollution and air pollution from HEW and a transfer out of Interior of those non-natural resource activities which logically belong in other departments." Indian affairs was clearly among those he had in mind. He said that "Following the pattern of the Indian health transfer, which was consummated in 1954, Indian education and welfare service functions might be transferred to HEW."[15]

Interestingly, the same memo did not recommend transfer of the trust territories from Interior, though those, too, were clearly non-natural resource matters. The reason was one of appearances. "Should this function be transferred we are convinced it should go to State rather than HEW. It is likely, however, that State will not relish the idea of having a new 'Office of Colonies.' . . . There are as many good reasons for this function in quiescence at Interior rather than making a transfer that might create a fresh protest in the United Nations and elsewhere."[16]

As it turned out, HEW did not relish its share of the reshuffling scheme either. Udall appointed an Interior task force to meet with HEW's Office of Education to consider the shift of education programs. The task force chair,

Associate Commissioner James Officer, reported to Udall that "Mr. Mylecraine [Walter Mylecraine, assistant to the deputy commissioner) opened the discussion by pointing out that the top officials of the Office of Education had held a meeting last week in which they agreed . . . that the Office of Education, with its many new programs, at the present time is not in a position and would prefer not to undertake the function of providing classroom education for Indian Children."[17]

It was probably not a viable idea in Indian country either. It was inevitable that new moves to transfer functions would be compared to the earlier ones and seen in the same light by Native Americans. The 1954 transfer of Indian health responsibility to the Public Health Service had taken place in the context of the termination effort, and the last time a department of natural resources had been considered was in the Hoover Commission report. As administration legislative plans were firming up in 1967, John Gardner, secretary of HEW, wrote the president, saying, "there are very serious obstacles in the way of moving the Bureau of Indian Affairs to HEW. . . . What I would like now to do, with your permission, is to offer Stu Udall all the assistance and resources that HEW can provide to help him in doing a better job under the present organization structure."[18] The proposal for transfer was never formally made to Congress, and the Bureau stayed intact and where it was.

"Views of the Reservation System"

With the cautious Bennett as commissioner, Udall was often "acting as his own commissioner" in the search for new directions. He turned again, as he had when he first took office, for new ideas from his close advisors, King and Officer. William King, by this time superintendent at Salt River, wrote Udall a lengthy memo describing ways in which his thinking had changed since the 1960 Officer-King report and suggesting new possibilities.[19] It is worth quoting at some length since it set out an approach and philosophy that was the core of the emerging new Udall policy direction—which came to be called self-determination. "One has to be a reservation administrator for only a short time," King wrote, "to recognize that the social organization that has developed within it is basically unhealthy." He thought the critical organizational problem was the "role of the superintendent. . . . As 'Big Daddy' he is still a major impediment to the assumption of Indian responsibility." The answer seemed to be that "much of the actual power of the superintendency ... must be shifted to an Indian power locus, logically the Tribal Council," and a "formula to achieve this step, which is both administratively sound and simple, is for the government to contract with the tribes to carry out many of the activities presently performed by the Bureau." The result hoped for was that "There would be a minimum change in services; there would be a maximum shift of power, authority and (most important) responsibility to Tribal entities. This simple step would transform Tribal organizations from mere administrative conveniences to the government (a condition much recognized by their more thoughtful members, and one which greatly impedes the development of much more than symbolic leadership) to organizations which could become the foundation for vital municipal growth."[20]

This was, of course, the same contract procedure used by the Community Action programs with which King was quite familiar. King said,

> Nothing I can think of has so accelerated the changing role of the Superintendent as has the OEO program. . . . The most important thing I have seen come out of the OEO . . . is that it has allowed Indians to redefine their relationship with the Federal Government. Tribes, in most instances, actually deal directly with OEO; BIA occupies a subordinate position as advisor and provider of technical services as requested. . . . We, in BIA, if we are wise, will learn a great deal from these positive aspects of the OEO program on reservations.[21]

Udall was sufficiently impressed with this reasoning to circulate the memo at a superintendents' conference in Santa Fe (with some personal elements and King's name removed) as "Views of the Reservation System by a Reservation Superintendent."[22] In his speech to the superintendents he touched on the memo and on the OEO contract model and called for similar new directions in the Bureau. He cited the King memo yet again in his "informal remarks" the next day.[23]

Though King seems to have been the first to put it on paper, others were coming to the same conclusions at the same time. The NCAI held a meeting of its own in Santa Fe, and Vine Deloria recalled that they intended to "pressure the bureau for changes, they had a specific idea in mind. The programs of the OEO had taken hold on the reservations and the idea of granting funds directly to the tribes for specific programs was very popular" (Deloria 1969:142). He also noted that "At the meeting, Udall wandered around holding a paper written by a superintendent from Arizona who advocated a strict contract method of providing services comparable to the OEO programs. It was a radical departure from traditional policies and no one could be sure that it could be sold to higher ups in the administration or Congress, but the tribes all felt it was the wave of the future" (142).

Given Udall's positive endorsement of the King memo and its stress on Indian self-administration, Deloria's claim that one of the reasons Udall had called the Santa Fe meeting "was to disqualify the tribes as sponsoring agencies in the War on Poverty and turn the community action funds over to the Bureau of Indian affairs for programming" is doubtful (1974:29). Udall was saying just the opposite in his remarks to the superintendents.[24] As early as 1964, Nash had observed that Udall "did not want the Indian Bureau to have full approval or disapproval power with respect to programs originated by Indian tribes in the form of proposals to the OEO," and there is nothing in the record to suggest Udall ever changed his mind.[25] There was, of course, no possibility of any transfer of OEO programs to Bureau control, since there was a general lack of sympathy at the OEO for any such role for the Bureau— and Udall knew that.

Deloria also later claimed that the NCAI "held a meeting concurrent with the Bureau at Santa Fe to thwart Udall's plans to continue termination; as a counter measure to his suspected program, the NCAI coined the phrase 'self-determination'" (Deloria and Lytle 1984:216). Deloria's recollection is a reflection of a general sense of alarm on the part of Indian leaders at the NCAI Santa Fe meeting. The spark for this fear was not Udall but strongly protermination comments of Senate members at Bennett's confirmation hearings.[26] "Members of the Senate Interior Committee criticized the BIA for not following through on Congressional directives regarding the termination of several tribes for which withdrawal programs had been requested. The report was a shock to both Indians and BIA personnel who had come to feel that termination was a dead issue" (Officer 1978:66).

However, it is impossible that "the NCAI coined the phrase 'self-determination'" at the meeting in April 1966 (Deloria and Lytle 1984:216). The phrase first came into common use in relation to "peoples" as a policy of President

Woodrow Wilson at the end of World War I, and had been very much a part
of the vocabulary of Marxism since the debates of Lenin and Rosa Luxem-
bourg on the "National Question" (Castile 1993; Knock 1992).

Native American leaders were aware of the concept as used by President
Wilson, if not the Marxists. In 1919 Robert Yellowtail of the Crow appealed in
the name of the principle of self-determination to Wilson to "not forget that
within the boundaries of his own Nation are the American Indians who have
no rights at all" (in Hoxie 1995:264). The OEO, pursuant to its theme of "maximum participation," had invoked the term frequently, and Sargent Shriver
had used it in a speech to the NCAI itself in the year prior to its supposed
coining by that organization (1965).[27]

Although the Indian leaders did not know it, Udall, before coming to
the Santa Fe meeting, had written to President Johnson denouncing the Senate report, saying, "It is my own view that the Senate Document which received publicity over the weekend is a one sided document. It does not accurately represent the temper of the Senate Interior Committee," and "I suspect
that the only answer is a concerted effort by all concerned to inject a note of
urgency into the new programs which will give our Indians an opportunity
to develop their talents and their resources."[28] Udall was not turning back
toward termination, although to some Congress seemed to be doing so.

The conference in Santa Fe got sidetracked into wrangles over the not
unjustified termination fears. As a result, little came immediately of the ideas
in the King memo or the endorsement by the NCAI of grant and contracting
approaches. However, the conference marked the shift to a discussion of a
new way of doing things. The NCAI editorialized, "One cannot help but recognize in the events at Santa Fe . . . a real turning point in the relations of
tribes," and went on, "The concept of the OEO programs which encourages
participation in planning and decision making by the people concerned is
most certainly the spirit with which tribes agreed to move to land reserved
for them which are now called reservations" (NCAI 1966:1).

New Directions

Later in April, Udall held a meeting at Interior with key staff and called for a
"working party" to put together a "new legislative program for next year—a
major piece of legislation with the President out front and the intent to do

the most thorough-going consultation on a legislative program."[29] He reported to the president in May 1966 on the need for new "foundation" legislation, saying, "We are already at work on such legislation but to use the consensus approach must fully confer with the Indians and the Congress before it is perfected." Here he first raised the issue of a presidential Indian policy message: "I believe the President should send a special message to the Congress next January on Indian development . . . and a history-making omnibus Indian bill."[30]

In June, Udall wrote to the president that the emerging omnibus bill "Would provide new 'tools' to enable the Indian people to enter the American money markets and use modern management and investment techniques. Would also enable the Indian Bureau and the Indians to strike off the outdated Indian trusteeship shackles and quicken the pact of economic development." He also tempted Johnson's sense of history by saying, "There has not been basic Indian foundation legislation since FDR's first term."[31] There was clearly every intention to consult with Indian leaders once some sort of working paper could be put together; however, Indian objections to the still-developing bill arose as early as July 1966.

A version of the Interior working paper was leaked to the NCAI and raised new fears of termination (Deloria 1969:182). Officer described it as "a tentative draft that nobody ever regarded as anything more than a document to elicit comment."[32] Clearly preliminary and covering a wide range of ideas (many tending toward increased self-determination), the discussions did have a definite "freeing" of resources theme that might have sounded like termination rhetoric to sensitive ears.

In September, Deputy Commissioner Taylor forwarded to the undersecretary "an outline for legislative discussion and copies of our July, 1966 and August 15, 1966 efforts at preliminary, partial drafting of legislation. The purpose of special Indian legislation is to modify the existing federal trust relationship over the property of Indians and Indian tribes to provide a means by which they will increasingly assume freedom and responsibility regarding their resources," including the "Right to sell, exchange or manage Tribal property."[33]

The idea of land sale was unsettling, and Commissioner Bennett somewhat belatedly set out to hold formal meetings with tribal members at nine separate locations in September 1966, at which he explained the plans and solicited ideas for new legislation. Deward Walker, an anthropologist, was asked by the American Indian Civil Liberties Trust to do an analysis of the nearly 2,000 recommendations received at these gatherings (Walker 1967). Walker commented on the Bureau's own report on these recommendations that it "fails to state adequately the principal emphasis in the recommendations, i.e., a strong desire for freedom from undue bureaucratic restraints, social and economic development, and maintenance of tribal organization, resources and associated rights" (21).

Walker explicitly suggested in his analysis, which was made available to the Bureau, that the omnibus bill provisions pertaining to the integrity of land would not find acceptance in Indian country and that "even a superficial reading of the numerous recommendations . . . makes it clear such proposals were foredoomed to rejection by the tribes" (18). The Bureau, in return, commented on Walker's report: "I don't think it was ever the intention of the Omnibus Bill to be all inclusive of the 1950 recommendations catalogued."[34] Whether the bill could have included them *all* or not, there were clear warning signs that the strong resource emphasis was raising terminationist fears.

"Outside" Task Force

Lyndon Johnson used task forces as a policy formulation vehicle to a greater extent than any other president, forming forty-three "outside" and ninety-two "inside" interagency policy planning groups (Graham 1987:177; Thomas and Wolman 1969). One source noted "the net result was a search for ideas not seen before or since in national politics" (Wood 1993:68). The Indians were not left out and were the subject of both one inside and one outside task force.[35]

The outside groups were designed to involve a wide range of nongovernment "expert" inputs in the planning process. The outside task force on Indian affairs was chaired by physician Walsh McDermott; the eleven other members were all to a greater or lesser degree bona fide experts.[36] Most participants had been selected from a list of nominees submitted to the president's staff by Udall. Some had long been active in Indian affairs, including anthropologist Sol Tax, attorney Richard Schifter with La Farge's AAIA, and educator Robert Roessel, who had just become director of the Rough Rock demonstration school. William Keeler, who had participated in Udall's 1961 task force, provided some continuity with this one. The rest of the task force members were in one way or another primarily development oriented.[37]

The outside task force deliberations on Indian affairs were not lengthy. The group held its initial meeting on October 11, 1966, and delivered its report, "A Free Choice Program for American Indians," on December 23, 1966.[38] During its brief life the group had little time for consultation with Native Americans, and very much in contrast with the extensive hearings of the JFK-era task force, its report listed only five Indian leaders with whom it held a single one-day session[39] (Keeler et al. 1961).

In their policy recommendations the group took special note of the growing impact of the OEO: "Except for the OEO program, neither mechanisms nor requirements for systematic Indian consultation exist either at the national or the local level." Further, "The OEO programs on the reservations have demonstrated that, given the proper incentives, communities with a reputation for apathy can be successfully induced to participate actively in designing and carrying out programs to improve their lot."[40]

Much of the report was, as always, concerned with reservation poverty and the need for more money for education and economic development to remedy it. However, it also incorporated some emerging new ideas that went beyond the simple call for more. Their description of the proposed presidential message gave the gist of their thinking.

Presidential Policy Statement.

1. The U.S. Government recognizes that, as the first Americans, the Indians and Alaskan natives, alone among its peoples, are under no social pressure to be culturally assimilated unless they choose to do so. In short, the United States concedes that the Indian is a special case.

2. A complete disavowal of "termination" as a governmental policy or goal. If "termination" ever is to come for a Tribe, it should come only after a slow process wholly initiated and carried forward by the Tribe. It should be stressed, in particular, that neither tribal progress in socio-

economic development nor any award by the Indian Claims Commission (so called judgment funds) should be used as a weapon to induce a Tribe to apply for "termination."

3. Indian lands, i.e., the Indian Estates, are inviolate. A similar statement should be made about the trust status of allotted lands. In the latter case only, there also has to be a statement of principles governing the rules of sale that must be so drafted as to fully protect *tribal* as well as individual interests.

4. Announce that substantial Indian participation is featured both at the national and local levels in the new instrumentalities proposed for improvement of Indian education and for the creation of jobs through Indian economic development.

5. (Perhaps and hopefully) announce that all of the major features of the three part program have been suggested and subsequently endorsed by an advisory group of Indian leaders formed from among the Chairman of Tribal Councils and including the President of the National Council of American Indians.[41]

Ignoring the last point, which might uncharitably be seen as suggesting simulating a Native American origin for the policies, the task force suggested presidential weight be thrown behind two basic issues. The first was to reassure the Native peoples of the permanency of the "special" Indian relation and renounce termination, *so as* to encourage economic and education development. The report was stronger on this disavowal of termination than was the 1961 task force (Keeler et al. 1961). The second theme was that of increased Indian participation and self-administration. Once termination fears were dispelled, the actions called for in the rest of the report were various forms of restructuring tending toward self-determination. The concept of "self-determination without termination" was beginning to take shape in this report.

The report, however, did continue to endorse the tribal "corporations," which were among the proposals raising the greatest termination fears. It was easy to see elements in this new economic structure that one author would later call "termination by accountants" (Morris 1992). Outside businessmen would have an important voice over tribal funds and lands, perhaps a controlling voice. It was not difficult to imagine that Indian lands might be somehow forfeit if bonds were to be issued, considering the language about the corporation issuing "guarantees" and the expressed possibility of being sued.

The report also incorporated emerging new ideas on Indian education. In addition to a range of quantitative recommendations aimed at making the Indian schools a "model system," there were structural innovations. The influence of the OEO Rough Rock experiment was clear: "It is essential to involve Indian parents in the education of their children and to give them an important voice—both at the national and local levels—in setting policy for those schools in which Indian children predominate. Indeed, wherever Indian tribes express the desire and experience to do so, they should be permitted to operate schools directly under contract."[42]

But their final recommendations on education said only, "The President should ask the Commissioner for Indian Affairs to see that an all-Indian School Board is established for each Federally operated Indian School." While "The School Boards must be given a real voice in setting policy and programs for the schools," they went on to say, "The Task Force realizes that this recommendation may be viewed as both impractical and threatening by many BIA school administrators."[43] They also recommended a "National Advisory Committee on Indian Education," half of whose members would be Native Americans. "The purposes of the Committee would be to . . . advise the Secretary and the Commissioner of Indian Affairs on educational policies and programs."[44] While suggesting some enhanced degree of Indian participation, they did not envision actual control or responsibility in Indian hands, either nationally or locally.

Their final concern was the most controversial among task force members themselves. As Udall had earlier suggested, "Primary responsibility for Indian affairs [should] be transferred from the Secretary of Interior to the Secretary of Health, Education and Welfare," and once there, "the possibility of transferring the Division of Indian Health into it should be seriously considered." Task force members William Keeler and Lewis Douglas so strongly disagreed that their dissent was indicated in three different places. Less controversially, the task force also recommended the creation of an "Inter Agency Committee on Indian affairs" for coordination purposes and an "Indian affairs advisory committee," which would have half its membership Native American.[45]

The omnibus legislative package that emerged embodied some of the advice of this task force but not all. The legislation proposed did not contain any of the strong language disavowing termination with explicit guarantees of Indian "estate" as recommended by the task force. The economic arrangements were put forward without the reassurances that would have calmed the sense of terminationist threat. The transfer of the Bureau, controversial in the report, was already largely a dead issue by the time the report was delivered.

Buy Indian

At the same time as these efforts to develop new legislation proceeded, within the Bureau Udall was encouraging innovation using existing authorization. James Officer, noting the increasing influence of the oeo contract model, said:

> The bia was doing some experimenting of its own in this area but in a very tentative and limited kind of way. . . . The law and order program had done some contracting with tribes to take over law and order responsibilities. . . . Also, the education branch had been conducting some experiments of its own having to do with the contracting of bus services, cafeteria services and things of this kind . . . in both cases . . . they had made use of the authority, contracting authority, which they thought existed in the so called Buy Indian Act.[46]

A draft of a memo sent by the commissioner regarding Section 23 of the Indian Service Omnibus Bill of 1910, usually referred to as Buy Indian, was entitled, "Policy Application of Buy Indian Act." It said, "The Act of June 1910 (36 Stat. 861, 25 usc47) . . . reads . . . 'So far as may be practicable Indian labor shall be employed, and purchases of the products of Indian Industry may be made in the open market in the discretion of the Secretary of the Interior.' The Bureau's policy in applying this Act shall be to acquire any and all products and services which can be provided by an individual Indian(s) or company which qualifies as 'Indian industry.'"[47] Among the Indian industries suitable for such contracting were "Indian tribes," that is, tribal governments. A variation of this draft was formally issued as policy in August 1968, but it had been de facto Bureau policy for some time.[48]

The Omnibus Bill

Still feeling that existing authority was too limiting, Udall continued to press for new foundation legislation. Task force recommendations and those ideas generated at Interior were reviewed, and discussions began with the Interior committees in January 1967.[49] The legislative package was finally sent by Udall to Congress in May 1967, as the "Indian Resources Development Act of 1967."[50]

The bill contained the idea of greater tribal self-administration but retained the unfortunate emphasis on the mechanism of corporations and the right to mortgage and dispose of resources. The Senate version (s.1816), headed, "A bill to provide for the economic development and management of the resources of individual Indians and Indian tribes, and for other purposes," stated, "It is the purpose of this Act to provide Indians with managerial, credit and corporate tools to enable them to participate more fully in American social, economic, educational, and political life; and to permit them to exercise greater initiative and self determination."[51] The self-determination phrase seems almost an afterthought.

The negative response of Indian leaders, already kindled by the leaked draft, was immediate. A meeting of some thirty tribal leaders, called by Bennett for an "Indian Conference on Policy and Legislation," sent a letter to President Johnson asking for more time for deliberation and said, "the managerial techniques of the proposed legislation effecting mortgage, hypothecation and sale of Indian lands," would lead "inevitably and inalterably to the prompt erosion and demise of the economic culture of the American Indians."[52] They did endorse some aspects of the bill, particularly the section on loan funds, but they also forwarded a resolution requesting that "the 'Omnibus Bill' considered at this meeting be rejected in its present form."[53]

Udall had predicted this reaction. Just before sending the bill to the hill, he wrote to Joseph Califano, saying, "Some Indian spokesmen will disagree with some of the provisions of the legislation. For this reason I recommend that Interior and not the President transmit the legislation to the Hill."[54]

The bill was introduced in May, and by October Udall was commenting in a memo to key staff, "While the House and Senate held brief hearings on the Indian Resources Development Act of 1967, there seems to be no substantial body of Congressional *or* Indian support for this legislation."[55]

Why did Udall push forward a bill that sounded so much like termination, which he knew would be found objectionable in Indian country? The cloaking of a shift toward increased tribal self-administration in language focused on economic development may have seemed politically necessary to Udall. Termination was on the wane, but it still had strong supporters in Congress, as was witnessed during Bennett's confirmation hearings. Attempts to please both Indian and such congressional constituencies with the same bill may have been doomed from the start.

Congress and Termination

Termination legislation HCR 108 remained on the books and actively on the mind of some members of Congress. Nash had attributed his resignation to demands made by the chairs of the Interior and Insular Affairs committees based on his resistance to termination (Nash 1986:197). Bennett's confirmation hearings had also brought forth strong Senate statements on termination. The House Interior and Insular Affairs committee, chaired through most of Udall's era by Wayne Aspinall, was less of a problem than the Senate. Udall felt, "They tended to be more what I would call pro-Indian."[56]

Where Nash had clashed frequently with the chair of the Senate committee, Clinton Anderson, Bennett faced his successor, Henry Jackson of Washington state. Jackson was something of a founding father of the termination policy as sponsor of the Indian claims legislation in 1945 (Fixico 1986:26). In 1964 he was just as strong a supporter, saying that the termination resolution was "merely an expression by the House and Senate that Indians should be subject to the same laws as other citizens and assume their full responsibilities at the appropriate time."[57]

The Colville reservation in his home state was the object of one of the most protracted termination struggles, one which he supported until 1971 (Dahl 1994). In 1964 he used the phrase "self determination" in relation to the Colville, but only as a synonym for termination: "What is disturbing to many members of the House and Senate is the footdragging on the part of the Bureau of Indian Affairs in recommending legislation for those tribes and groups who, by the Bureau's own admission, are not receiving material benefits from the government, yet are restrained by Federal law from exercising the right of self determination. The Colville tribes in our state are a specific example of this situation."[58]

In a matter of such small political weight as Indian affairs, a single determined congressman could be crucial. Much of the initiative for the termination policy in the 1950s could be credited to the efforts of Senator Arthur Watkins and Representative E. Y. Berry (Fixico 1986; Burt 1982). In the Johnson administration, Henry Jackson was a powerful senator, a warhawk important to the administration in support of its troubled foreign policy—and so a man not to be ignored by Interior.

However, both Vine Deloria and Udall's staff believed that it was not so much Jackson but one of his Senate Interior Committee staffers, James Gamble, who was the prime mover in keeping the termination effort alive in the '60s. Udall observed: "Jim Gamble (James H. Gamble), who Senator Anderson brought in (Clint Anderson, NM) was about as unsympathetic and hostile to Indians as anyone in the county. So he was there throwing his weight around almost as though he were a Senator, trying to block anything."[59] Udall's aide Oren Beatty said of Gamble, "He has very fixed views on Indian affairs and he runs the subcommittee. It's just that simple. The Senators in my mind are just figureheads." As to why the initiative was left in Gamble's hands, Beatty suggested of the senators themselves that, "they all just viewed it as a losing proposition; you can't solve it; it's going to cost money; it won't show any results even though you do spend it."[60]

Vine Deloria noted: "Rarely does a judgment bill come before the committee but what Gamble tries to have a termination rider attached. So powerful is Gamble that Jackson [Senator Henry Jackson] might be characterized as his front man" (Deloria 1969:78). Whether this vision of a single staffer as key was correct, the fact remains that throughout the Johnson era new Indian policy proposals had to pass muster with both a Congress still tilted toward termination and a Native American constituency opposed to any hint of it. Not an easy task.

In the midst of the omnibus bill debate, Senator George McGovern had introduced a Senate resolution which effectively, but not explicitly, repudiated the terminationist HCR 108 (SCR #11). This was debated more or less simultaneously with the omnibus package, and the resolution, unlike the bill, did at least pass in the Senate, very late in the administration (September 1968).[61] It was never taken up by the House, and HCR 108 remained on the books. This resolution had no significant impact on policy but did put on record the fact that there were contending schools of thought on termination in Congress. Congress was no longer single-mindedly bent on getting out of the Indian business.

Indian "Activism"

Udall faced not just a lack of Indian support but active Native American opposition to his bill. Vine Deloria summed up what seems to have been a general Indian perspective on the omnibus bill: that it "suggested that Indians might consider mortgaging their lands to get enough money to embark on development schemes. . . . If the project did not succeed, the bureau could walk away from its responsibilities, leaving the tribe not only bankrupt but potentially landless" (1984:224). The NCAI editorialized against it, calling it the "Ominous" bill (NCAI 1967:8). By the time of the 1968 presidential campaign, a Nixon Indian campaign staffer was making political hay by saying, "The Senate Bill, s.1816 or Indian Resources Development Act, which resulted from the 1960 Democratic Platform, is a Bill of devious means for obtaining Indian land."[62]

Udall's use of language that tended to sound like termination might, in part, have been due to an expectation that there would be little Indian resistance. Indian views had not been critical in determining Indian policy up to this time, as witness allotment and termination.

The new level of active Native American opposition, surfacing to help sink the omnibus bill, was a part of a new general energizing of the Indian leadership in the cause of resisting termination. Jim Officer noted earlier Indian opposition to proposed "heirship" legislation. "The defeat of the Legislation also made clear to Congress and the Executive department that the fight against termination had enabled Indians to assemble a strong lobbying force for the first time in their history" (1984:83). In later years, Udall said, "I was glad to see young Indians being militant. I thought we needed this for several years and I thought it was the passivity of the Indians, the way they accepted everything, that caused so little to be done, that this was one of the reasons at least."[63]

The National Congress of American Indians (NCAI) was the principal rallying point for this lobbying, though it had previously been a very low key organization (Hertzberg 1971:271). Vine Deloria was able to galvanize considerable unified tribal support by acting as a sort of termination Paul Revere. Still, Deloria later oddly noted: "The battle over the Omnibus Bill was the last unified resistance by the older tribal leaders. Thereafter they buttered their own bread with the Johnson administration, and later with the Nixon administration, endorsing whatever policies they were asked to endorse" (1974:32).

Deloria's statement is questionable. The omnibus struggle was not the last but the first stirring of what was to be a rising tide of activism by tribal government leaders throughout the '60s and into the '70s. Much of the media attention shifted to the more theatrical actions of youthful "new Indians," who may have seemed to Deloria in 1974 to be supplanting older tribal leaders, but the elected leaders of Indian tribes never ceased to play an important role (Steiner 1968).

There were moves toward organizing increased militancy among younger Native Americans, notably the formation of the National Indian Youth Council (NIYC) in 1961 (Hertzberg 1988:316). At the time of the omnibus bill struggle, these young activists still had little audience outside of Indian country and not all that much inside it. The new media-oriented (rather than lobbying-oriented) style of Native American activism that was emerging was partly a byproduct of the civil rights movement. As early as 1958 the Lumbee of North Carolina had gained national attention as a result of confrontations with the Klan (Sider 1993:101; Dial and Eliades 1975:158).

Though the influence of the civil rights movement in sparking higher levels of Indian activism cannot be doubted, the Indians were also independent to a considerable degree in their activist origins. The central issues for Native American protest were very different. As Vine Deloria put it, "The white man signed no treaties with the black. Nor did he pass any amendments to the constitution to guarantee the treaties of the Indian" (1969:173). The Native Americans were beneficiaries of the ethnic climate created by the civil rights movement, but the Indian political renaissance was something of a parallel movement, not directly derivative.

Native American organizations like the NCAI did not participate in either the 1963 or 1968 civil rights mass marches on Washington, and the NCAI explicitly refused to endorse the 1968 "Poor Peoples" march (Deloria 1969:169–

95). Some Indians who did participate criticized the NCAI for its stand and provoked an editorial response: "So we challenge the Johnny Come-lately group with the same question they recently asked us 'Where were you when we needed you?' It is fairly easy to get out into the streets and raise hell. In fact it doesn't take any sense at all. But to work steadily day after day on programs and unspectacular legislative problems is another thing altogether" (NCAI 1968:9).

Indian political protest, in the form of staged confrontations to make a point, had begun over fishing rights in 1954, before such things as sit-ins had become commonplace in the civil rights movement. Robert Satiacum and other Puyallups challenged Washington state fishing laws with what inevitably came to be called "fish-ins" (Cohen 1986:67). This uniquely Indian protest spread to other Northwest tribes and generated considerable action in the courts, but little national or federal attention was paid until ten years after it began.

The Northwestern Indian fishing activism finally got greater national media attention in 1964 when the National Indian Youth Council (NIYC) sent delegates to participate in the fish-ins, adding a national component to what had been a local struggle. Still more important in catching the media eye was the participation of celebrity "friends" of the Indian. Marlon Brando made a cameo appearance with Robert Satiacum, inviting token arrest, as did civil rights activists such as Dick Gregory (Cohen 1986:73; Thompson 1979:378). The celebrities, however, moved on to other causes and after a brief moment in the media sun the fishing dispute fell back into obscurity and into a long series of federal and state court decisions which were not fully resolved until 1974.

In the '50s, Watkins and his congressional companions got their termination legislation through Congress, with scarcely a single dissenting voice being heard during the process. In the dispute over the omnibus legislation, Indian input was weak but directly audible in Congress. By the end of his term, Udall observed of this beginning, "They have in recent years begun to acquire the constituency and the political muscle to influence their relationship with the Federal Government in directions and at speeds favorable to them." The Indian voices, however, were still in disarray, and Udall noted his failure to coordinate them, saying, "Our failure to obtain from the 90th Congress an Indian Resources Development Act . . . demonstrates that the Indians themselves must be fully in accord before we can begin even to lay the necessary legal foundation for reservation economic growth" (1968:554–55).

Alaska

Despite the setbacks of the omnibus bill, Udall suggested to the president in December 1967 that "It is my intention to make and implement a maximum of pro-Indian decisions during my remaining time as Secretary . . . whatever the cost or criticism. I intend to put a pro-Indian stamp on the record of this Administration."[64] Specifically, he suggested, "Nothing would give me greater satisfaction than to work out a liberal settlement for the Alaska Native on their aboriginal claims next year."[65] A task force on Alaska Native affairs had met in 1962 to consider the problems of Indian land title occasioned by Alaskan statehood in 1959, but little had been done (Keeler et al. 1962). Udall had earlier indicated to Bennett his desire to "Tackle the native land claims issue head on."[66]

By March 1968 the administration was proposing a land settlement of approximately 10 million acres (with the Alaskan Federation of Natives asking for more than 40 million) and offering approximately $250 million as a share of federal outer-continental-shelf oil and gas revenues in cash compensation, plus a twenty-five-year right to "subsistence" use of other lands.[67] Ultimately, the House and Senate committees and the Alaskan Native groups were unable to agree on an acceptable compromise during the LBJ administration. The final settlement came in the Nixon years and was far more generous than Udall had proposed and thought liberal.

RFK Redo

In August 1967, a Special Subcommittee on Indian Education was created, not by the Committee on Interior and Insular Affairs but by the Committee on Labor and Public Welfare. This was at the initial request of Senator Paul J. Fannin of Arizona but when formed was under the chairmanship of Robert F. Kennedy[68] (Szasz 1974:150). What exactly the political motivation of this end-run around the Jackson-dominated Interior Committee might have been is open to speculation. It is probably not a coincidence that at this point Kennedy was becoming a serious presidential contender and was staking out an independent position on ethnic issues.

Kennedy was separating himself from Johnson and trying to create an independent political identity, so "an increasingly critical Robert Kennedy found fault with something in almost every proposal LBJ put forward" (Califano 1991:260). His sudden interest in Indian education is otherwise remarkable, given that his only previous involvement in things Native American occurred in his days as attorney general and took the form of a serious gaffe, as noted in Chapter 1. Now, having become a carpetbagger senator from New York, he could and did claim an interest based on the large Indian population of his adopted state.[69] The positive aspect of this jockeying for ownership of the Indian issue was as an affirmation that Indian affairs were beginning to take on a degree of political importance. It was now worthwhile for presidential contenders to embrace the Indian cause more actively.

From beginning to end, the Kennedy committee was highly critical and condemned virtually all prior educational work of the Bureau.[70] Kennedy's opening remarks as chairman set the tone when he declared the situation of the Indians "a national tragedy and a national disgrace," and suggested the answer was remarkably simple: "We have chosen a course of learning as obvious as it has been ignored: we are going to listen to the Indian people speak for themselves about the problems they confront."[71] He chose to ignore the moves that the Bureau itself already had undertaken to involve Indians in education, such as the Rough Rock school.

One of RFK's biographers discussed his interest in Indians in a chapter titled, "Tribune of the Underclass," where they are listed right after "braceros and bindlestiffs" (Schlesinger 1978:793). Kennedy seemed intent on using the Native Americans as a surrogate to stress his commitment to the broader issue of this more inclusive "underclass." He linked education to this larger issue, saying, "The American vision of itself is of a nation of citizens determining their own destiny; of cultural difference flourishing in an atmosphere of mutual respect; of diverse people shaping their lives and their children's. This subcommittee today begins examination of a major failure in this policy."[72]

Kennedy appeared on national television to denounce the Indian situation and to bash the administration. Officer noted: "References to BIA on the program were unkind and some inaccurate."[73] In this same vein, RFK appeared before the Senate Interior Committee during its deliberations on Senate Concurrent Resolution #11.[74] His testimony there was equally critical of the administration. When he announced his candidacy for president, he said the administration's "disastrous divisive policies" could change "only by changing the men who are now making them," Indian policy presumably included (Califano 1991:265). Kennedy's committee continued to deliberate without reaching any conclusions during the remainder of the LBJ administration.

Indian Civil Rights

The Indian Civil Rights Act was the only significant piece of foundation Indian legislation to pass during the LBJ era. This was not generated by Udall, Interior, or the task forces but by yet another non-Interior congressional committee. It came about largely through the efforts of Senator Sam J. Ervin, who chaired the Subcommittee on Constitutional Rights of the Judiciary Committee. In 1961, the committee had begun to consider extending the protections of the Bill of Rights to cover the relations of Native Americans to their tribal governments.[75] This six-year effort, described as a "labor of love," sprang from Ervin's interest in the Cherokee and Lumbee in his home state of North Carolina (Burnett 1972:602).

As a southerner with a record of resistance to civil rights, his effort to graft his plan onto the 1968 Civil Rights Act was suspect. "Senator Ervin's goal was either to amend the Civil rights bill into defeat or to have it pass with his Indian rights provisions attached" (606). The simple blanket extension of the Bill of Rights which he first proposed was modified after many objections by the Bureau and the tribes. "Notably absent are limitations similar to the establishment of religion clause, the guarantee of a republican form of government, the privileges and immunities clauses, the provisions involving the right to vote, the requirement of free counsel for indigent accused, and the right of a jury trial in civil cases" (Getches et al. 1993:499).

Ervin's bill did pass as part of the 1968 act, and even as modified it was a mixed blessing for tribal self-government. Despite alterations to protect unique tribal forms of government, the new law created challenges to tribal authority (Wunder 1994). One of the more dramatic instances was on the Navajo reservation, over the right of the tribe to expel the OEO legal services director (Iverson 1981:95–96). Tribal government seemed weakened by inter-posing federal courts between itself and Indian citizens. It was not until 1978 that the bill's impact was much narrowed with the Supreme Court decision *Santa Clara Pueblo v Martinez*, establishing that tribal governments retained a large degree of sovereign immunity from such suits in federal courts (Pevar 1992:245).

A more positive result of the debate over the bill was the successful effort by the Bureau to include in the act language which amended PL 280, requir-ing tribal consent to states' assertions of jurisdiction (Officer 1978:67). In-dian reaction to the civil rights bill was mixed: the PL 280 sections were per-ceived as anti-termination, but much of the rest was seen as threatening sovereignty. The Pueblos in particular were alarmed by a perceived threat to their religious form of government.[76] In terms of the trend toward self-deter-mination, it was at best a case of one step forward and one step back.

Inside Task Force

Even as the omnibus bill was being debated, Joseph Califano appointed Lee White, a JFK holdover and now chair of the Federal Power Commission, to head an Interagency Task Force on American Indians, in August 1967.[77] White was the White House specialist in civil rights, and the other task force mem-bers represented the major agencies that had some hand in Indian matters—Interior, HEW, Commerce, Labor, HUD, Treasury, OEO and the Bureau of the Budget. There was also a White House staff representative, Matthew Nimetz. Their brief was to try to coordinate efforts and create a cohesive Indian policy approach for the administration. This was not a second-guessing of Udall or the outside task force but a normal stage in the process of in-house coordi-nation and filtration in the LBJ administration (Thomas and Wolman 1969).

By October 1967 they issued their report in "administratively confiden-tial" form, limited to only 36 copies.[78] The task force's secrecy caused suspi-cion in Indian country, but it was normal procedure with all LBJ task forces to keep things close until ready for public airing. Their report, entitled "Ameri-can Indian Program for FY 1969," looked beyond the ongoing debate on the omnibus bill, which they'd assumed would become law, but neither they nor Udall anticipated the decision by LBJ not to run.[79] Udall had even asked Officer to do research on presidential inaugurals with an eye to having LBJ include Indians in his second inaugural.[80]

The report did not propose a new legislative program but said, "With imagination and strong leadership, the principal difficulties can be attacked within the existing organization set-up and under existing statutory authorizations."[81] But within existing legislation they did propose some new directions and procedures. The summary stressed "measures that put a premium on Indian self help, self growth and self determination."[82]

Their most innovative recommendations were those that tended in the direction of increased Indian self-administration and restructuring of the federal-Indian relationship. Most of these were included in their recommendations for the content of a presidential message:

> A major Presidential address on Indian policy to (1) acknowledge the Indian's right to retain his identity; (2) announce creation of a National Commission on Indian Opportunity; and (3) pledge Federal support for Indian participation in decisions affecting him, and especially in the educational process on which Indian development ultimately depends— e.g., Indian parent school boards at all Federal schools . . . To give highest visibility to a "people oriented" philosophy, the Bureau of Indian affairs with the Office of Territories should be put under an Assistant Secretary of the Interior for Indian and Territorial Affairs; and BIA's field organization should be restructured to insure closer contact with Indian families and problems.[83]

In general, they recommended actions that the executive branch could take independently of Congress. "Portions of the above program, which stresses self determination rather than termination of Federal support, could be embodied in new legislation. . . . However, the Task Force does not feel that the needed statutory amendments justify a full-blown legislative program."[84]

The impact of the OEO was noted: "The uniqueness of the CAP approach— funding tribal councils directly—has brought a new Indian leadership to the forefront; this largely explains the overwhelming Indian acceptance of the program. For the first time, Federal funds have been entrusted to the complete discretion of Indian tribal councils."[85] They proposed to build on this success. While they recommended spending increases, they said, "More fundamental in this case than money for houses or materials for highways are the decisions and cooperative abilities of the Indians themselves."[86]

Officer had correctly predicted the general character of the report: "The Task Force Report will probably at best be a document which identifies and recommends greater financial support for the best programs now carried on by all the participating agencies." He also observed to Udall that there was a great deal of anti-BIA sentiment on the task force, based (in the case of one member) on "Primarily from reading novels relating events which were hoary when Helen Hunt Jackson wrote *Ramona*."[87] In the end, however, very little Bureau-bashing was evident in the final document.

The Forgotten Remembered

By early 1968, "There was a sense of siege in the White House. It was increasingly difficult to find public forums for the President that avoided disruption from demonstrators opposing the war or demanding more money and programs for blacks and poor people" (Califano 1991:257–58). However, in this atmosphere, rather than retrench and bury new proposals such as Indian self-determination, Califano said, "The President could not hurl programs at Congress and the Public fast enough. He was irritable and impatient when I did not have a draft special message in his night reading to go to Congress the next day" (260). Among this final hurling of messages and proposals, Califano included the "Forgotten Americans," the long-proposed message on Native Americans.

The final version presented by Califano for President Johnson's approval was based on Interior drafts and written by Matthew Nimetz and Ervin Duggan, Califano aides. In the memo transmitting it to Johnson, Califano said, "The main theme of the message is a change in approach from paternalism to full partnership and full choice for the Indians. Udall and Bennett believe this is the most positive statement ever made by a President about the Indians."[88] Johnson approved it and sent it to Congress on March 6, 1968. He did not meet with Indian leaders on the occasion, but Vice President Hubert Humphrey and Secretary Udall met with a gathering at Interior on that day.[89]

The message was, above all, an endorsement of the policy of self-determination that had been slowly percolating through Interior and the task forces.

LBJ made it official policy and also renounced termination, saying, "I propose a new goal for our Indian programs: A goal that ends the old debate about 'termination' of Indian programs and stresses self-determination; a goal that erases old attitudes of paternalism and promotes partnership self-help. . . . I propose, in short, a policy of maximum choice for the American Indian: a policy expressed in programs of self-help, self-development, self-determination."[90] He acknowledged the OEO: "Within the last few months we have seen a new concept of community development—a concept based on self help—works successfully among Indians. Many tribes have begun to administer activities which Federal agencies had long performed on their behalf."[91] On education there was a clear echo of the Rough Rock demonstration: "To help make the Indian school a vital part of the Indian community, I am directing the Secretary of the Interior to establish Indian school boards for Federal Indian schools."[92]

The programmatic steps proposed to bring about the self-determination goals, however, were not so dramatic. The money requested was only a ten percent increase over the previous year's budget (less than the task force had recommended). The only new structural change was the establishment, by executive order, of a National Council on Indian Opportunity, to be chaired by Vice President Humphrey. Most of the rest of the message simply deplored the Indian condition and sounded the usual call for more—for education, housing, health, jobs, etc.

Several controversial proposals fell by the wayside. Notably absent was any mention or endorsement of the transfer of any portion of the Bureau to HEW, or of the elevation of the Bureau to assistant secretary status within Interior. The only specific legislation addressed was in the form of endorsement of the items already pending—the Indian Civil Rights Act, Alaskan Native Claims, and the Indian Resources Development Act. There was a call for modification of PL 280, granting states the right to assert jurisdiction: "I urge the Congress to enact legislation that would provide for tribal consent before such extension of jurisdiction take place."[93]

Udall declared at the meeting with Indian leaders that the change in policy goals expressed in the message were "comparable to only one period: The first years of the New Deal with the John Collier Administration where President Roosevelt changed the whole focus of Indian action."[94] In terms of goals he was essentially correct, but what was lacking was some analog of the 1934 Indian Reorganization Act, which gave teeth to the Roosevelt policy. The goal of self-determination was clearly established, but no very clear path to its achievement was spelled out except through existing mechanisms—and that with little new money.

There was to be little time for the administration to do much more in the way of implementing its new policy. The Indian message was shortly followed by LBJ's, "I shall not seek and will not accept" announcement (Califano 1991:270). Vice President Hubert Humphrey had little time for his new role on the National Council on Indian Opportunity as he began his own campaign for the presidency. Indian members for the NCIO were, however, commissioned—Roger A. Jourdain, Wendell Chino, Cato Valandra, Raymond Nakai, William J. Hensley, and LaDonna Harris.[95]

LBJ thought that his gesture of withdrawal from the presidential race would allow him greater latitude to press Congress for support of his social policies. Instead he found himself in a fight to save his existing Great Society program against a cost reduction campaign led by Wilbur Mills, chair of the House Ways and Means Committee. He was also assailed by representatives of the very constituencies he sought to help. Joseph Califano noted: "The President's fight to protect the Great Society from Wilbur Mills and the conservatives was not helped by the Poor Peoples Campaign that camped out in the nation's capital during the Spring of 1968. . . . Abernathy excoriated the administration and Congress and called the social and legislative advances of the prior five years a record of 'broken promises' " (286–87). Caught between those who wanted much more and those who wanted much less, little political progress could be made in the last days of the lame duck administration.

In the end, the omnibus bill never got out of committee, and the Alaskan Native Claims legislation bogged down in a struggle with the Bureau of the Budget over the magnitude of the settlement. Even the implementation of Indian school boards was delayed by the BOB's insistence that they be strictly advisory.[96] Marburger, in his brief tenure as assistant commissioner of education, did organize a National Indian Education Advisory Commission that the Bureau consulted on policy in Bureau schools (Szasz 1974:155). The Indian civil rights proposals—including modification of PL 280 to require Indian consent—attached as titles of the 1968 civil rights bill were the only items to become new law (82 U.S. Stat. 73).

If not as much in the way of foundation legislation had emerged as Udall had hoped, a new policy climate had been created which made an overt return to termination politically unlikely. Appraising that climate, Officer observed in a 1968 address to the NCAI, "no matter who is elected President in November, the relationship between Indians and the Federal government is in for some kind of redefinition—perhaps a drastic one" (Officer 1968:17). Indian voices had been heard for good or ill in the scuttling of the omnibus bill, and from here on Indian participation would be increasingly important in the policy process. Officer urged the NCAI that "the time has come for this organization to take a positive approach to new legislation aimed at freeing the Indians to make more decisions for themselves" (20).

In the historical literature, Udall and Johnson have received scant credit for their contribution to Indian affairs. Rebecca Robbins has called Johnson's message a " 'duty' speech," and suggested, "clearly his heart or mind, or that of the administration was not in it" (1990:32–33). Deloria observed that "Udall proved a tremendous disappointment to the Indian people in his years as head of the Interior Department. Too many times he was totally unresponsive to Indian proposals" (1969:254). Margaret Szasz said of the era, "What encouragement Indians did receive came primarily from Congress and the Office of Economic Opportunity (OEO). Udall's supervision of the Indian Bureau in the 1960s deserved little credit for the growth of self determination, in spite of his public demands for policy changes" (1974:157).[97]

Udall more accurately appraised his era, perhaps even overmodestly, in an article, "State of the Indian Nation," written as he was leaving office in 1968. He observed:

> The staff of the venerable Bureau of Indian Affairs has come closer to a general acceptance of the fact that Indians are not only capable of making critical decisions without constant supervision by Federal Bureaucrats, but must be given the opportunity to do so. I do not assume credit for the latter development although I have encouraged it. Rather it has

been most influenced by changes in the mood of the country and of the Congress—changes induced by the war on poverty and by a more critical analysis of the problems of America's minority groups.

I will leave office in January hopeful that the trend toward diminishing the high degree of Federal paternalism in Indian affairs has been so well set in recent years that it will be difficult to reverse. Henceforth, the pace and direction of change in this regard will, I believe, largely depend on the desires of the Indians. (1968:554)

He further prophesied that "President-elect Nixon, if we are to judge from his campaign statements, seems inclined to continue the kind of Federal policy enunciated by President Johnson" (8). As it happened, he was a good prophet. Major shifts in federal Indian policy had been inexorably set in motion and would come to legislative fruition in the Nixon and Ford administrations.

New Federalism and a New Era

> The Time has come to break decisively with the past and to
> create the conditions for a new era in which the Indian future
> is determined by Indian Acts and Indian decisions.
> —President Richard M. Nixon, Special Message to the Congress on
> Indian Affairs, July 8, 1970

A "new Nixon" appeared during the 1968 presidential campaign, much changed in his stance on Indian affairs, as in many other matters. Without any mention of the "Forgotten Americans" message of Lyndon
Baines Johnson or its theme of self-determination, Nixon brought up the
new goal in a campaign statement to the NCAI: "A Brighter Future for the
American Indian."[1] In 1960 he had said, "the constructive Indian programs
of the past eight years will be continued, expanded and intensified," even
though those years had been dominated by programs of termination.[2] In
1968, after eight years of Democratic control and a policy trend moving away
from termination, he nonetheless managed to imply Democratic fault, saying, "The Indian people have been continuous victims of unwise and vacil-
lating Federal policies and serious, if unintentional mistakes," and, "Their
plight is a bitter example of what's wrong with the bankrupt old approach to
the problems of minorities."[3] He went on to make a series of policy pledges,
including an explicit renunciation of termination: "The Special relationship
between the Federal Government and the Indian people and the special responsibilities of the Federal Government to the Indian people will be acknowledged." He went on, "Termination of tribal recognition will not be a
policy objective and in no case will it be imposed without Indian consent."[4]
He also promised that "The Right of self determination of the Indian people
will be respected and their participation in planning their own destiny will
be encouraged." To this end he would "see to it that local programs and Fed-

eral budgets are operated with minimum bureaucratic restraint and in full consultation with the Indian people who should achieve increasing authority and responsibility over programs affecting them." With specific reference to education, he said, "Independent school boards, funded at government expense, must be urged for each government run school." The rest was yet another promise of more, in economic development, health, and so on.[5]

As Udall and Officer had predicted, in 1968 the political climate in Indian affairs had clearly changed. Nixon now renounced what he once had defended and embraced the shift toward self-administration. Given the momentum established during the Johnson years, it would have taken a compelling negative political motivation for any new administration to turn away from what had been so well received in Indian country. There was no such counter-current, and as it happened, the theme of self-determination turned out to fit very well into the general political patterns established in Nixon domestic policy.

Nixon and the "Chief"

President Richard Milhous Nixon, like Presidents Johnson and Kennedy before him, had no track record of political interest in things Indian. California did have recognized Indian tribes, but Nixon seemed to have had no direct personal involvement with them. He was not involved in any congressional committees which dealt with Indian affairs either in the House or Senate.

His major biographers had nothing to say on the matter of his role in Indian affairs either before or during his presidency (Aitken 1993; Ambrose 1989, 1991; Morris 1990). None of his "Six Crises" prior to his presidency involved Native Americans, and he did not discuss them in his other autobiographical works (Nixon 1962, 1978, 1990). But while his books had nothing to say about his Indian policies, all of them devoted space to the important impact on his life of his Whittier College football coach, "Chief" Wallace Newman (1962:402; 1978:19–20; 1990:104–7).

The influential coach was of Native American ancestry, identified by one biographer as a "mixed blood born on the La Jolla reservation" (Morris 1990:134).[6] Nixon aide Leonard Garment more improbably identified him as a "full blooded Cherokee" (1997:225). In those ethnically less sensitive times it was the almost inevitable fate of any Native American to be called "Chief," but as Bernstein noted of Indian soldiers in World War II, "The word was not the equivalent of a racial slur. . . . 'Chief' signified something other than condescension; it signified respect" (1991:56). That was certainly true in this case.

The extent of Nixon's inclusion of Native Americans in his domestic policy agenda (given their numerical voting insignificance) may have been influenced by the simple happenstance that a man very important to him personally was of Native American heritage. Once elected, Nixon had many good political reasons for courting larger traditional democratic ethnic constituencies in his efforts to build a "New Majority" for the Republican Party (Safire 1975:486). His chief of staff, H. R. Haldeman, noted that, "p wants to build up 'forgotten minorities' idea" (1994:212). The Indians were certainly among the most forgotten, but it may have been Chief Newman who caused Nixon to remember them.

In his first presidential term Nixon did not spend a great deal of his official time on Indian affairs, any more than did Johnson or Kennedy. His more personal concern for Native Americans seemed to surface in private and unguarded moments. In the dawn hours of May 8, 1970, Nixon left the White House with only his valet for an impromptu mingle with students who had gathered at the Lincoln Memorial to protest his Cambodian bombing policy. He talked with them about many things, including his concerns about ethnic relations, and said, "What we have done with the American Indians is, in its way, just as bad as what we imposed on Negroes. We took a proud and independent race and destroyed them. We have to find ways to bring them back into decent lives in this country" (Safire 1975:206). In a press conference the next day, aide Ron Ziegler quoted Nixon as saying, "the Indians in this country are the most mistreated of all our people."[7] Louis Bruce, Nixon's first BIA commissioner, confided to Robert Hecht "that Nixon simply thought that Indians had gotten a raw deal in history and wanted to help them" (Hecht 1991:301). Similarly, Garment noted of his plans for new Indian programs that "Nixon felt an empathy for Indians, America's home grown victims, losers, and survivors. I sensed from the start he would support us" (1997:225).

Whether it was the Chief, or a practical concern with the political clout of the minorities issue, or a genuine concern for the plight of Native Americans, Nixon did in fact indicate to his key domestic policy staff that he would look favorably on new Indian policy initiatives. They took that cue as a mandate to pursue a very active program in Native American affairs. His principal domestic policy aide, John Ehrlichman, recalled:

> Nixon had a very benign attitude toward Indians. We used to smile behind our hands about it because he was fond of talking about Chief Newman who was his football coach at Whittier College, who was an Indian. And he used to go on and on, he could rhapsodize about this brave Native American who instilled in his football students the ideals of manhood and Americanism and all this stuff. And that may or may not have been what really lay behind this.
>
> On another occasion in private Nixon said to me, 'You know, Indians are the only manageable minority we have.' He said, 'We can accomplish something with and for Indians. They're numerically convenient, they are identifiable, they're not radicalized (this was before AIM), and so we ought to have some good programs for Indians. We ought to do something for Indians. They'll be grateful, people will see we're doing things, that we're not prejudiced against minorities, and so forth. So anything you can come up that does good for Indians, let's do it.' Now, that was the climate.[8]

The mixture of practical political motivation and gut-level benevolence on the part of the new president was evident in a memo from his chief of staff Bob Haldeman written in the very first month of the administration. "RN would like somebody to make a study of the Indian Bureau, and particularly Bobby Kennedy's approach to the Indian Problem, and to come up with some recommendations for us. He feels very strongly that we need to show more heart, and that we care about people, and thinks the Indian problem is a good area for us to work in."[9]

The use of the Indians to "show heart" on the issue of minorities was also suggested by other administration staff. Leonard Garment noted "negative" perceptions of "this administration in the black and Spanish speaking community," and suggested "Reference to the new Indian program as a model of our concern for some of our nation's underdogs."[10] Other observers thought that there was in the administration "a feeling that the Indian offers a chance to demonstrate that private enterprise and minority capitalism might be the best solution to the problems of poverty, whether Indians, Negro, Puerto Rican or Appalachian" (Strickland and Gregory 1970:433).

Why the poor standing with other minorities and the need to use the Indians as surrogates? The Nixon administration did move forward on the civil rights issues more directly important to larger ethnic constituencies. The problem was, in part, a problem of perception. Wicker noted that in regard to desegregation, many thought that "if Richard Nixon had had anything useful to do with it, his hand had been forced by the courts, he had complied reluctantly, and anyway, why hadn't he done it a year earlier" (Wicker 1995:505). It was also a matter of timing, as Hoff observed: "Any administration following Johnson's was bound to suffer from the fallout over rising expectations" (Hoff 1994:81).

Josephy Report

As a result of the presidential request forwarded by Haldeman, Alvin M. Josephy was commissioned to make a report on Indian affairs for the White House. The report was produced exactly one month from the date of request and did not involve any new research or consultation with Native Americans.[11] In the staff memo forwarding the report, they observed "a Senate Subcommittee, headed by Ted Kennedy, is to begin hearings next Tuesday on Indian Affairs, more or less picking up where Bobby Kennedy left off last year. This will no doubt create some immediate stir on this subject. This leads me to recommend that we announce as soon as possible—and surely before Tuesday—that we have this report in hand and are giving serious consideration to the Indian problem."[12] Such an announcement was made the day before the Indian education committee renewed its hearings, saying, "The President has received and has under consideration a study of the Bureau of Indian affairs," and indicating that it was "highly critical of the structure and operations of the Bureau."[13]

This pattern of stealing the Democrats' political lunch by preemptive strike was to become a common tactic of the Nixon White House. A Haldeman aide, Stephen Bull, later passed on the Josephy material to John Ehrlichman, saying, "At the time that we received this report, information came to light that a Congressional Committee was about to initiate hearings the following Tuesday (February 18). In order to deflate this effort for our own purposes, a press release was issued the Monday prior."[14] That purpose having been accomplished, "We still have this Josephy report which we bragged about last month and have done virtually nothing with it. . . . I am forwarding the entire Indian file to you with the question 'what next?'"[15]

Josephy's report recognized, as did everyone by now, the need to renounce the termination policy. Despite the fact that Nixon had already specifically renounced it in his campaign, Josephy suggested he do it yet again, "making clear that the new administration has no intention of disrupting the Indian peoples by new directions in policy" (Josephy 1971:97). The basic problem, he suggested, was the BIA itself. "The top priority is for a change in the administration of Indian affairs to accelerate Indian progress . . . utilizing and not impeding the Indian's development of self determination" (108).

In the end, nothing much was done with this report's specific suggestions, but it did provide some starting points for familiarizing the newcomers with background and the issues involved. Leonard Garment did not even mention the report in his account of the formation of Nixon Indian policy (Garment 1997). The Josephy report was largely interesting as an indication of what was then common coin among those knowledgeable about Indian affairs. Analyzing it, William King said, "This is a fairly innocuous document which contains its share of good suggestions."[16] He also suggested that Josephy "views contracts, it seems, as do most Bureau personnel, as innovative programs to be added to the panoply of existing programs." In his own opinion, "Further emphasis on tribal service contracts could do more to change the Federal-Indian systems along the lines sought by Mr. Josephy, than by leaving the administrator-administered confrontation intact, and making the existing system which serves it more 'efficient.'"[17]

King, who had done much to originate the self-determination policy, offered some of his own views to the new administration about the climate in Indian country. "There is virtually total consensus that Indians increasingly should control their own individual and collective destinies. . . . The objective seems at last obtainable by the Bureau's contracting away some of its programs. . . . Properly planned and executed—initially with full Indian consent and with subsequent full Indian involvement—no activity suggested in the past 100 years so thoroughly could redefine the Indian-federal relationship."[18] Outgoing commissioner Robert Bennett also prepared a summary listing of "Legislative activity and problems" for the new administration, but it made no new proposals.[19]

The Kennedy Report

A second report came to the attention of the administration in that first year. The Indian Education committee, originally chaired by Robert Kennedy and now by Edward Kennedy, finally issued a report in November 1969: "Indian Education: A National Tragedy—a National Challenge." The title kept the phrase "national tragedy" that Robert Kennedy had used on the first day the committee had met some eighteen months earlier, suggesting the committee had started with certain assumptions and retained them to the end.[20]

In the report, the committee members repeatedly declared themselves to be "shocked" at what they found. "What concerned us most deeply as we carried out our mandate, was the low quality of virtually every aspect of the schooling available to Indian children. The school buildings themselves; the course materials and books; the attitude of teachers and administrative personnel; the accessibility of school buildings—all are of shocking quality."[21] They went on to make a laundry list of sixty often unrealistic recommendations, including setting up a rival subcommittee to Interior, on the "Human Needs of American Indians." Margaret Szasz noted that "Not surprisingly, the Kennedy report was ill received by the Bureau of Indian affairs" (1974:152).

One of the Bureau educators, Madison Coombs, wrote a refutation of the Kennedy conclusions: "The Indian Student is *not* Low Man on the Totem Pole" (Coombs 1970). Doubting the integrity of the Kennedy study he said, "they obscure the encouraging advances which Indian people are making in education, largely through their own efforts. . . . No people can enjoy being told repeatedly that they are the lowest of the low when they are trying to work their way up—and especially when it isn't so" (2). Yet another and considerably more objective "National Study of American Indian Education" was conducted in this same time period (1968–70) under funding from the Office of Education. The results were published as *To Live on This Earth: American*

Indian Education (Fuchs and Havighurst 1972:295). While critical of the Bureau programs, this work was more measured and took exception to some of the same basic research the Kennedy staff had accepted as gospel.

The Nixon administration did not do much with the Kennedy report. Its major influence may have been to reinforce the administration's desire to do better than Kennedy's in Indian affairs. William Safire noted what he called the "Kennedy Criterion" and said, "Nixon's standard as a modern President, conscious or not, was John F. Kennedy. The Kennedy 'myth' appealed as it appalled; how, the Nixon men asked each other, could so much legend be made out of so little accomplishment?" (Safire 1975:152). The efforts to best the Kennedys in Indian affairs simply added to Nixon's other more laudable motives for supporting innovation in Indian affairs.

The Domestic Council and New Federalism

During the administrations of LBJ and JFK the initiatives for change in Indian affairs within the government came mostly from Interior, Udall, and his close staff. In the Nixon administration, the activists were more often to be found in the White House itself. Described as the "Imperial Presidency" for his concentration of power, Nixon had set out to centralize control over the executive branch (Schlesinger 1975). This process took much management and decision-making power away from the various cabinet departments—including Interior (Nathan 1975; Greene 1992).

The principal White House mechanism devised to coordinate its control of the domestic side of policy was the Domestic Council. It was designed as an internal analog of the National Security Council and was largely managed by John Ehrlichman (Reichley 1981:239; Kessel 1975). Nixon brought in two rather divergent figures as his personal domestic policy advisors—the conservative economist Arthur Burns and the liberal Democrat Patrick Moynihan (Reichley 1981:68). His former law partner, Leonard Garment, another liberal Democrat, had a special brief on civil rights and minorities. These "White Hats," as William Safire titled them, guided the president toward a surprisingly liberal domestic legislative agenda, including Moynihan's "Family Assistance Plan," which amounted to a guaranteed minimum income program (Safire 1975:99; Burke and Burke 1974).

However liberal in some aspects, Nixon was by no means endorsing the preceding Democratic Great Society. The OEO, centerpiece of that effort, was acknowledged for its contributions by Nixon in his initial 1969 national message on plans for domestic policies, but he also announced its overhaul. "OEO is to be a laboratory agency where new ideas for helping people are tried on a pilot basis. When they prove successful, they can be spun off to operating departments or agencies."[22] Donald Rumsfeld ran the agency for Nixon, diligently spinning off its components—Project Head Start to the Office of Education, for example (Levitan and Hetrick 1971:91). Nixon was prevented by Congress from dismantling the agency completely, but it was converted in 1974 into the less activist Community Services Administration (Matusow 1984:270; Hoff 1994:60–65).

The Native American Community Action programs were among the successful spin-offs. At first Leonard Garment suggested that they not be taken out of the OEO but that the entire Bureau be moved *into* the OEO, and "What the President would tell OEO to do is turn Indian affairs on reservations into Indian hands as much as possible."[23] Like many other schemes to relocate the Bureau, that move was not to be. After the OEO itself declined, "The Indian Division of OEO was transferred intact with all staff, programs and budget, moving to the Office of Human Development," where it became the "Office of Native American Programs."[24]

The Nixon administration announced a general domestic policy theme it called "New Federalism" as "the first major reversal of the trend toward ever more centralization of government in Washington, D.C., . . . a New Federalism in which power, funds and responsibility will flow from Washington to the States and to the people."[25] William Safire composed a New Federalist paper: "This much we knew: Power should be permitted to seek the level where the problem can most fairly and expeditiously be handled. 'Power to the people' was a slam bang slogan; local control and 'participatory democracy' were fashionable ideas after forty years of the accretion of power to the central government; and decentralization was certainly the direction Nixon had in mind" (Safire 1975:220).

Indians were not the only minorities to benefit by this thrust toward local self-government. Where the JFK administration had regarded the peoples of the trust territories as "primitive," the Nixon administration "established 'home rule' (local voting rights) in the District of Columbia, Guam, American Samoa, and the Virgin Islands" (Hoff 1994:94).

A central element of New Federalism was the use of "block grants" (Conlan 1988:23). This was often described as revenue sharing: "taking the 'categorical grants,' which had been doled out by Washington and mother-henned all the way by central government, and changing them to 'bloc' grants, dropping specific guidelines so as to let local government direct the money and accept responsibility for its decisions" (Safire 1975:223).

Early on, several members of the administration proposed to promote Indian self-administration by this means. "The enactment of the proposed Indian revenue sharing program would, with a single stroke, provide the resources needed to assure a degree of self-determination for every Indian group in the nation."[26] Neither Indian nor any other form of revenue sharing was to get through Congress, but the Nixon administration would move in the same direction by other methods.

John Ehrlichman, head of the Domestic Council, seemed like Nixon to have been personally benignly inclined toward Indian matters. Ehrlichman was one of the few major figures in the administration to discuss Indian affairs in his writings, saying, "We had inaugurated some praiseworthy Indian policies—self determination being our central theme—and we were gaining some recognition, thanks to Bobbie Greene Kilberg, Len Garment, Brad Patterson and the other White House staff people who urged Nixon at the right times and in the right directions" (Ehrlichman 1982:103).

Ehrlichman's main contribution while in office was to support the initiatives brought to him by this staff, but after leaving the White House he took a very active personal interest at the sharp end of Indian affairs. He sought, for example, to do public service on the reservations when sentenced for his Watergate involvement (Wicker 1995:519). Though that request was denied, Patterson noted that on his own "he spent some time on the Navajo reservation. He chose to do this as a sort of penance. . . . I got this call from John, 'I'm calling out here from Black Mesa. You know, do you suppose you could find a used four-wheeled drive jeep that we could use out here as an ambulance?'"[27] In a letter to Leonard Garment, Patterson remembered, "The man who sat at the right hand of the President of the United States is now worried about the adequacy of the Pinon school."[28]

Leonard Garment had "the status of resident liberal conscience on civil rights matters" (Safire 1975:574). Although most of his recommendations went through Ehrlichman and the Domestic Council, he had a degree of direct access to—and in certain special areas considerably more influence on— Nixon than his rank as "special consultant" might suggest. "Nixon knew that Garment was an important counterweight in the White House" (Safire 1975:574). Garment recalled, "I had certain delineated areas. I was responsible for minority issues, which included civil rights" (Garment 1987:101). Later, he wrote, "I gradually became White House counsel to power impoverished parts of the federal government, resident advocate for the great unwashed of the executive branch" (Garment 1997:156).

Garment had an executive assistant, Bradley J. Patterson Jr., a very experienced government career man. "He knew how and by whom policy was formed in the federal government" (157). The two soon came to include Native Americans in their wider "minority" brief and between them shaped much of the Nixon Indian policy. Patterson noted that he was "considered a resident overseer on Indian matters here in the White House. . . . On Indians my role has been more like 90% and his (Garment) was 10 [sic] in terms of time, man hours. Obviously he came in on the key points, and he was in every case my supervisor."[29]

Ehrlichman noted of the White House domestic policy staff in regard to Indian affairs that:

The activists on my staff were Bobbie Kilberg and Brad Patterson. Leonard Garment had sort of his own boutique assignment in the White House, civil rights and minorities, but he didn't report to me. And from time to time they would come up with inspirations generated often from the outside. Bobbie was connected with LaDonna Harris and a lot of others and Brad was somewhat connected with the Indian lobbyists and people of that kind. And they would come in with good ideas.

And somewhere early on the whole self-determination thing was broached. Where do we stand? And we took the most liberal available view. It was just as simple as that.[30]

Bobbie Greene Kilberg was a White House fellow assigned to

Ehrlichman's deputy Kenneth Cole, who became part of the Domestic Council staff. LaDonna Harris, wife of Oklahoma senator Fred Harris, was an active supporter of Indian causes and president of Americans for Indian Opportunity.

When he first took up his work for the president in minority affairs, Garment noted, "I knew what most New Yorkers knew about the Indians' social problems, which was virtually nothing" (1997:223). The Nixon message on Native Americans was initially stimulated, in Patterson's recollection, by yet another Indian report, *Our Brother's Keeper: The Indian in White America* (Cahn 1969). The report was even more sweepingly negative than the Kennedy effort. Discussing the Bureau, it said that "Our Brothers Keeper has fabricated an artificial world for the Indian—a world that degrades, alienates and destroys him" (188). It repeated every possible charge against the federal government, including blame for introducing scalping (176). Like the Kennedy report, it offered little beyond blame, even calling itself a "report without recommendations" (188). Patterson recalled in an interview with this author:

> Garment said, 'Come on Patterson, let's do this.' So we knew nothing about Indian affairs, no background, no history, no nothing. No expertise. Babes in the woods. I mean we had a brain, and we had general American history but no expertise, no scholarship. So Garment arranged a meeting . . . Agnew and Garment and I and Agnew's staff, Bob Robertson, listened to these Indian people talk about . . . the problems of Indian affairs. And we were impressed—they made a very impressive presentation and we in effect came out of that meeting saying, 'Well, let's do something about it.'
>
> Just around that time into our office comes a memo from Ehrlichman which says, 'We're gathering ideas for a presidential policy initiative in 1970 that he can announce in the State of the Union message. Things he's planning to do, messages he's planning to send to Congress during 1970, and he wanted to mention in the State of the Union message.' So he said, 'You got any ideas?' And this memo went all around the White House. And Garment and I took one look at this memo and

said, 'Here's an idea, John. What about a special message on Indian Affairs?' And that went to Ehrlichman, and within days the word came back, 'Good idea, get going on it, you do it.'

And then we began to spread out and talk to people, and we talked to Josephy and we talked particularly to these people who were coming into the Bureau of Indian Affairs like Louis Bruce and Sandy MacNabb and Ernie Stevens.... We worked on this.... Bob worked his field hearings and taking these ideas out in the Indian communities around the field, and by June we had a draft message. We had a memo to the President. And it was a very good memo proposing a whole raft things to be in a message.... Ehrlichman of course took it to the President, and it was approved. And then it was sent back.... it went to the speech writers.... Lee [Huebner] got the assignment. I remember him coming into my office, and we spent two hours at least on my giving him the background of this memo and what all this was about and what we were trying to do. That was the origin of the Nixon message of July 8, 1970, which set the agenda.[31]

Things were probably less linear than Patterson's account might have suggested, but it clearly reflected the key role of the White House staff. Garment indicated that the opening paragraph of the message was contributed by yet another player, Pat Moynihan (1997:226). While indicating that they had consulted with Interior, Patterson noted, "There were four of us—Ward, Robertson, Garment and me in the White House. Handled the whole thing. ...Obviously, we showed it to Interior ... consulted with, called them in, but nothing in the initiative was theirs."[32] Bobbie Greene Kilberg had independently suggested that "I think the time has come to begin considering a Presidential message on Indians" in March 1970.[33]

In my interviews with Patterson and Ehrlichman, I pointed out the start of a self-determination theme in the LBJ presidency, but both denied any connection. Bobbie Greene Kilberg did raise the LBJ message in her call for a Nixon version, but only negatively: "I am fearful of being left in the position of President Johnson who, in light of his March 1968 Indian message, is viewed by much of the Indian population as just another easy talker with a record of

unfulfilled promises."[34] All of the White House staff were new to Indian affairs and had little knowledge of what had gone before, but it seems unlikely
there was no awareness of a policy Nixon himself had addressed in the campaign.

When I asked where the phrase "self-determination" itself came from,
Patterson said, "Oh, I think that was probably the Indian people themselves
came up with it."[35] By 1969 the phrase had indeed become pervasive in Indian country and occurred frequently in the Cahn document as well as the
Josephy report. To the White House newcomers it probably did seem to be
coming from everywhere, especially from the Indian people. Whatever the
source of the phrasing, the new administration's Indian program had taken
rough shape by April, had been proposed to the president by June, and had
been transformed into a "message" by July.[36]

National Council on Indian Opportunity

Under LBJ, the newly created NCIO was stillborn, coming as it did at the very
end of his administration. Vice President Spiro Agnew resuscitated it, though
there was some consideration of eliminating it for lack of funding authorization.[37] Originally composed of the secretaries of Agriculture, Commerce, HUD,
Interior, Labor, and the OEO, plus six appointed Indian representatives, it was
expanded to eight Indian members by Nixon.[38] Robert Robertson was the
NCIO executive director.

Ehrlichman did not feel that much in the way of policy was made by the
NCIO staff. "I'd say in general, the Vice President and his commission were
not players."[39] The NCIO did become an important sounding board for the
collection of Native American inputs. Robertson often held meetings in Washington with Indian representatives, but the formal field hearings at nine locations around the country that Patterson referred to above were not held
until *after* the Nixon Indian message.

The NCIO staff were instrumental in encouraging the formation of the
National Tribal Chairmen's Association. This was proposed but failed to be
endorsed (by two votes) at the NCAI conference "On Indian Self Determination," March 8–12, 1971.[40] In April, a group of tribal chairs formed the organization, which subsequently received support and funding through the NCIO

(Tyler 1973:262). "Membership is limited to the chief elected official of each Federally recognized tribe," creating a forum for a "government to government" interchange (Taylor 1983:139).

Approaching the 1970 congressional elections, "Some candidates were sending word that Agnew would not be welcome in their districts or states" (Ehrlichman 1982:103). Hoping to get some mileage out of their "praiseworthy Indian policies," with which Agnew was associated through the NCIO, Nixon ordered, "Let's put Agnew on at least six Indian reservations between now and November. . . . Let's tie him to Indians. And," he said, as if determined to solve all of his problems at once, "Pat [Nixon] should also do Indians" (103). After the positive reaction to the message, Indians were apparently taking on the character of a "safe" constituency. Ehrlichman commented, "It was a safe place to put Agnew because Indians are ladies and gentlemen, so they weren't going to throw anything at him."[41]

Interior and the Bureau

Nixon's choice for interior secretary, former governor of Alaska Walter Hickel, also turned out to be remarkably sympathetic to Indian issues, although he was initially greeted with considerable suspicion by Native Americans. At the 1969 NCAI meeting Deloria said, "Not since George Armstrong Custer's sensitivity-training session on the banks of the Little Big Horn had so many angry Indians surrounded a representative of the United States government with blood in their eyes" (Deloria 1975:165). The Custer metaphor seems to have been popular, presumably because of Deloria's book *Custer Died for Your Sins* (1969), because Hickel observed, " 'If you liked Custer, you'll love Hickel.' This was the slogan with which a group of militants greeted me" (Hickel 1971:165). Hickel noted, "At the root of the hostility was fear that the Republican administration, which I represented, would reactivate the policy of the Eisenhower years known as termination"—everyone apparently having forgotten both Truman's role in forming the policy and the Nixon campaign's disavowal of it (165).

The disruptions at this NCAI meeting, and at one the previous year, also marked the beginning of a tension between the reservation-based NCAI and urban Indian "militants" (Hertzberg 1988:320). "NCAI President, Wendell

Chino, had to take the microphone to plead with the militants to 'offer the Secretary due courtesy as an official of this great country of ours. The Secretary really has the concern of the Indian at heart'" (Hickel 1971:166).

Hickel had brought an aide with him, Morris Thompson, a Tanana Athabascan, who served in the new position of special assistant to the secretary for Indian affairs. "I wanted someone working closely with me so I would have direct access to an Indian thought or an Indian idea" (165). Hickel also set out to fill the job of commissioner and other key BIA positions with Native Americans. Since Bennett's appointment by LBJ, there was a growing commitment to making the BIA more of an "Indian's Agency," starting self-government at the top. Affirmative action was a Nixon-era innovation, and so this trend was continued (Hoff 1994:90).

Initially, Hickel had considerable trouble coming up with Indians for his staff. "It was next to impossible to find a Republican Indian in the United States, especially after the Eisenhower termination years" (Hickel 1971:167). The administration would not allow him to staff with the more abundant Democratic Indians. One Republican he did find was the Navajo Peter McDonald, but he was deemed to be unacceptable for other reasons. "We finally found an acceptable Republican Indian . . . His name was Louis Rooks Bruce. He was a Mohawk and Oglala Sioux. Bruce was a founding member and a secretary of the National Congress of American Indians" (Hoff 1994:168).[42] Bruce was not a home-grown product of the Bureau like Bennett, nor in fact very well known in Indian country at all, having been a dairy farmer and businessman for most of his career (Cash 1979:334).

The staff of the Bureau shortly ended up in a state of considerable disarray, which lasted for most of Nixon's first term. The selection of Bruce as commissioner took until August 1969, and yet more time was required to find a team of second-tier Native American staffers. In the process there was a degree of restructuring, eliminating the posts of deputy commissioner and six assistant commissioners, shifting some area directors, and creating a group of "field administrators," all of which tended to strengthen the hand of Bruce[43] (Nickerson 1976:66). Garment observed, "What this will really do is permit Bruce to shift—by transfer or retirement—close to seventy-five men who have personified the out of date philosophy of the BIA of yesterday."[44]

Hickel announced to the NCAI "the creation of a new team to run the BIA. In the seventeen top posts under the Commissioner, fifteen were Indian men and women" (Nickerson 1976:179). Indian preference in employment in the Bureau had been around for a hundred years, but under Bennett and now under Bruce, this policy began to create a predominantly Native American agency at the higher levels. Steve J. Novack has argued a downside to this trend: "preferential hiring inadvertently perpetuated Indian dependency," because federal programs had become the largest employers of Native Americans (Novack 1990:654). It also began to create internal problems with those non-Indians being replaced.

Feraca commented in a chapter titled "We're Getting Rid of All These Honkies," that "Immediately upon Bruce's confirmation . . . the Indian preference policy reached new levels of stridency" (Feraca 1990:161). Indian preference, previously largely confined to initial hiring procedures, was expanded in September 1971 when Bruce proposed a policy (which became official in June 1972) "that Indian preference be applicable to the filling of all vacancies in the Indian service whether by initial appointment, promotion or reinstatement. . . . Where two or more candidates who meet the established qualification requirements are available for filing a vacancy, if one of them is an Indian, he shall be given preference in filing the vacancy."[45]

As Bruce began to make controversial changes at the BIA, he encountered congressional opposition. Senator Henry Jackson objected to Bruce's reorganization efforts, and eight days after they were announced, he "requested a halt to the BIA reorganization plan to allow the Senate Subcommittee on Indian affairs time for review of the proposed changes" (Champagne 1992:48). Hickel, however, was supportive of Bruce from the start. In a speech to the NCAI in October 1970, he said "to the new team: Have the courage of your convictions. Go ahead and make mistakes! As long as your aim is better conditions for all Indians, I will back you 100 percent" (Hickel 1971:180). Before the new team could make many decisions, correct or incorrect, Hickel himself was out of office.

Hickel appears to have had little clout at the White House. John Ehrlichman thought of him as a "small timer," and "found him difficult to work with simply because he was less experienced and less informed than his colleagues" (1982:98). Another insider noted that "Hickel rarely got to see Nixon because the President neither liked or respected him" (Safire 1975:192). In May 1970 he committed a political gaffe by releasing a letter to the press "charging that Nixon lacked 'appropriate concern' for dissenting young people who were protesting the war." Ehrlichman said, "By May 21 it was definite: Rogers Morton would replace Hickel, the President told me." In November, Hickel was out (Ehrlichman 1982:98–99).

Fred Malek, chief of the White House personnel office, was given the job of "clearing out Hickel's staff . . . insisting as Haldeman had ordered, that Hickel's staff be out of their offices by the end of the day" (Reichley 1981:244). This included his Indian affairs aide Morris Thompson but did not immediately reach down to the Bureau itself, nor to Assistant Secretary Harrison Loesch.

Rogers Morton, a moderate Republican congressman from Maryland, head of the Republican National Committee in the administration, became the new secretary of the interior. Nixon observed in his memoirs, "I had immense respect for Morton and we saw eye to eye on nearly all issues" (Nixon 1978:313). With the confidence of the president, in January 1971 Morton began to make substantial changes at Interior, including revamping the Bureau structure.

In March 1971, Nixon sent a message to Congress on plans for more general and extensive executive branch reorganization, including the creation of a new Department of Natural Resources, much as Udall had proposed. This was to include Indian affairs "until such time as an acceptable alternative arrangement could be worked out with Indian leaders and other concerned parties."[46]

Bradley Patterson proposed that the Bureau be moved whole to HEW, where "I foresee a BIA which aggressively contracts out its service functions to those Indian tribes and communities which request this contracting."[47] The NCAI at a "National Conference on Indian Self Determination" indicated "general support" for the Nixon legislative package, but proposed the Bureau become an entirely freestanding "Department of Native Affairs."[48] The creation of the new department was never approved by Congress, and the BIA stayed put.

In a meeting in Portland, Oregon, Nixon observed, "frankly, I have not been satisfied with BIA and I don't think the Secretary of the Interior is. . . . I have told him we should look at the whole bureaucracy with regard to our handling of Indian affairs and shake it up and shake it up good."[49] Bruce and his new Bureau team soon became the focus of the shaking. They had become known as the "young turks" for their activist approach. "Primarily young Native Americans oriented toward rapid reform, they had not reached their positions of influence and power in the bureau by moving up the normal bureaucratic ladder" (Cash 1979:335).

Alfonso Ortiz pointed out that many of them had instead gained their administrative experience in the OEO reservation programs and were "known collectively as 'Bruce's Braves'. . . . All were graduates of the War on Poverty" (Ortiz 1986b:19).[50] Like the OEO itself, they tended to be disdainful of the federal bureaucratic establishment and its procedures. To stabilize daily administration and to act as a counterbalance to the active but inexperienced newcomers, Morton reinaugerated the post of deputy commissioner and elevated John O. Crow, the thirty-year BIA veteran, giving him administrative responsibility parallel to that of Bruce (Cash 1979:337; Nickerson 1976:69). The result was yet another new level of internal factionalism of Old Indians vs New Indians.

Remarkably, despite the almost constant staff reorganization and virtual civil war, the Bureau did manage to move forward to implement the new policies put forward in the presidential message. But although it could make some progress on implementation, the internal disarray weakened whatever voice it might have otherwise had in formulating administration policy. As a result of the furor at Interior, Garment and others in the White House were left with the Indian policy ball by default.

Nixon's Indian Message

The Nixon Indian message was put together by White House staff, but it included ideas collected from a variety of sources, including ideas incubated at Interior during the prior administration. The message's central theme of self-determination—plus the explicit renunciation of termination—had already been enunciated in LBJ's message and echoed in Nixon's campaign statement, but unlike the LBJ message, the Nixon message was immediately followed by an implementing legislative package.

In the first substantive section of the message, Nixon sketched his New Era proposals under the heading "Self determination without termination." He declared unequivocally that the "policy of forced termination is wrong" and suggested that it was counterproductive because "the fear of one extreme policy, forced termination, has often worked to produce the opposite extreme: excessive dependence on the Federal government." He declared that "This then must be the goal of any national policy toward the Indian people to strengthen the Indians sense of autonomy without threatening his sense of community."[51] How was this to be achieved? Nixon suggested a series of very explicit actions and proposed legislation or executive action for each of them.

Rejecting termination was his first proposal. "I am asking the Congress to pass a new Concurrent Resolution which would expressly renounce, repudiate and repeal the termination policy as expressed in House Concurrent Resolution 108 of the 83d Congress." He also said, "I hereby affirm for the Executive branch—that the historic relationship between the Federal government and the Indian communities cannot be abridged without the consent of the Indians."[52] If the goal of this was to calm fears of continuing termination efforts, it is hard to imagine how it could have been more definitively worded.

Nixon also spelled out the practical steps leading to self-administration/self-determination:

> In my judgment, it should be up to the Indian tribe to determine whether it is willing and able to assume administrative responsibility for a service program which is presently administered by a Federal Agency. To this end, I am proposing legislation which would empower a tribe or a group of tribes or any other Indian community to take over the control or operation of Federally funded and administered programs in the Department of the Interior and the Department of Health, Education and Welfare whenever the tribal council or comparable community governing group voted to do so.

He stressed this was "a wholly voluntary matter" and that "The 'right of retrocession' is guaranteed," so that if a tribe "later decided to give [a program] back to the government, it would always be able to do so." He further reassured that, "No tribe would risk economic disadvantage from managing its own programs; under the proposed legislation, locally administered programs would be funded on equal terms with similar services still administered by Federal authorities."

For those in Congress who might fear he was simply giving away the keys to the treasury, he assured them that the bill "would also contain accountability procedures to guard against gross negligence or mismanagement of Federal funds." For the states, "This legislation would apply only to the services which go directly to the Indian community," and for the Bureau employees, "If they chose to hire Federal employees who had formerly administered these projects, those employees would still enjoy the privileges of Federal employee benefit programs."

The seminal role of the OEO in promoting self-determination was acknowledged as a means of assuring that the plan was already demonstrably a good idea. "For over four years, many OEO-funded programs have operated under the control of local Indian organizations and the results have been most heartening." So finally, "The time has now come to build on these experiences and to extend local Indian control—at a rate and to the degree that the Indians themselves establish."[53] Compared to these two sweeping sections, the rest of the message was important but anticlimactic.

The Pueblo of Taos had for some sixty-four years sought restoration of "sacred lands" around Blue Lake. Nixon declared, "The restoration of the Blue Lake lands to the Taos Pueblo Indians is an issue of unique and critical importance to Indians throughout the country. I therefore take this opportunity wholeheartedly to endorse legislation which would restore 48,000 acres of sacred land to the Taos Pueblo people."[54]

The message acknowledged problems in Indian education without mention of the dreaded Kennedys despite RFK's chairing of the Indian Education subcommittee. It continued the self-determination theme, suggesting that "at least a part of the problem stems from the fact that the Federal government is trying to do for Indians what many Indians could do better for themselves." Nixon cited the Rough Rock school and other examples of local control as successes and declared, "We believe every Indian community wishing to do so should be able to control its own Indian schools. This control would be exercised by school boards selected by Indians and functioning much like other school boards throughout the nation."

To move in this direction, he announced the creation by executive order of a "Special Education Subcommittee" of the NCIO, composed of Indian educators whose "objective should not be self perpetuation but the actual transfer of Indian education to Indian communities." Adding a little financial backing to the aim, he said, "I propose that the Congress amend the Johnson O'Malley Act so as to authorize the Secretary of the Interior to channel funds under this act directly to Indian tribes and communities."[55]

He suggested economic development provisions which contained odd surviving remnants of elements that made up the defunct omnibus bill in order to "help Indians develop their own economic infrastructure." He said, "To that end, I am proposing the 'Indian Financing Act of 1970.'" It would add to the existing "Revolving Loan Fund," asking it "be increased from approximately $25 million to $75 million." He also proposed "loan guarantees" but avoided the pitfall of the omnibus bill by suggesting these be purely federal with no hint that Indian lands would be put at risk. He did suggest long-term leasing of Indian lands, asking that "legislation be enacted which would permit any tribe which chooses to do so to enter into leases of its land for up to 99 years," but again side-stepped the threatening aspects of leasing by stressing "Long term leasing is preferable to selling such property since it enables tribes to preserve the trust ownership of their reservation homelands."[56]

He also addressed Indian health: "I will request the allocation of an addition $10 million for Indian Health programs." But in addition to the simple more, he said, "These and other Indian health programs will be most effective if more Indians are involved in running them."[57]

He addressed urban Indians: "The BIA's responsibility does not extend to Indians who have left the reservation, but this point has not always been clearly understood." He said that a group of several agencies led by the OEO "will expand support to a total of seven urban Indian centers in major cities which will act as links between existing Federal, State and local service programs and the Urban Indians."[58] In effect, he proposed not an extension of BIA services to the cities but an attempt to hook up the Indians with programs that already served other urban poor. In January, Assistant Secretary Harrison Loesch had issued a strong directive along these lines.[59]

Nixon recommended an "Indian Trust Council Authority" based on "an inherent conflict of interest. The Secretary of Interior and the Attorney General must at the same time advance both the nation's interest in the use of land and water rights and the private interests of Indians in land which the government holds as trustee." Nixon suggested, "I am calling on the Congress to establish an Indian Trust Counsel Authority to assure independent legal representation for the Indian's natural resource rights."

He also recommended a new position of assistant secretary. "Indian affairs in the Interior falls at this point under the Assistant Secretary for Public Land Management—an officer who has many responsibilities in the natural resources area which compete with his concern for Indians. A new Assistant Secretary for Indians and Territorial Affairs would have only one concern."

The message ended with a recitation of deeds done so far in the seventeen months of the administration and suggested that "The recommendations of this administration represent an historic step forward in Indian policy. We are proposing to break sharply with past approaches."[60] Unlike JFK's campaign claim of a sharp break, this one is true.

Nixon met briefly with Taos Indian leaders on the occasion of signing and sending this message to Congress but had no published remarks other than the message itself. A formal press conference was held by Vice President Spiro Agnew and Leonard Garment. Agnew's comments were pro forma. Garment took questions, and in his comments gave widespread credit for preparing the message, saying, "it drew together issues, concepts and themes with respect to the reaffirming and strengthening of the context of Federal trust and treaty responsibility while at the same time, enlarging Indian independence and self assertion and it drew together those things that had been working their way through the various departments of the government for several decades."[61]

The administration moved promptly to send up a package of legislation to implement the proposals spelled out. White House staffer Arnold Weber, however, noted that congressional action was not expected to be imminent: "there is little reason to anticipate further Congressional action on the President's proposals prior to adjournment. There is general consensus we should be prepared to resubmit a legislative program at the outset of the 92d Congress."[62] Garment noted that after the momentum that led to the message, "Most of the administration's Indian reform initiatives . . . got bogged down in the congressional stalemate machine" (1997:227).

Commissioner Bruce immediately suggested steps to be taken in the Bureau "in support of this policy."[63] These were later elaborated by him into a formal policy stance for the Bureau:

In keeping with the President's legislative proposals ... my staff and I
began working to restructure the Bureau at all levels so that its policies
and programs would reflect more closely the thinking and feelings of
Indian people. Five policy goals were announced in November 1970 to
guide the bureau in its new administration of Indian affairs:

(1) transformation of the BIA from a management to a service organization;

(2) reaffirmation of the trust status of Indian land;

(3) making the BIA area offices fully responsive to the Indian people
they serve;

(4) providing tribes with the option of taking over any or all BIA program functions, with the understanding that the bureau will provide
assistance or reassume control if requested to do so; and

(5) working with Indian organizations to become a strong advocate
of off-reservation Indian interests. (Bruce 1976:243–44)

Regarding the Buy Indian act, through which the Bureau had continued to
implement self-administration, Nixon noted in his message, "Two Indian
tribes—the Salt River tribe and the Zuni tribe—have recently extended the
principle of local control to virtually all of the programs which the Bureau of
Indian Affairs has traditionally administered for them," as an example of his
own new directions.[64] In 1968, the Bureau had begun stressing utilization of
the Buy Indian law, and experiments had been underway since 1966.[65] The
Salt River tribe had been among those involved in the very earliest contracting experimentation under Superintendent William King and had moved a
considerable distance toward self-administration, as had the Zuni (Hoikkala
1995).[66]

The language of the "Zuni plan" adopted by tribal resolution made plain
the self-determination theme. "The purpose of this agreement is to maximize the involvement of the Zuni people in the management of their affairs
on the reservation. It is designed to place Bureau of Indian Affairs programs
on the reservation under the administration and direction of the Pueblo government, with the exception of non-delegable trust responsibilities placed in
the Bureau of Indian affairs by the Congress of the United States."[67]

By the time of the president's speech, both the Zuni and the Salt River
tribes were contracting for most services, and in August the Bureau was look-

ing at the Zuni agreement for still more ways "to provide the Pueblo with greater flexibility in the use of appropriated funds in their administration of Bureau activities at the Pueblo."[68] Similar contract arrangements were made with the small newly recognized Miccosukee of Florida (Covington 1993:270).

The need for new contracting legislation remained since there was some considerable doubt about the limits of the mandate given by what one solicitor called the "Buy Anything" act.[69] A legal opinion, "Scope and applicability of the 'Buy Indian' Act," suggested: "Although the 'Buy Indian' act grants no substantive authority to contract, the Bureau of Indian Affairs has cited it as the enabling legislation for several existing and projected programs."[70] The Bureau was obviously pushing the limits, and Nickerson suggests that in June 1970 the contracting came to a halt in a legal dispute with the General Accounting Office (Nickerson 1976:69).

Despite the wrangling over his legal authority, Bruce moved forward very aggressively to extend the participation of Native American leaders in the planning and administration of BIA programs. One of his turks, Alexander (Sandy) MacNabb, was given charge of the drive for contracting with tribes, but Bruce himself was much involved (68). In August 1970 he sent out guidelines for program planning for the coming fiscal year to all area directors and superintendents, and simultaneously sent copies of it to all tribal chairmen.

In his letter to the chairmen, Bruce referred to the president's message and said, "It gives you a clear idea of the administration's policies for Indian people." He also said in reference to the enclosed BIA staff directive that "Superintendents have been told to coordinate their plans with you. After these plans have been developed, please write me a letter giving me your frank opinion on how accurately your wishes and priorities are reflected." Finally, he said, "I want you to see the BIA change from an organization which manages your affairs to a service operation designed to assist Indian people in achieving their goals. You are the only people who should make decisions as to the future of your communities."[71]

Addressing the superintendents on "BIA Program Development," he reminded them that the president's message "expresses the general policy guidance," and he reinforced the self-administration theme, saying, "I place absolute top priority on achieving Indian participation in program development." He also said, "The long term goal that I seek through joint budget development is to give Indian leadership the opportunity to initiate a process of negotiating with local BIA administrators for the tribes to take over and administer a range of programs which we have traditionally administered for them."[72]

The way to this was, of course, contracting. "Contracting with tribes to take over and operate existing BIA programs . . . must be given the very highest priority. Initially this may be accomplished under the 'Buy Indian' contract." He called on the superintendents to reassure tribes that none of this would lead to termination and that "retrocession" was guaranteed and that "our contracting program seeks only to finally place program control where it should have been years ago—in the hands of the Indian people themselves— while keeping full Federal funding and retaining the umbrella of Federal trusteeship."[73]

Congress and Indian Policy

The intentions of both Bruce and the president seem plain, but Bruce had to continue using existing legislation for contracting with the tribes throughout his term as commissioner. The self-determination bill was not even brought up for committee hearings until May 1972. Nixon was, of course, a Republican president confronted with a Congress in which the opposition party controlled both houses. The only hope of passing significant legislation was in putting together bipartisan coalitions for particular bills (Genovese 1990:37). Ehrlichman observed: "In his dealings with the Congress he necessarily allied himself with Senior, conservative Democrats to win critical legislative votes" (1982:196).

When his legislation was "liberal," Nixon ironically had more trouble building such coalitions, the Family Assistance Plan being a case in point. Wicker noted that "Democrats—the political majority in Congress—were unwilling that a Republican President (Richard Nixon of all people) should get credit for such a fundamental reform" (1995:537). Patterson observed, "Some Democratic liberals gagged at the thought of helping the hated Richard Nixon get credit for 'reform' of anything" (Patterson 1988:194). Bobbie Greene Kilberg reported that in regard to Indian legislation, "our favorite Democratic Senator. . . has been informing both the Democrats on the committee and certain interested Democratic non-committee members that supporting our legislation would only make the President and the Republican party look good. 'Why should we help the Republicans?' "[74]

Nixon and his team also suffered from some lukewarm support from Senate Republicans. Leonard Garment noted in 1971 that "there has been little Congressional action on our program ... the Indian community has become very restless about this. Part of our problem lies with Senator Allott and his displeasure with our proposals. While he has agreed to introduce on request some of our bills, he is basically hostile and will not push any of them."[75]

On Indian matters, the Senate Interior committee generally continued to be a greater obstacle than the House. Lloyd Meeds of Washington, who succeeded Wayne Aspinall as the House interior chair in 1971, was supportive of Indian policy initiatives. The chair of the Senate Interior committee, Henry Jackson, a conservative Democrat, was less cooperative. Nixon had attempted to have Jackson become his secretary of defense and he was a key "coalition" partner on defense policy (Safire 1975:10). But while Nixon and Jackson frequently saw eye to eye on foreign policy, Jackson's biographers referred to his grilling of Hickel during his confirmation as "a harbinger of Jackson's general disagreements with Nixon over domestic issues" (Prochnau and Larsen 1972:244).

As a Democratic senator with presidential ambitions of his own, Jackson had purely partisan motives for keeping a little daylight between himself and Nixon, and domestic policy was where he drew apart. Another senator seeking to distance himself from Nixon was the vastly more liberal senator George McGovern of South Dakota, who was the chair of the Indian affairs subcommittee. He was, of course, to be Nixon's Democratic opponent in the 1972 presidential race, and, like Jackson, he had partisan motives of his own to keep Nixon's proposals from gaining too much credit (Safire 1975:592).

Other western senators continued to be a problem. Clinton Anderson of New Mexico, who had been the chair, remained on the committee. Another senior conservative Democrat important to the administration in defense matters, he was the principal opponent of administration attempts to return land to Taos Pueblo (Bodine 1978; Gordon-McCutchan 1995).[76] Anderson had a commendable record as a conservationist, but unlike Udall, he seems not to have had a comparable concern for Native Americans (Baker 1985).

Patterson and Ehrlichman both regarded Jackson and Anderson as the principal stumbling blocks to the administration's proposals. "I think they felt . . . those Indians were their Indians. They belonged to them. Many of these western Senators, you know, like Anderson, Church and Jackson, they felt like those Indians were part of their private property. Nobody else should monkey with them."[77] Ehrlichman commented on resistance to the administration's proposals: "Well, there was all kinds of resistance. Largely on the Democratic side. If I were you I'd check around and see why it never got out of committee. My hunch is you'll find people like Clinton Anderson, Scoop Jackson, sitting astride of this stuff."[78]

Giving It Back to the Indians

Despite problems with a Democratic Congress, the Nixon administration did move significant legislation through to law. Though the basic reorganization of Indian affairs stalled, other Indian initiatives made their way successfully through Congress or were accomplished by executive order.

The earliest of the items promised in the message to become law was the return of Blue Lake to Taos Pueblo. Although one author has called the Family Assistance Plan "Nixon's Good Deed," in Indian affairs that title might better go to the Blue Lake Restoration (Burke and Burke 1974). Secretary Hickel observed, "We were fighting great legislative powers, and our argument was based on the need of a people small in number. We were fighting the issue on its pure clean merit" (1971:174).

Recalling Nixon's comments on the signing of the bill restoring the land, Ehrlichman said:

> [I]t was the high point for me, because eventually I moved to New Mexico and lived there for a long time and that was continually a theme that I encountered. People would say, 'Oh, yeah, you were a part of that,' you know. But he really rose to the occasion and he made a big ceremony out of it and spent a lot of time with the elders and then, from that point on, that was pointed to as one of those seminal moments of Native American relations. And when you would go to other reservations they would point to that as the evidence of the administration's commitment, and the good guys won."[79]

The Taos struggle had been going on since 1906 when the land was first taken from the tribe and made part of the new national forest system (Gordon-McCutchan 1995). Tom Wicker described the idea of supporting the pueblo as having been introduced directly to Ehrlichman by aide Bobbie Greene Kilberg and carried forward in the Senate struggle primarily by Ehrlichman himself (1995:591–92). But Wicker's account had it occurring a year after it actually did (and spells Kilberg "Kilbrig," to boot), so his version needs to be treated with caution.[80] Patterson, who was the team leader on the message, was a little vague on the origin of the Taos initiative in his account:

> Then we picked up from somewhere about Taos Blue Lake, and that was some land that, as you know, sacred land, and the Forest Service took it and the Indians said we want it back and the Claims Commission said, yeah it's yours. You should have it back but we can't give it to you—all we can give to you is money, and the Indians said to hell with the money, we want the land. And then an uneasy truce for a while with the Forest Service and bills have been introduced and passed, I think once or maybe twice in the House, giving it back, but the Senate under Mr. Jackson's committee, in his committee, and the very liberal Frank Church . . . would not pass any bill, approve any bill giving it back.[81]

There was certainly a Senate struggle, with Anderson and Jackson as the principal opponents and Jackson quoted as saying to the White House, "We have to decide whether it is ABM [Anti-Ballistic Missile], or whether it is Taos Indians we opt for."[82] As Patterson told the tale,

> The first big victory was in December. . . . The Senate Interior Committee, good old Mr. Jackson and Mr. Church and these others, recommended again a leasing arrangement and that was something the Indians would not accept and we would not accept. So we went with Fred Harris, and LaDonna worked with Fred and I worked with the Republicans, Chuck Percy, old friend of mine from University of Chicago days, and Barry Goldwater . . . and when that bill came to the floor of the Senate, we overturned it on the Senate floor and rejected the Interior's Committee report and advice. . . . So then the movement got going. . . . Lloyd Meeds, was the House guy, and he was a real supporter. We paid

calls on him, and on the Senate side, and we tried to keep working and did a lot of lobbying ourselves. . . . Anyway, we beat 'em all and signed that bill. So that established a momentum and a reputation . . . We felt real good about that.[83]

At the signing ceremony, Nixon commented in his formal remarks, "Both Democrats and Republicans joined together to get it through the Congress. . . . This bill indicates a new direction in Indian affairs in this country, a new direction . . . in which there will be more of an attitude of cooperation rather than paternalism, one of self determination rather than termination, one of mutual respect."[84] After remarks by Taos cacique Juan de Jesus Romero (in Tiwa), Nixon departed from his formal text to make some personal comments. He referred yet again to the influence of his football coach, then contrasted this signing with the trillion-dollar budget bill he had to deal with next, saying, "On this occasion, as we look at that $1 trillion, we want to remember that the Indians in the United States of America have contributed something that no trillion dollars could ever possibly estimate."[85]

The simple act of returning the Taos lands probably did, as several of the participants thought, create a positive climate in Indian country and did more than any speech making to show that the president was sincere in his policy declarations. Land, even more than money, talks to people who have done nothing but lose it for generations.

One result of the land return was to stimulate other groups to press their own similar long-standing claims. The Yakima, for example, had also lost part of their lands to the park system by action of President Theodore Roosevelt, and the question arose as to whether the land could simply be restored by executive order or whether it would require legislation like that for Taos. Patterson got an opinion from the attorney general: "the opinion came back from Mitchell, Agriculture's wrong, Interior's right, the President can rectify this document by executive action. Right away we sent a memo to the President and he drafted and signed the memo saying give the land back. . . . And the Yakima was restored."[86] The president's remarks were brief on this occasion.[87]

The biggest land action by the administration was, of course, the settlement of the Alaskan Native Claims. As noted in the previous chapter, the political struggle here was complex and lengthy (Anders 1994; Arnold 1978;

Berry 1975; Lazarus and West 1976). Hickel, as governor, had been involved in the negotiations with Udall that had failed during the LBJ administration. As secretary, he pressed for a settlement—presumably to "unfreeze" the lands for the non-Indians, though he suggested he acted because the Indians had a "moral claim" (Hickel 1971:176). The urgency of a solution had increased since the 1968 discovery of the Prudhoe Bay oil fields and the plans to build an Alaskan oil pipeline, and the only real argument was over the size of the settlement (Berry 1975).

Both Patterson and Wicker described the rather remarkable way in which an amount was finally reached (Patterson 1988:36–37; Wicker 1995:520). The White House staff began work on the problem at the end of 1970. Garment prepared a position paper in which he suggested "our task is to maximize our consultation, maximize our reasonableness and minimize any inconsistencies with the philosophy in the President's July 8 Message, which has already won us much praise among Indian and non Indian."[88]

A meeting was held March 11, 1971. There, the White House staff presented their proposal, which was opposed by Morton and the Office of Management and Budget (OMB). At that time Ehrlichman indicated that the package was "what the President wanted. . . . Then Morton caved" (Wicker 1995:520).

Patterson elaborated on the sequence of events in his interview with this author:

> Arthur Burns was counsel to the President, sort of co-equal to Ehrlichman at the time, and in 1969, Burns in his capacity as domestic policy adviser, before Garment and I were there, early 1969, put together an Alaskan Natives Claims bill and a very modest one, $100 million dollars, 10 million acres . . . and the Indians didn't want that. Alaskan natives thought that was very unfair. Bobbie (Kilberg) was convinced of this too and she came to our office and said, "Let's make a promise to review that." . . . I remember writing a twenty-five-page memo to Erlichman to the President on Alaska Native Claims and the issues we had with OMB.[89]

And then there was a meeting in Erlichman's office—famous meeting. And the head of the OMB was there, and Morton, Garment and me, and Erlichman and nobody from BIA, just Morton. . . Erlichman said,

"Now just a minute, Mr. Patterson. I just want all you folks to know that I've discussed this with the President and he wants to continue to be forthcoming." And Morton said, "Oh, hell, let's make it 40 million acres and a billion dollars."[90] (See also Patterson 1988:36–37)

The bill became law on December 18, 1971. The kicker in this story was that Nixon had indeed given Ehrlichman a general guideline to be "forthcoming" on Indian affairs but not specifically on the sums for the Alaskan settlement. In fact, Ehrlichman only got specific approval of the settlement ex post facto (Wicker 1995:520).[91] In Patterson's version, Ehrlichman had only spoken to the president "very briefly, he later acknowledged" (1988:36). Patterson also indicated that there was some attempt to crawfish on the terms, but that he nailed it down with a memorandum on what had been agreed.[92]

The Indian Trust Counsel Authority, proposed to provide independent legal representation for these land disputes and other Indian trust issues, was one of the items in the 1970 message that got stalled; indeed, it never was enacted into law. Nixon had observed that "No self respecting law firm would ever allow itself to represent two opposing clients in one dispute. . . . There is considerable evidence that the Indians are the losers when such situations arise."[93] Like the efforts of Bruce to advance self-administration with existing authority, the White House staff did what it could to address the problem that the legislation was meant to cure, by altering procedure in the executive branch.

A case where the holder of Indian land taken into trust was being sued by the Internal Revenue Service for tax evasion was brought to the attention of the White House staff by the defendant's attorney. "Your Mr. Nixon made a statement about guarding Indian trust rights. Well where is the federal government's defense of my client? The only federal presence we see is the prosecution" (Patterson 1988:60). Garment then "called a session in his office with the solicitor of the Department of the Interior and senior officials from Justice and the IRS. He asked the solicitor if the latter could draft a legal statement in defense. . . . Garment then turned to the assistant attorney general and reminded him about the president's message of a year earlier. 'You are to take that Interior Department defense statement . . . and attach it right along with your brief for the prosecution'" (61). To the extent that it could, the administration tried to operate on the basis of such split briefs.

Senator Henry Jackson and Self-Determination

Late in the first Nixon term, Henry Jackson, a stout proponent of termination since its beginning and a stumbling block for much of the Nixon legislation on Indian affairs, began to shift his ground. In 1971 he finally abandoned
his quest for termination and joined in sponsorship of a resolution repudiating it—but the resolution still used the term "self-determination" as something of a synonym for termination. "While S. Con. Res. 26 repudiates termination of Federal relations of Indian people as a national policy, it also
embraces a self determination concept to permit Indians to exercise various
options. Should the Congress approve S. Con. 26 as it is now written, the
majority of a tribal government would not be prevented from requesting
legislation to terminate their Federal relations with our government." While
switching to this more "optional" approach, he explained his past support: "I
sponsored legislation in the past at the request of the Colville Tribal business
council to terminate the Federal relations of that reservation. I have not introduced such legislation in this session of Congress primarily because the
Tribal business council has not requested such legislation."[94]

This shift may be connected to his preparations to make a try for the
Democratic presidential nomination in 1972. He did make such a run, and
though his candidacy began to fade in the February Florida primary, he stayed
in the race right into the convention as what one critic described as the 'ABM'
[Anybody but McGovern] candidate" (Ognibene 1975:23). Like any presidential candidate, he sought to create for himself a national profile on key issues.
While Indian bashing may have played well in Peoria (or in Jackson's case,
Walla Walla) it did not do so well on the national stage. Gross observed of
Jackson that "he was generally viewed as anti-Indian until his political aspirations became, as one respondent phrased it, 'presidential.' American political traditions, it seems, require presidential candidates to be sympathetic to
'the Indian problem'" (1989:79). Jackson—or his staff—seem to have been
coming to this conclusion in the months leading up to November 1972, and
for the first time Jackson allowed self-determination legislation to come up
for hearings in his committee in May. It was also at about that time that he
appointed a Native American to the committee staff, Forest Gerard, whom
he rather indelicately referred to as "my Indian" (Ognibene 1975:16).[95]

At the hearings, Jackson sponsored s.3157, "to promote maximum Indian participation in the government of the Indian people." The bill was a slight variation on the administration's own s.1573 and s.1574, which had been before the committee since April 1971. In his testimony, Harrison Loesch summed up the difference: "the administration prefers s.1573 and s.1574, the administration bills, to s.3157 simply for reasons that the administration believes the final control of Indian programs should be in the hands of the tribes rather than in the hands of the Secretary, and that is the gist of the matter."[96]

The difference was in fact not great; the Jackson version simply allowed the secretary of the interior greater "discretion" in granting contracts. Both bills specifically eschewed any intention of termination, but the administration version allowed for complete retrocession, which s.3157 did not. Only three Indian spokesmen appeared at the hearings. All supported the Jackson bill, and none commented on the administration version except William Youpee, president of the NTCA, who, when pressed in questioning, said, "most of the reservations kind of feel this would maybe eventually lead to termination." But he still endorsed the Jackson-sponsored bill.[97]

The committee reported favorably on its own version of the bill in July, recommending passage.[98] In his formal statement at the hearings, Harrison Loesch noted that despite the administration preference for its own bills, "This is not to say that s.3157 would not provide useful authority to this department in involving Indians more fully in the conduct of Indian programs."[99] Despite these breakthroughs, the concurrent resolution, the self-determination bill, and the bulk of the Indian legislation proposed by the administration still did not manage to make their way into law. s.3157, despite a voice vote approval by the Senate on August 2, 1972, was not considered by the House.[100]

Indian Education

As in the LBJ administration, one of the major pieces of legislation to become law in the first Nixon term was not administration sponsored or supported. The Kennedy Indian Education committee report of 1969 took some time filtering through Congress, but finally in June 1972 it stimulated the so-called Indian Education Act of 1972. The act is in fact simply Title 4 of the much broader Education Amendment Act of 1972 (Prucha 1990:263). The legislation was not supported by the administration, in part because it had some tendency to balkanize Indian programs. The president did sign it into law on June 23, 1972, but with little enthusiasm.

The administration's own proposals on Indian education dealt primarily with self-administration for reservation schools and greater Indian control over the Johnson O'Malley funds, federal "head money" to public school districts enrolling Indian children. The provision of this Kennedy-inspired act ignored those proposals in favor of a parallel system of federal support for Indian education in public schools. It also created a new Office of Indian Education in HEW to administer the funds allocated to those schools (Szasz 1977:199).

The bill, whose larger focus was special aid to the disadvantaged and to minorities, treated Indians largely as just another ethnic group rather than in terms of the "special relation" of tribes to the federal government. It extended its educational aid to urban Indians, who, as Nixon noted in the message, were not part of the federal trust responsibility. De facto, it broadened the definition of "Indian" to include all Indians, whether members of federally recognized tribes or not (Prucha 1984:1141). Tribes were, however, among the entities that could participate in the program's funding.

The Bureau's mission was actually little changed as a result of this legislation. It continued to have the responsibility to fund the reservation schools as before, including the new tribally contracted and controlled schools like Rough Rock. It also retained responsibility for administration of the Johnson O'Malley funds for public schools. The primary impact of the act was on the nonreservation, nonrecognized urban Indians never before under Bureau auspices.

The act also attempted to broaden Indian policy participation by creating a new "National Advisory Board on Indian Education," with which the new Office of Indian Education must consult (Szasz 1977:199). The provisions of this whole program were not implemented until well into 1973, since, while Congress appropriated funds, the administration "reserved them"— that is to say, refused to spend them.

Szasz described suits filed by Indian groups to free this funding and implied that "the determination of the Indian people is what led finally to that result" (200). In fact, the Indian fund impoundment did not take place in a vacuum. It was part of a broader struggle between Congress and the president, which Ambrose described as his "war with Congress," during which he was "reserving" a great deal more than this one program (Safire 1975:682; Ambrose 1991:62). The Nixon administration was not in favor of this particular bill, but the withholding of its funding was not in any way a reflection of a turn toward an anti-Indian stance.

The only other significant piece of Indian education legislation to become law was the Navajo Community College Act, in December 1971. In 1969, the founders of the path-breaking Rough Rock school had gone on to start a Navajo Community College at a boarding high school at nearby Many Farms with OEO support (Iverson 1981:121). Without proper facilities and operated on a shoestring, the effort was not a great success, but it stimulated interest, as the Rough Rock school had done. The federal legislation ensured that the community college, soon to move to Tsaile Lake, would get the same level of funding as equivalent BIA schools such as Haskell Indian Junior College (Szasz 1977:178).

A New Era?

In his January 1972 State of the Union address, Nixon recalled his promise of a new era and reprised what had been accomplished thus far in Indian affairs—pointedly not including the Indian Education Act:

> Some parts of this program have now become effective, including a generous settlement of the Alaska Native Claims and the return to the Taos Pueblo Indians of the sacred lands around Blue Lake. Construction grants have been authorized to assist the Navajo Community College, the first Indian-managed institution of higher education. . . . We are also making progress toward Indian self determination on the administrative front. A newly reorganized Bureau of Indian Affairs, with almost all Indian leadership.
>
> I again urge the Congress to join in helping Indians help themselves. . . . As Indian leaders themselves have put it, the time has come for more rain and less thunder."[101]

He reiterated his commitment a few days later in his first budget message of the new term: "We will step up our efforts to promote self determination for Indians on reservations and to assist them in their economic development. . . . Outlays for programs benefiting Indians on reservation will reach $1.2 billion in 1973."[102]

As the new term opened, the administration was clearly still committed to change in Indian affairs. Native Americans at this point had every reason to be optimistic that the shift to greater self-determination set in motion in the '60s would take on more solid form in the '70s. In January 1972, after considerable internal debate, Morton, Loesch, and Bruce finally managed to put forward their united plan, "A Way to Go in '72," which continued to strongly stress the self-determination theme.[103]

Nixon's first term was a considerable popular success, largely based on his foreign policy initiatives. His single most popular accomplishment was to reduce the American troop involvement in Vietnam from over a half million men to 20,000 (Ambrose 1989:655). He was overwhelmingly re-elected by a 60 percent majority, opponent George McGovern winning only Massachusetts and the District of Columbia. Ambrose suggested that "Nixon's 1972 victory must be recognized as tremendous vote of confidence that reflected a deep and wide spread approval of his leadership in the first term" (653). He was certainly well-regarded in Indian country by this time.

With a clear mandate Nixon approached the new term with a renewed focus on domestic policy. While much of his New Federalism, including his Indian initiatives, had stalled in the first term, "Nixon expected to make his domestic policy contribution in his second term. He planned to return to state and local governments the power they had lost over the past four decades. . . . He also intended to reorganize the Federal government starting at the top. . . . He called his program the New American Revolution" (Ambrose 1989:657). The Indian self-determination theme continued to fit in as a small-scale example of these larger intentions, and Native Americans could expect to benefit from these new initiatives.

5

The Media's Chiefs

It is a good day to die.
—Russell Means, *Where White Men Fear to Tread*

*N*ative American political activism, virtually nonexistent in the 1950s, had begun to have some impact in the 1960s as the rising tide of the civil rights movement raised the clout of all ethnic constituencies. The movement also provided Native American activists with models of the tactics of civil disobedience, confrontation, and demonstration. However, it was only right before the second Nixon term that some largely urban Indian "street theater" first received sustained national-level media interest. The curtain had actually gone up on this political theater with the events surrounding the "occupation" of Alcatraz in November 1969, but not much of an audience gathered until the march on, and trashing of, the BIA building in November 1972, just as Nixon won his second electoral victory.

At this time, there were more Native Americans than ever before active and influential in the mainstream policy process, both inside and outside the administration. Louis Bruce, as BIA commissioner, brought a high level of internal Indian activism with his turks at the Bureau and maintained very active cooperation with tribal government leaders. On the outside, many individual Indian leaders, such as Vine Deloria and LaDonna Harris, were by now regularly consulted by the White House staff. National Indian organizations, especially the NCAI and NTCA, were routinely involved in legislative proposals by the Nixon staff (Patterson 1973:54).

Newly strengthened by OEO contracting, individual tribal chairs were more and more aggressively seeking to "get something for the people" in Washington (Bee 1979). To that end, tribal delegations regularly journeyed to Washington recognizing, in direct reversal of Speaker Tip O'Neill's dictum,

"All politics is local," that for Native Americans, "all politics is Federal" (O'Neill 1994). Most of these Indian inputs came through the normal political process—lobbying the administration, letter writing campaigns, testifying before Congress, litigation in the courts, and so on (Bee 1982, 1992). An American Indian Press Association had begun in 1971, whose news releases are to be found throughout the Nixon staff files (LaCourse 1973:43).

However, in the second Nixon term the face of Indian affairs seen by the public shifted to the control of those who embraced the politics of confrontation. There were many "happenings" staged to catch the public eye—Cornell estimates fifty demonstrations over the five years after the seizure of Alcatraz—but most received little sustained national attention (Cornell 1988:190).[1] Two events were exceptions: the "Trail of Broken Treaties" in November 1972 and the occupation of Wounded Knee in February 1973. Both briefly captured the hearts and minds of the national media and for a time overshadowed the normal political process.

There have been many accounts of these dramas. Unfortunately, most of them are highly partisan (Akwesasne Notes 1973, 1974; Burnette and Koster 1974; Churchill 1993; Churchill and Vander Wall 1988, 1990; Deloria 1974; Forbes 1981; Johnson 1996; Lazarus 1991; Lyman 1991; Matthiessen 1983; Smith and Warrior 1996; Taylor 1983; Weyler 1982). In this chapter I want to relate these events to their impact on the shifts in federal Indian policy occurring during the second term of the Nixon administration, especially in the context of how they were reacted to and seen by the White House staff, the principal framers of new policy.

Alcatraz

The only noteworthy activist incident in the first Nixon term was the long-running occupation of Alcatraz Island. An undetermined number of Indians—300 (Deloria 1974:37), 80 (Patterson 1988:72), 78 (Josephy 1971:186; Smith and Warrior 1996:18), or 89 (Mankiller 1993:191; Johnson 1996:1)—landed on the abandoned federal prison island of Alcatraz during the night of November 19, 1969. The group was composed primarily of young students from the San Francisco area, with some outside leaders like the Mohawk Richard Oakes. Apparently the original intention of the occupation was to raise funds to replace a recently burned local Indian center.[2] They announced themselves as the "Indians of All Tribes" and insisted that they were reclaiming the is-land under 1868 Sioux treaty provisions allowing Indians to reclaim aban-doned federal lands.

As Vine Deloria noted, "The claims were mythological," since there were no such provisions (Deloria and Lytle 1984:236). The treaty arranging for Sioux allotments on the reservation did contain a phrase allowing Sioux to homestead federal land "which is not mineral land, nor reserved by the United States for special purposes other than Indian occupation," but the courts had denied its applicability to universal reclamations by any Indians of any fed-eral land (Lazarus 1991:290). When similar claims had been raised in 1964, then Attorney General Ramsey Clark suggested of the treaty language that it did "no more than put the Indians in the same position they would have been had they been citizens."[3]

The demands of the occupiers continued to escalate, as did the group-announced aims. "We hope to reinforce the traditional way of life by build-ing a cultural center on Alcatraz Island. We hope to build a college, a reli-gious and spiritual center, a museum, a center of ecology and a training school" (Josephy 1971:188). Rather a lot to fit on a small island.

Although there was an initial move by the General Services Administra-tion (GSA) to simply boot the occupiers off by force, Leonard Garment, fore-seeing the publicity implications of some Bull Connor–style media images, intervened (Patterson 1988:73).[4] "The last thing I wanted was a Federal shootout with a garrison of Indians" (1997:225). Coordinated by Garment, the administration adopted a policy of restraint, opening negotiations first through Tom Hannon of the GSA and soon through Robert Robertson of the NCIO. A wide range of proposals were made to the occupiers, but all of them were rejected.[5]

The sit-in did get some publicity for a time, including visits for photo ops by celebrities—Anthony Quinn, Jane Fonda, Jonathan Winters, Ed Ames, Merv Griffin, and Candace Bergen, among others (Mankiller 1993:191). Demo-crats, including the dreaded Kennedys, made what political use they could of it. Garment noted, "Ethel Kennedy has interested herself in Alcatraz in a big way."[6] Local newspaper coverage was enhanced by an act of "creative" jour-nalism by the San Francisco Chronicle, which helped to keep its hot local story alive by providing a generator for the Indians after the GSA turned off their power.[7]

Ultimately the group's demands were not met. Indeed, by their nature they could not be met. Inasmuch as the occupiers were not "tribes," Deloria noted, "the government had no legal relationship with the activists by which it could have justified giving them the lands they demanded" (1974:39). There were proposals put forward by Robertson to make the island a park with an "Indian theme," but all such proposals and many others were flatly rejected by the occupiers (Bluecloud 1972:67).[8] Eventually, the GSA turned over the administration of the island to the Department of the Interior, and the island became a public park.[9]

Meanwhile, the government requested that local Indian groups form "a group representative of the total Bay Area population," which they did, and Garment and other officials met with this group.[10] With Garment's encouragement, the OEO made a $50,000 "planning" grant to the newly formed Bay Area Native American Council (BANAC) to study Indian needs in the area.[11] None of these actions brought closure to the occupation of the island.

Despite some incidents—mostly over attempts by the Coast Guard to maintain navigation aids—no serious confrontations occurred. After nineteen months the drama simply sputtered to a close. The main leadership had abandoned the island, which continued to be occupied only by a shifting group of about twenty toward the end. Local Indian organizations were no longer actively supportive, and the press had lost interest in what was now a stale story. Garment judged the time was ripe for the removal of the remaining occupiers and sought John Ehrlichman's approval.[12] Federal marshals peacefully scooped up the remaining handful on June 11, 1971. Patterson noted, "It finally disintegrated into just a matter of petty crimes and squalor, and then the Marshals moved in and took them off."[13]

What had been accomplished? Johnson, in a recent study of the Alcatraz events, rather sweepingly suggested that "As a result of the Alcatraz occupation, either directly or indirectly, the official government policy of termination of Indian tribes was ended and a policy of Indian self-determination was adopted" (Johnson 1996:217). This attributed far more impact to Alcatraz than seems reasonable. Prucha, for example, observed that Alcatraz's impact was limited, that "The occupation of Alcatraz was a symbolic gesture, on the periphery of government attention and concern" (Prucha 1984:1117). Patterson suggested a similar White House staff perspective: "it was obviously purely a demonstration, it was purely a PR thing. It wasn't territory, it wasn't land, it wasn't Alcatraz as such. . . . The whole thing was symbolism from beginning to end."[14] There is no indication that official Washington, beyond Garment and Patterson, took much notice. Secretary Hickel, for example, saw no need to take note of it in his book, which does otherwise discuss his involvement in activism and things Indian (Hickel 1971).

One effect was to touch off some copycat demonstrations for similar restoration of federal lands, but the demands made were, as at Alcatraz, not only incapable of satisfaction but largely irrelevant to actual problems of the Indian people. Deloria noted, "Tribal government grew wary of the staying power of the activists . . . clearing title to lands was a complicated procedure, certainly nothing that could be achieved in a weekend of television appearances" (1974:40). Alcatraz was a harbinger of the "New Indian" events to follow, in that the number of Indians involved was small, both the demonstrators and the locale were urban, and the intended audience was the media and the general public, not the tribal populations supposedly being represented.[15]

The Counterculture and the Activists

The occupation of Alcatraz may have been pure symbolism, as Patterson said, but it did contribute to a trend toward raising the public profile of things Indian. The newly demonstrative Indians did not so much create a favorable climate for Indians as they took advantage of one that had recently come into being for other reasons. The '60s saw, among other things, the rise of the counterculture, and what many simply called "the movement." Anderson wrote, "Social activism swelled during the sixties and by the end of the decade the movement was attacking nearly every institution—from armed forces to religion, from business to government" (1995:4). The civil rights movement momentum joined with that of the anti–Vietnam War protest and gave rise to many offspring, including group-specific movements of "liberation"—blacks, Chicanos, Women, Gays, and Native Americans. All sought "power"—Red power in the case of the Native Americans (Anderson 1995:335; Josephy 1971).

Things Indian rapidly became among the "groovy" icons of the movement (Matusow 1984:298; Anderson 1995:268). Brand noted that "the new counterculture loved the old. There was a big increase in sales of books about

Indians. . . . Canvas teepees appeared at every counterculture enclave. The most common headgear on young men and women was a headband. The San Francisco Human Be-In, a pivotal event in 1967, was subtitled 'A Gathering of the Tribes'" (Brand 1988:570).

Nothing much had really changed in Indian country itself to precipitate all this new interest. As Sam Deloria commented, "Indians did not discover they were Indians in the early 1970's. We were not reborn; we were simply noticed" (quoted in Philp 1986:204). For the urban Indian activists the relationship was symbiotic: "As time and confrontations progressed the Indians could increasingly count on logistical as well as moral support from young Whites. The 'Indians of All Tribes' who took possession of Alcatraz in 1969 relied largely on San Francisco Bay area artists and students for food, water and transportation to the Island" (Brand 1988:571). But for the reservation peoples the hip had less attraction. Matusow noted, "Real Indians were not much impressed. In the spring of 1967, when [Allen] Ginsberg and Richard Albert met Hopi leaders in Santa Fe to propose a Be-In in the Grand Canyon, the tribal spokesmen brushed them off, saying, according to the *Berkeley Barb*, 'No, because you mean well but you are foolish. . . . you are a tribe of strangers to yourself'" (Matusow 1984:298). Peter Nabokov quoted Hopi Peter Numasa as saying, "Why are you here? Why do you behave this way doing anything that comes into your head? We do not like the way you are behaving. It's not our way. It's improper" (1991:390).

The tide of urban Indian activism arose just as the hippie movement was itself running out of steam (Matusow 1984:305). The self-proclaimed freaks had, however, created a momentum in straight places by stimulating the interest of the general public in matters Indian. There were simply not enough hippies buying books to make Vine Deloria's *Custer Died for Your Sins* a best seller in 1969, or Carlos Castañeda's *Teachings of Don Juan* in 1968, or Dee Brown's *Bury My Heart at Wounded Knee* in 1971. It was the public at large that had become newly interested in and newly sympathetic to Native Americans as the '70s began. The widespread public awareness of the symbolism of Wounded Knee as portrayed by Dee Brown surely played a part in the location's later selection by the militants for their self-styled "second battle of Wounded Knee."

Indians in the '70s were clearly "in" for whatever reason, and a great many writers set out to supply the public with "authentic" Indian insights into everything from spirituality to the environment (Kehoe 1990). Unfortunately, except for a very few of the newly popular writers such as Vine Deloria, none of this new pop literature focused on the real problems of the real Indians. It had little relevance to the changes in federal Indian policies except as it generated a kind of generalized public sympathy for things Indian (Castile 1996).

The American Indian Movement

It was in this larger atmosphere that the Indian activist group known as the American Indian Movement (AIM) formed and began to gain attention, putting forward its own versions of Indian insight for the media and the public. The militant and confrontational AIM was not a reservation-based movement; like most other elements of "the movement" it had its origins in an urban setting and its audience in the media. Clyde Bellecourt and Dennis Banks appear to have conceived the idea for AIM while in Stillwater State Prison, but it first took shape in 1968 on the streets of Minneapolis (Warrior and Smith 1996:129; Weyler 1982:35).

Most of the early members of AIM were young and urban; many were of Chippewa or Ojibwa descent. Some shared the rough social background of their leaders. Russell Means, a Sioux, has left the best of several autobiographies, which, while flowery and self-justifying, gives some glimpses of the life experiences that motivated these angry young Native Americans (L. Crow Dog and Erodes 1995; M. Crow Dog and Erodes 1990; Stern 1994; Means 1995).

AIM's first focus was its own urban environment, an "Indian patrol to monitor police activities in predominantly Indian sections of the city" (Lazarus 1991:291). Whether consciously or not, they were following in the footsteps of the Black Panthers who in 1967 had "enlisted young supporters who established breakfast programs and self defense groups to combat what they claimed was police or 'pig' brutality" (Anderson 1995:176). AIM also adopted the "in your face" or "mau-mauing" techniques of the black militants to produce its urban street theater (Castile 1976; Wolfe 1970).

AIM attracted little more than local media attention until it took its show on the road. One insider noted that Means "revealed his bizarre knack for staging demonstrations that attracted the sort of press coverage Indians had been looking for; the capture of the Mayflower II . . . a brief occupation of Mount Rushmore" (Burnette and Koster 1974:196). Except for the final action at Wounded Knee, very little of their campaign of confrontation took place on the isolated reservations, inconvenient to the media.

Even in AIM's more obscure moments, the FBI took notice. An FBI report, "The American Indian Movement: A Record of Violence," indicated that the FBI had tracked and listed some twenty-one separate "incidents" involving AIM between May 1971 and November 1973.[16] The report took a dubious view of AIM and indicated that the "FBI investigation is based on information which indicates activities which may involve violations of Title 18, U.S. Codes Section 2383 (Rebellion or Insurrection), or 2384 (Seditious Conspiracy)."[17] Ward Churchill has said a good deal about the relationship between AIM and the FBI—some of it useful but much of it sounding like the conspiracy plot of an Oliver Stone film (Churchill and Vander Wall 1988, 1990).

The Trash-in at the BIA

Not a great deal of media or administration attention was paid to the usually small-scale efforts of AIM until the "Trail of Broken Treaties," when AIM brought its road show into the political Broadway of Washington, D.C., on November 2, 1972. Russell Means noted, "Until then AIM had been little more than rhetoric. . . . We tried to make the Trail of Broken Treaties an all-Indian project" (Means 1995:226). The idea of a caravan of Indian people converging on Washington, according to Means, was originally conceived at the Rosebud Reservation Fair the last weekend in August by a number of Indian leaders, prominent among which were Robert Burnette and Dennis Banks. "Out of these discussions came the idea to take as many Indian people as we could to Washington, D.C., and air our complaints at the BIA" (223). Burnette claimed personal credit for the idea (Burnette and Koster 1974:198).

A conference to discuss the scheme was held in Denver from September 30 to October 2, which had some support from a wide range of Indian organizations, but the NCAI convention shortly thereafter (October 18) declined to endorse the planned march on Washington (Akwesasne Notes 1973:2; Taylor 1983:35). On October 6, the activists departed in car caravans from Los Angeles, San Francisco and Seattle, converging on the state fairgrounds in St. Paul, Minnesota (Akwesasne Notes 1973:3). There, according to Russell Means, a series of workshops led to the writing up of the "twenty points" document of their grievances by Northwest Coast fishing rights activist Hank Adams, who appears to have been the amanuensis of the group (Means 1995:227). While Robert Burnette and others had arrived early to make arrangements—meeting, for example, with Robert Robertson of the NCIO on October 20—the main force of the caravan arrived in Washington in the dawn hours of November 2 (Akwesasne Notes 1973:9).[18]

They had given fair warning of their coming, writing to the administration to ask for a hearing of their grievances by the president. Dennis Banks, styling himself "Chairman, Caravan Committee," wrote to the president on October 4, announcing with typical hyperbole that 100,000 Indians would arrive on November 1, and on their behalf he "requests to be addressed personally by the President."[19] Robert Burnette, as "Co-Chairman, Trail of Broken Treaties," sent another statement, received on October 18.[20] Burnette later declared that Banks's letter was "unauthorized" (Burnette and Koster 1974:201).

Leonard Garment replied for the president, regretting that he would not be available and offering instead to see if "arrangements can be made for an administration representative to meet with you." He also recounted the president's accomplishments in Indian affairs, adding, "But his major proposals requiring legislation remain before the Congress. The President supports them as much today as on the day he sent the message."[21] Neither in this demonstration nor at Wounded Knee did the AIM protesters ever acknowledge the positive LBJ or Nixon policies, simply lumping them in with all that had gone before in their denunciations.

Burnette's letter, perhaps more official, was certainly more rambling, with a presentation of some of the later twenty points and some review of the history of Indian policy. The letter was sprinkled with demands such as, "We therefore demand that a new Indian Reorganization Act be introduced into Congress."[22] To this letter Garment also responded, referring Burnette to his earlier letter to Banks. He repeated that "The problem is that Congress has not enacted the Trust counsel and other major pieces of legislation which the President submitted; we trust that the Caravan will call this to Congress' attention."[23] There is an echo here of Ralph Abernathy's demands at the end of the LBJ administration, in that they "were asking for more when he hadn't been able to persuade Congress to pass what he had already requested" (Califano 1991:287).

Bradley Patterson noted the arrangements made by the White House for the impending caravan arrival. The Park Service issued demonstration permits and "BIA on its own offered them the use of its auditorium for evening leadership meetings. . . . Loesch, Robertson and BIA senior staff will be willing to meet with small leadership groups peacefully." He warned, "The leadership of AIM is clearly confrontation minded, Alcatraz style," and that "If they try confrontations, trashing, etc., we all agree that should be handled by the police."[24]

It turned out not to be so simple. Up to this point the administration was reacting normally. Other than a meeting with the president, the protesters were promised most of what they asked, within the limits that had become an accepted and institutionalized political mechanism for dealing with such protests developed after years of Vietnam and civil rights demonstrations.

In outline, the events in Washington of the Trail of Broken Treaties occupation are simple to relate. On November 2, some of the caravan members meeting in the BIA auditorium seized and occupied the entire BIA building. Negotiations on demands were called for and held with a variety of federal officials, ultimately leading to an agreement on November 7 on terms that led to the vacating of the building by November 9. In between, there was a great deal of fierce rhetoric of the "It is a good day to die" variety. The building itself was trashed, but there were no actual violent confrontations. Beyond this outline, though, little was agreed upon by sources, not even simple facts like the numbers of demonstrators, which ranged from "thousands" to a few hundred (Akwesasne Notes 1973:8; Josephy 1984:239; Weyler 1982:50).

The confrontation began when, arriving in Washington in the early-morning hours of November 2, elements of the caravan went to the BIA building—ostensibly in protest of the conditions of the housing they had found arranged for them. While meeting in the BIA auditorium Means said that, "Spontaneously and with no thought of consequences we took control" (1995:231). In light of his own accounts of very similar prior seizures and confrontations by AIM, this claim of total spontaneity seems disingenuous. In September 1971 AIM members had abortively attempted to storm the same Bureau building and "arrest" John Crow, and just prior to departing for Washington, they had briefly seized the area offices in Minneapolis (Means 1995:192; Josephy 1984:238). Leonard Peltier was quoted as saying, "the plan was to hold a sit in of the building until we got results. We never planned no occupation" (Matthiessen 1983:53). The distinction between sit-in and occupation is elusive.

Most accounts attempted to link the immediate motivation of the seizure to unhappiness over broken government promises, especially over the accommodations offered. There were frequent references to rats—which in Means's version reached the "size of a small dog"—in a church basement where the Indians were to be housed (Akwesasne Notes 1973:8; Josephy 1984:239; Lazarus 1991:300; Means 1995:230; Warrior and Smith 1996:150; Weyler 1982:49). Vine Deloria omitted the rats but shared some of his outrage at the government with the caravan leaders: "those responsible for housing had wasted their time enhancing their images as glamorous Indian leaders, and had done little to secure rooms" (1974:54).[25]

Robert Burnette, co-chair of the caravan and in charge of doing the arranging, indicated that the government had never been asked nor expected to provide housing, and only on November 2 did the newly arrived AIM members demand government-supplied accommodations (Burnette and Koster 1974:204; Warrior and Smith 1996:150). A White House chronology indicated that on October 20 and 27 the caravan representatives explicitly indicated that they had made suitable arrangements of their own for lodging.[26]

Be it due to rats or bureaucrats, and whatever the actual degree of prior planning and source of motivation, the demonstrators barricaded themselves in the building and called for negotiations over their twenty-points document and other demands. Initial plans by Harrison Loesch and Robert Robertson to simply have the protesters evicted by security police were forestalled by Bradley Patterson, who requested and got directions from the president—presumably through Ehrlichman—to seek a court order rather than use immediate force (Garment 1997:231; Patterson 1988:77). Harlington Wood, one of those in the Justice Department who framed the request for the court order, said, "Our petition had two purposes; to put a little federal judicial pressure on the Indians to leave voluntarily; and to seek judicial support in the unfortunate likelihood that force would have to be used to reclaim the building" (1995:40).

Garment noted that "A predictable gang of protest celebrities dropped by: Stokely Carmichael, Benjamin Spock, Marion Barry, others" (1997:231). After sporadic discussions over the next few days, a crisis was reached on November 6 when police were poised to enforce the court-ordered eviction and the occupiers were preparing to burn down the building (Means 1995:233). Garment, alerted to the impending crisis by Bruce and Egil Krogh, called back the police at the last minute and made a final offer to negotiate: "Leonard Garment, Frank Carlucci, Secretary Morton and Commissioner Bruce are willing to meet with the leaders of the Trail of Broken Treaties tonight or any other time, at a location that is mutually agreeable."[27] A meeting was held that evening at nine o'clock in Garment's office, with Hank Adams acting as the principal negotiator for the occupiers, and a series of agreements were quickly reached and signed on November 7 and 8.[28] Garment noted of Adams that "He, too, was looking for a way out, one that would not humiliate the Indian occupiers" (1997:232).

In a series of written statements signed by Garment and Carlucci, they agreed to form an "Interagency task force to review Federal Indian policy and Indian needs."[29] In addition to some minor and general items, they also agreed that "the written proposals of the Trail of Broken Treaties would be analyzed and responded to by the administration," and that "we will recommend that there be no prosecution for the seizure and occupation of the BIA building."[30] None of the actual legislative proposals being considered by Congress were even mentioned or discussed in the demands of the demonstrators.

Not part of the written agreement was a government decision to provide travel money in the amount of $66,650. "Funds available in the Office of Economic Opportunity were determined to be eligible for the purpose."[31] Defending the expenditure, Frank Carlucci said, "Since the court had ordered the government to pay for housing and feeding the Indians after their vacation of the building, it was decided that the most prudent and economical course of action would be to use funds to encourage their immediate departure rather than accepting an indefinite obligation for their maintenance."[32] Bought off or simply given fair travel allowances, by November 8 the occupiers began to leave; they were all gone by the next day.

No source disputed that the interior of the BIA building was destroyed. Garment said, "It was as if a massive nonincendiary explosive charge had been detonated on the premises" (1997:234). Documents soaked in gasoline carpeted the floors. Thousands of pounds of other documents were carted away, many ending up in the hands of Lumbee in Robeson, North Carolina (Sider 1993:117). Means reported, "That night, we rented two U-Haul trucks and backed them up to the entrance. With a crowd of people standing around to block the feds' view, we spirited three thousand pounds of BIA documents out of the building. We told the cops the trucks were carrying our bedrolls" (Means 1995:235). While the views and grievances of the Native Americans attracted a degree of sympathetic coverage in the press, in the end the destruction of the building and the document theft became the focus of press attention, as both Burnette and Means had apparently feared (Akwesasne Notes 1973:30; Burnette and Koster 1973:216; Means 1995:235).

Dennis Banks declared: "We have destroyed the BIA" (Akwesasne Notes 1973:26). The BIA was, in fact, up and running within three weeks, but for the Bureau staff—as well as for their building and files—the results were certainly destructive. Commissioner Bruce and many of his turks—as well as the more conservative Harrison Loesch and John Crow—were dismissed as a direct outcome of the demonstration. To the White House staff, Loesch and Crow seemed to have taken a too provocative and outspoken hard line with the demonstrators. Patterson noted of initial meetings with the demonstrators that, "They are especially offended by Loesch who three weeks before had issued a menacing instruction to the entire Bureau of Indian Affairs 'not to provide any assistance or funding, either directly or indirectly'" (1988:76).

Deputy Commissioner Crow had publicly said of Commissioner Bruce, "he couldn't administer anything," and, "one of us has got to go" (Akwesasne Notes 1973:45). In the end, both of them went but for very different reasons. Morton issued a secretarial order, #2950, on December 2, 1972, in which the authority of both the commissioner and the deputy was "hereby suspended and withdrawn until further notice." Two days later he amended the order to include the assistant secretary for public land, thus removing Loesch's authority.[33]

Bruce submitted his resignation November 8, 1972, and it was formally accepted on December 8.[34] While Crow and Loesch were blamed for their strictness, Bruce's fault lay more in being perceived as having had excessive sympathy for the demonstrations. During the initial negotiations he had spent a night with them to show support; afterwards, he was ordered to stay away by Secretary Morton.[35]

Not only these higher-level folk left the Bureau. "Departing with them ... were several of the BIA newcomers whose recruitment had been so heralded just two years before," i.e., the turks (Officer 1984:90). Officer further noted that, "In all its stormy history, the Bureau of Indian Affairs had never been in greater disarray than during the first few months of 1973" (1984:91).

Garment recommended they "Install a 'Trustee in Bankruptcy'—or a group of Trustees—as a temporary team to shake the BIA down and shape it up into a part of the Executive Branch again."[36] Secretary Morton temporarily put Richard Bodman, assistant secretary for management and budget, in control to begin a process of reorganization which included having the commissioner reporting directly to the secretary and removing the assistant secretary for public lands (Loesch) from the chain of command.[37] There shortly followed another stage of reorganization during which Marvin L. Franklin, "Asst to the Sec. for Indian affairs . . . senior official for Indian affairs within Interior . . . [would] immediately assume direct responsibility for all Department programs concerning Indian and Alaskan Native people on an interim basis"[38] (Akwesasne Notes 1973:46). The Bureau was in receivership.

In frustration, the NTCA passed a resolution that called upon the president to direct the secretary of the interior "to get on with the substantive work that has accumulated over the past four years while BIA has been so busy reorganizing, restructuring, or realigning."[39] It was not until December 3, 1973, that a new commissioner, Morris Thompson, Hickel's one-time Indian affairs aide, was put in charge and the Bureau began to function on its own again (Smith 1979). The practical result of all this was that no new initiatives or activism were to come out of the Bureau for the remainder of the Nixon era.

Some commentators on all this have tended to credit the AIM activists

and their demonstrations with somehow forcing the positive changes in Indian policy that had emerged in the Nixon administration (Nagel 1996:227).
Churchill, for example, observed, "In retrospect, there can be no serious question that the 1972 Trail of Broken Treaties occupation of the Bureau of Indian
Affairs Building in Washington, D.C., . . . did more to bring Indians into the
BIA than all the petitions and letters of 'more responsible' and 'legitimate'
tribal officials over the preceding fifty years" (Churchill 1994:45).

This particular appraisal of the occupiers' impact is demonstrably untrue. Commissioners Nash, Bennett, and Bruce had long before moved
strongly toward Indian inclusion in Bureau staffing. In the Nixon administration, Hickel had pushed for Native American staffing from the beginning,
and by June 1972, months before the occupation, Bruce had announced so
sweeping a preference policy as to produce a lawsuit by non-Indians. The
Supreme Court case, *Morton v Mancari*, upholding the legitimacy of the
administration's preference program, was not decided until 1974, but the decision simply affirmed what was already being done. Contrary to Churchill's
assertion, the one undeniable direct impact of the 1972 occupation was the
dismissal of Bruce and his turks, and so, at least temporarily, there were fewer
Indian activists in the Bureau, not more.

Most attempts to link the Nixon-era policies to the impact of militant
Native American activism face the hurdle of timing. The core self-determination theme had been enunciated by LBJ in 1968 and reaffirmed by Nixon in
the presidential campaign. The major Nixon Indian policy initiatives and
legislation were put forward in July 1970, and they did not significantly change
later. It was not until more than two years after the delivery of Nixon's message that the Trail of Broken Treaties brought Indian activism to any sort of
significant level of notice.

The "responsible" and "legitimate" tribal leaders slighted by Churchill
did not rally to the caravan's cause. The administration's view, enunciated by
Secretary Morton, was that "the protesters do not represent America's reservation Indians."[40] During the occupation, Bob Robertson of the NCIO solicited and received statements of nonsupport of the demonstration from the
National Tribal Chairmen's Association (NTCA), NCAI, and the NCIO, as well
as from a large number of individual tribal chairs.

The statement of Charles Trimble of the NCAI denounced the destruction of the BIA building and disassociated the NCAI from the caravan, but Trimble also blamed the administration for "apathy" (Akwesasne Notes 1973:39). The NTCA board issued a position paper which said, "The Board protests negotiations with any such illegitimate group and affirmatively urges that all negotiations relative to the status and problems of Indian tribes be carried on by the government with the recognized and legally elected tribal leaders of which the National Tribal Chairmen's Association represents the vast majority."[41]

Garment's files on the Trail of Broken Treaties contained many statements by individual tribal chairs and councils, most having in common the NTCA concern of nonrepresentation (Akwesasne Notes 1973:23–24). For example, the statement to the press by Clarence Hamilton, chair of the Hopi, said: "The AIM people are only talking for themselves. They were formed from the urban Indians, not for the benefit of the reservation tribes. We had just reached a point of confidence between the BIA and the Indians and now look."[42] If a purpose of the occupation was somehow to unite and mobilize the energies of Native American leaders, it failed to do so.

But while disapproving of the activists' violence and repudiating their representativeness, many Native leaders had some similar grievances, and a good many took the opportunity to take their own swipe at the BIA. The Navajo Tribal Council condemned the occupation and AIM, while its chair, Peter McDonald, shared out some of the blame to the failings of the BIA of past and present (Akwesasne Notes 1973:38).

The caravan probably aimed more at influencing the administration than it did Native American leaders. If so, the caravan's timing was odd, arriving just before the presidential elections on November 7. There was little likelihood of commanding high-level attention, since Nixon was occupied on the campaign trail. Nixon's chief of staff, H. R. Haldeman, took no note of the AIM events in his diary, neither when they began nor throughout November 2 to November 9 (Haldeman 1994:643–48). However, some notice must have been taken by November 15, when there is an entry indicating that Nixon had at least momentarily soured on Indian affairs. "The VP raised the question of Indian affairs and said he's very interested in that, the P said it's a loser and the VP should not be tied to a loser" (1994:651). This irritable Nixon comment was very much in contrast to Ehrlichman's 1970 note of the president's endorsement of a positive role for the vice president in Indian affairs (1982:103).

After the demonstration, Ehrlichman considered the negative impact of AIM and its occupation. Referring to a plan of his own to bring the Bureau more directly under the White House, Ehrlichman observed of Nixon's attitude, "Once they sat-in at the BIA and poured gasoline all over the carpets and strewn the papers around and made threats right on the eve of the election, he turned hard set against the idea."[43]

However, the souring does seem to have been momentary, and calmer voices prevailed. Joan Hoff wrote that "Agnew . . . offered some of the calmest advice to Nixon after a small group of disgruntled Native Americans trashed the offices of the Bureau of Indian Affairs in 1972: 'It is important that we not allow all of the progressive policies of your administration with regard to Indian affairs to be submerged by the unlawful activities of a few urban militants who are not representative of the Indian community'" (Hoff 1994:29).[44]

Despite some temporary loss of enthusiasm as the result of AIM joining the long list of activist detractors that bedeviled him, there is no indication that Nixon withdrew his long-standing benign support of Indian affairs. Ehrlichman was out of office shortly after the election, but Garment and Patterson were unfazed, perhaps even energized by the confrontation. "We believed that progress would come via the comprehensive Indian reform proposals the White House had tabled before the T.B.T. caravan got started" (Garment 1997:236). They continued to pursue self-determination and to consult with the same Indian leadership as before, the tribal chairs and national Indian organizations.

In January, Garment replied to the twenty-points proposal submitted during the occupation with a cover letter to Hank Adams saying, "we hope that the wanton destruction in the Bureau of Indian Affairs building and the theft of many of its contents will be seen as the distracting and divisive act that it was—an act which served only to impede the progress already being achieved by the combined efforts of the Administration and the responsible Indian community."[45] The twenty points (see Means 1995:228–29 for a summary) were presented in full along with Garment's responses and a rebuttal commentary by Hank Adams in Akwesasne Notes (1973:63–87). There is little point in reviewing them all in detail, since none of them were ever the basis for any Nixon policy shifts. Number six, one of the shorter items, shows the general character of the exchange:

6. ALL INDIANS TO BE GOVERNED BY TREATY RELATIONS. The Congress should enact Joint Resolution declaring that, as a matter of public policy and good faith, all Indian people in the United States shall be considered to be in treaty relations with the Federal government and governed by doctrines of such relationship.[46]

To which Garment replied:

The Treaties that were concluded and ratified with Indian tribes are still in force and will be respected by the United States. But as explained in points 1 and 5, we are a Union and, since 1871, no longer negotiate new treaties with our citizens as if they were foreign entities.

American Indian people have many needs and concerns; these needs and concerns are being addressed and must be addressed further by both the Executive and Legislative branches of our government. We, in this Administration, want Indian people to continue to work with us in formulating and carrying out specific proposals and actions to meet the pressing economic, legal, educational, health, and housing problems of Indian people.

To call for new treaties is to raise a false issue, unconstitutional in concept, misleading to Indian people, and diversionary from the real problems that do need our combined energies.[47]

Many of the other points were similarly sweeping, calling for the complete restructuring of the federal-Indian relationship, the restoration of total sovereignty, and the return of vast areas of land. Most of Garment's responses, like the one above, tended to point out the lack of realism. In general, he suggested what the actual legal and constitutional possibilities for constructive change might be, stressing the actual legislative proposals being debated. Attorney Glen Wilkinson commented on the exchange: "This impresses me as a forthright, fair and scholarly reply to the 20 proposals submitted."[48] It was less well received by the proposers, and in his rebuttal Hank Adams used words such as "imbecilic" to describe Garment's commentaries (Akwesasne Notes 1973:67).

In August, Garment sent a memo to the president as the agreed upon report of the "task force to investigate Indian grievances." He indicated that of one hundred Indian organizations contacted since January for input, only six had responded and, "We consider it significant that the National Congress of American Indians, the National Tribal Chairmen's Association and tribal governments have not responded. Perhaps this may be viewed as their way of disassociating themselves with the Trail of Broken Treaties." He concluded: "In summary, while the responses are too few to be considered representative of the Indian people, they do indicate that many of the issues will be best addressed by the continuation of the present policy of self determination. Therefore, we do not recommend any policy change at this time."[49] The demonstration failed to sway the administration from its policy course. Edward Lazarus commented, "In the end, the Trail of Broken Treaties changed nothing" (Lazarus 1991:303).

The Occupation of Wounded Knee

The administration was not yet done with AIM; there was a final act three months later, when Wounded Knee, a small hamlet on the Pine Ridge Sioux reservation, was occupied from February 27 until May 8, 1973.

Covering a longer period than the Trail of Broken Treaties, this event is equally simple to sum up. A group of about two hundred, led by AIM, occupied and fortified the hamlet. They were quickly ringed by federal marshals and FBI agents. Negotiations were called for, demands kept shifting, and several agreements were aborted. Desultory gunfire was exchanged, but no frontal confrontation ever occurred. In May, an agreement was finally reached: the occupation would end and those under indictment would submit to arrest. In return, the government would look into charges made against the Pine Ridge tribal government, and White House officials would meet with "traditional chiefs" to discuss the 1868 Sioux treaty. The occupation ended on May 8, and the treaty discussion took place on May 17.

Tom Holm suggested that "At the center of the decision to occupy Wounded Knee was a controversy over Oglala Sioux tribal leadership" (1985:138). Ostensibly, the affair was precipitated by the oppression wreaked by the administration of a new Pine Ridge tribal chairman, Richard Wilson.

Means observed: "With hundreds of armed men, he began to act like Haiti's Duvalier or Nicaragua's Somosa" (Means 1995:237). At Wounded Knee, Chairman Wilson took the symbolic place of the rats "as big as cats" which had precipitated the trash-in at the Bureau.

A "full blood" tribal chair, Gerald One Feather, had been replaced by a "mixed blood"—Richard Wilson. The supporters of the ousted faction accused Wilson of a wide range of malfeasance, including misuse of his auxiliary police force—invariably referred to as "goons" (Warrior and Smith 1996:196). Some of the opposition formed the "Oglala Sioux Civil Rights Organization," which sought the impeachment of Wilson, but that move was voted down by the tribal council. OSCRO called in AIM support and appealed to the BIA to go over the tribe's head and replace Wilson (Means 1995:251). The BIA refused and, fearful of another building occupation at Pine Ridge, fortified their headquarters with extra guards (251).

The anti-Wilson dissidents turned elsewhere after they were thwarted in appeals to normal political process. "To the traditionals, the real power on Pine Ridge . . . lay with our eight traditional chiefs and holy men" (252). Seven of these leaders held a meeting "to hear the complaints of their people," and women at the meeting asked, "Where are our men today? Where are our defenders?" (252). The answer was not long in coming. "Grandpa Fools Crow, speaking for them all, said 'Go to Wounded Knee. There you will be protected.' . . . It was suicidal to go to the BIA building. . . . At Wounded Knee, on ground consecrated with the blood of our ancestors, we would make our stand" (253).

Seen in a vacuum (as many other sources other than Means presented it), this version of events made for a persuasive heroic tale, the noble AIM struggling against the Caligula-like Wilson on behalf of the downtrodden traditional (Burnette and Kostler 1974; Means 1995; Matthiessen 1983; Weyler 1982). Hoxie, however, has observed in his study of Crow leadership that "Painting a picture with only two colors—one for surrender and the other for unbending opposition—gives a severely constricted vision of social change within the reservation world" (Hoxie 1992:42).

Things at Pine Ridge were complex. Lazarus noted of the impeachment attempt that "Opponents initiated impeachment proceedings, but like *every one of his predecessors,* each of who had suffered attempted impeachment,

Wilson weathered the storm" (Lazarus 1991:302; emphasis mine). Hertzberg noted that in Sioux politics accusation of corruption was "a charge made frequently by those opposed to whatever council was in power at the time" (1988:322). In the realm of Pine Ridge tribal politics, indeed in tribal government politics writ large, wide-ranging accusations of wrongdoing and moves to impeach were well-nigh automatic responses by an ousted faction. In tribal politics it had become something of a tradition, just as, since Nixon, it has become a wider U.S. political tradition that every sitting president be suspected of "gate" crimes of one sort or another.

Against this backdrop the Pine Ridge situation in 1973 was less remarkable. Such factional infighting as swirled around Wilson was epidemic in tribal government and has been described by scholars for many other reservations (Bee 1979, 1981, 1990; Clifton 1970; Dobyns 1981). Bee wrote that regularly in tribal government, "Dissidents might pester office holders into resigning (repeated demands for audits of tribal books is a popular technique), or they may choose the more formal means of a recall election" (1982:37). Bee also noted of his study of Quechan governmental struggles, "The typical grounds for a recall attempt were alleged acts of personal misconduct, which could cover anything from allegations of misappropriation to failure to approve a personal loan. But, of course, those seeking recall portrayed these essentially particularistic, one on one alleged acts as universalistic transgressions against the tribe as a whole" (1990:57).

Wilson was accused of nepotism, but "Gerald One Feather, the previous full blood incumbent, apparently alienated his natural constituency because he had been *insufficiently* generous in handing out tribal jobs on the basis of kinship and blood quantum" (Lazarus 1991:302; emphasis mine). Loyalty to kin supporters was expected, and the actual grievance was simply that for the first time a mixed blood was favoring a new set of kin over the long-entrenched full bloods (Warrior and Smith 1996:196). There is no means at this long distance of sorting out whether Wilson was, in fact, guilty of any of the charges. In the end, after extensive investigations, he was never found guilty of any wrongdoing (Weyler 1982:95).

The root causes of the disputes over tribal self-government on Pine Ridge, as on most reservations, dated from the 1930s and the Indian Reorganization Act (Biolsi 1992, 1995). As Tom Biolsi has shown, on Pine Ridge there was a complex and ever-shifting tension between the factions labeled "mixed blood" and "full blood," or "old dealers and new dealers," after the IRA constitution (Biolsi 1992:153). Bee observed, "The points of contention vary from reservation to reservation; one of the oldest and most common is a 'traditional' vs 'modernized' cultural identification. This may be portrayed in biological terms; full bloods vs mixed bloods" (1982:36). AIM's variant of this was the "traditional chiefs" versus the "hang around the fort" Indians (Means 1995:250).

By 1973, such tribal factional struggles may have been intensified by the very success of the new programs of the OEO (Bee 1990:57). Deloria noted that "During the 1960's the War on Poverty brought many new patronage jobs to the reservation and the tribal chairman's position became even more critical in reservation politics. . . . So the fight for tribal chairman became nearly an armed conflict between opposing groups of Sioux" (1974:70). Between 1968 and 1972 the annual tribal budget for Pine Ridge was estimated by one source as increasing from $100,000 to $3,000,000 (Roos et al. 1980:92). The increased intensity of the dispute over Wilson's administration was made more comprehensible by the fact that at that moment, due to Indian policy changes, there was more to be disputed.

At Pine Ridge the out faction simply wanted in, which was nothing new in tribal affairs. So how did a normal faction fight become a national media circus? Within a short time the Wounded Knee scene lived up to the '60s slogan "The whole world is watching" (Gitlin 1980). Patterson noted that "Three hundred news people cover the story, among them reporters from a dozen foreign countries, including the USSR" (Patterson 1988:79). The National Council of Churches representative on the scene, John P. Adams, noted, "Every square foot of ground inside Wounded Knee was mined, not with explosives, but with political sympathy. . . . National television networks parked vans within the Wounded Knee district so that their representatives could live within the occupied area and cover the events from day to day with the battle zone" (Adams 1976:107).

What was different in Pine Ridge politics from every prior faction fight was AIM. At the Trail of Broken Treaties, AIM had shown itself to be good copy; it promised a good story here as well. Means and its other showmen soon delivered, shouting death-defying rhetoric, waving arms about, taking hostages, and fortifying perimeters. All of this drew the media to cover a dispute that would otherwise have had the national attention accorded to a hard-fought town council race in Walla Walla.

For openers, AIM said, "The only two options open to the United States of America are: 1) They wipe out the old people, women, children and men, by shooting and attacking us; 2) They negotiate our demands" (Matthiessen 1983:66). In a similar vein Means later said, "This is our last gasp as a sovereign people. And if we don't get these treaty rights recognized, as equal to the constitution of the United States—as by law they are—then you might as well kill me, because I have no reason for living" (75).

The content of the initial demands reflected AIM's national media focus more than they did the local issues. "Chairman William Fulbright must call Foreign Relations Committee hearings on the violation of Indian treaties, Senator Ted Kennedy must start a Senate investigation of the BIA, and Senate Indian Affairs Committee Chairman James Abourezk must initiate an investigation of all the Sioux reservations" (Patterson 1988:78). Abourezk, who had just become chair of the Select Committee on Indian Affairs and who was something of a political maverick, did in fact meet briefly with the protesters, along with South Dakota Senator George McGovern (Abourezk 1989:206). None of the other representatives or senators agreed to a meeting, and the subsequent negotiations were largely in the hands of the Justice Department (Wood 1995).

As talks proceeded and the Justice Department negotiators indicated a willingness to investigate local grievances against the tribal government and to withdraw their roadblocks, AIM demonstrators responded by upping the ante. On March 11, "they [the traditional chiefs and headmen] declared the formation of a new independent Oglala Nation, reviving the treaty of 1868 as the basis of their relationship with the Federal government. They also asked OSCRO and AIM to form a provisional government for the Oglalas, called for the abolition of the BIA tribal council government, announced their intention to send a delegation to the United Nations, and asked the Iroquois Six Nation Confederacy of the Northeast for recognition and support" (Josephy 1984:248).

What AIM wanted was publicity, not resolution. Attempts to join the UN and declarations of total Oglala independence were good theater for the media but were never taken seriously by anyone. The escalating rhetoric of impossible demands overshadowed the mundane real grievances and problems of the local people. Lazarus cited Sioux lawyer Ramon Roubideaux, who was involved in the negotiations, as saying that AIM "was more intent on keeping the pot boiling than getting anything settled" (Lazarus 1991:308). Means himself suggested that after the government had taken down their roadblocks as a gesture of good faith, "Without a confrontation to focus public attention on Wounded Knee, the government could ignore us. The war would be over and we would lose. I decided to start a fire fight so the marshals would put the roadblocks back up and we could continue the battle" (Means 1995:271).

AIM's tactic of ignoring the local elected Sioux government and appealing for direct federal intervention was of course a repudiation and undermining of tribal self-determination. Hertzberg noted that "the two national organizations that spoke for tribal Indians, the NCAI and the National Tribal Chairmen's Association, opposed the occupation. For them, the principle of upholding the right of elected tribal governments to run their own internal affairs was at stake. . . . If tribal governments could be seriously threatened or overturned by an urban based Indian movement from outside the reservations combining with dissident factions from within—factions that existed on every reservation—then tribal government itself would be endangered" (1988:322). These other tribal leaders were not so much in love with Wilson as aware that all that they had fought for—to establish tribal self-government—was at risk. If the feds could simply be invited by fiat to overrule any elected government by the demand of "chiefs" whose only constituency was the media, the result would be what one source called a "media coup d'etat" (Smith 1973).

In place of the elected constitutional government, AIM offered in exchange only a vague "traditional" government. In their attempts to "return" to the 1868 treaty, what they obviously intended was complete sovereignty, but that is not what that treaty was about. Ruth Landsman has observed of the Mohawk "the treaty is also a symbolic construct displayed and interpreted in the public arena . . . the treaty has in modern times been invested with meaning different from those it held at its original writing" (1987:110).

No one familiar with the federal Indian policies of the nineteenth century could possibly imagine that the 1868 treaty was intended to create a permanent, self-governing, sovereign Sioux state. Lazarus said of AIM that "their notion of tribal governance did not exalt self determination but rather presumed a return to the treaty era when a bureau superintendent controlled reservation affairs while paying token respect to the prerogative of tribal elders" (1991:309). The treaty to which they wanted to return had nothing in it about forms of tribal self-government, but a great deal about the duties of the "agent" to enforce the usual paternalist assimilationist schemes of compulsory education for children and self-betterment through land allotment for adults. It was a document of its times, from the provision of rations to trivia like wool stockings for women (Lazarus 1991:433–49).

Chairman Wilson noted, "they are not just against me personally but against a tribal government that takes charge; they really don't want their own people to run the affairs of the reservation. They have more faith in being run by outsiders than in their own people, they believe in paternalism" (1976:64). Harlington Wood said, "Our negotiations were intended to eliminate the guns, restore order and enforce the law with minimum loss of life. It was not to enable the Department of Justice to take charge of the reservation" (Wood 1995:81). Stanley Lyman, BIA superintendent at Pine Ridge, thought that Justice had already gone too far in its dealings with AIM: "they appear to deal with Indians as the BIA must have done twenty-five to thirty years ago. I am referring to the fact that they do not consult at all with Indian tribes and elected Indian leadership. . . . They rush out and try to get ahold of their 'chief,' as they call him, and tell him what they have already decided, and try to get him in on their side" (1991:19).

Conspicuously missing in the AIM rhetoric was any acknowledgement that the Nixon administration was moving toward greater self-administration. Governor Lewis of Zuni Pueblo, one of the most successful in taking over self-administration, wrote to Nixon about the AIM positions: "The basis of all these are demands for things, most of which are presently being met or for which plans are being made to correct or change. . . . these so called 'spokesmen for Indians' or 'Indian leaders' just do not understand what is going on in the true reservation world. Furthermore they appear to be unwilling to work peacefully, anonymously and hard to bring about beneficial change."[50]

One observer even thought perhaps AIM and the Nixon negotiators were somehow in cahoots. Wax wrote, "The real danger at Wounded Knee was seldom perceived—a further Federal sell out. The Nixon administration played its usual adroit public relations game. It talked of Indian autonomy and rights." However, "AIM's activities undermine the legitimacy of tribal governments (and their national Indian associations). They also further discredit the Bureau of Indian Affairs which was some protection. So the Nixon administration can not only tolerate AIM but even support it quietly with cash." He went on: "Meanwhile, the plans of the Nixon administration for looting reservation resources could proceed" (Wax 1973:137). I think this falls in the Churchill-Stone conspiracy theory category.

Although representatives of the Department of Justice, Ralph Erickson, Harlington Wood, and finally Interior solicitor Kent Frizzell did most of the on-the-spot negotiating, policy was clearly set from the White House (Wood 1995). Patterson said that when the occupation first occurred, "The White House is immediately notified and again Garment is point man for the decision making process at that level. Again, knowing the President's views, he sets the policy . . . no violent counterattacks. The well trained marshals, agents, and police act with professional restraint" (Patterson 1988:78). Garment gave credit for the decision to avoid any frontal assault to Col. Volney F. Warner's portrayal of the probable costs to all concerned (1997:240). The White House kept a close eye on the situation and apparently even maintained some backchannel contacts through Indian leaders Robert Burnette and Hank Adams in the negotiating process (240; Burnette and Koster 1974).[51] The administration's approach, and the extent of Leonard Garment's involvement in framing it, are clearly set out in an internal White House memo of Garment's to Ken Cole, then domestic council chief:

> The core of the question is how to get that bunch of armed headline hunters out of Wounded Knee without loss of life. Since moving in with adequate force would mean a large loss of life, there is really only one option left:
>
> Prevent reinforcements, make the perimeter as leakproof as possible, offer to meet with the leadership *after* they evacuate the place, pile up Grand Jury indictments for the certain arrests that both they and we know are going to follow, and if they don't come out now, hold the status quo until diminishing adherents, declining media attention and internal let down convince them they have had their day.[52]

Which is precisely how it all devolved. In the end, the government policy of restrained watchful waiting led to a spluttering close to the drama rather than to Armageddon. Vine Deloria said in summation,

> The Federal government proved to be incredibly patient with the AIM militants. It was apparent that several Federal laws had been broken, and the conservative Indians demanded that the government use force to remove the armed occupants of Wounded Knee. The administration felt however that the saving of lives was more important than enforcing the laws in a rigid manner. To prevent bloodshed, it conducted prolonged negotiations with the embattled Indian protesters, thereby winning the gratitude and confidence of the great majority of Indians whose strongest concern was to prevent any loss of life.[53]

Garment gave much credit to the roles of Hank Adams and Col. Volney F. Warner: "the Indian and the soldier, were the individuals who did the most to prevent the Second Wounded Knee from ending like the first one" (1997:242).

For the media it had all dragged on too long. "Press coverage dropped. ... When the lights were turned off in the theater, the show ended and the audience went home. After seventy-three long days of dangerous confrontation, Wounded Knee II was over with little, if any resulting benefits for the Native Americans" (Wood 1995:89). The agreement to end the occupation gave only what had long been offered, a promise to look into the finances and civil rights record of the Pine Ridge government and to review the larger-scale treaty issues after hearing the complaints of the traditional chiefs at a special meeting with White House representatives (Lazarus 1991:310). Wood observed that "Wounded Knee II came to an end on terms not much different than what the government had originally proposed" (Wood 1995:89). An agreement had in fact been signed a month earlier, on April 5, that included only small variations from the form of the final terms.[54]

On May 7, many of the occupiers slipped quietly away from a village now as devastated as the BIA building had been after the departure of the Trail of Broken Treaties forces. The next day, by agreement, the key figures surrendered to authorities (Josephy 1984:251). None denied the sad state of the village, but views as to blame were wide ranging. One version said: "They left behind a thoroughly destroyed village. Indian homes had been used for slaughterhouses, whorehouses and toilets. The stench of the village itself, the twisted girders of the burnt trading post, the charred remains of several homes, and the pornography-smeared churches mutely testified to the asininity and frustration of the affair" (Dollar 1973:7). By way of counterpoint, Means said, "Before allowing the press back into Wounded Knee, the feds pulled what they thought was a great public relations stunt. They trashed all the homes, then showed them to the media and said that was what AIM and the Oglala people had done" (1995:293).

The Impact of Wounded Knee

In terms of the local grievances that ostensibly initiated the occupation, little was gained. The government dutifully looked into the charges against the tribal chairman as agreed. On civil rights violations, "Some fifty complaints were brought to the government's attention. The Civil Rights Division of the Department of Justice and the Federal Bureau of Investigation investigated all of them." In regard to misuse of funds, "the United States . . . contracted for an outside firm (Touche, Ross) to do a complete audit." None of these actions led to any prosecutable case.[55] Wilson was convicted of nothing and served out his term and was even reelected in 1974 (Josephy 1984:252).

In the 1974 race Russell Means ran against Wilson, and despite the fact that the "Sioux had never reelected a president to a second term," Wilson won (Lazarus 1991:309).[56] With hindsight it seems possible that Wilson won because Means divided the "traditionals" vote with former chair Gerald One Feather, who also ran, and alienated enough of them to allow Wilson to win in the runoff. Wilson served until 1976 and was then defeated by another mixed blood, Al Trimble, who was finally able to reconcile both factions (Lazarus 1991:329). In the end nothing changed in the Sioux form of government.

On the larger treaty issues, Garment wrote (with a rather ominous misspelling) to the "Headsmen and Chiefs of the Teton Sioux" that "As was promised in my letter to you of May 4 and in the agreement of April 5, we are sending five White House representatives to meet with you for the purpose of examining the problems concerning the 1868 treaty, and so that you may outline to them your views."[57] The delegation consisted of Patterson and Kilberg (directly attached to the White House staff), Charles Soller and Craig Decker (attorneys from Interior), Leslie Gay of the Bureau, and R. Dennis Ickes from the civil rights division of Justice.[58]

On May 17, the self-designated traditional chiefs held their meeting with these representatives. The partial transcript in Akwesasne Notes indicated the unbridgeable gulf between the Indian representatives and the White House team. Fools Crow began by saying, "I want Mr. Patterson to say yes or no on this matter. Can we be reinstated back to the 1868 Treaty?" (1974:252). Patterson was, of course, unable to give a simple yes or no. He noted, "When 'Chief' Fools Crow demanded that the Black Hills be returned to the Sioux forthwith, the author had to tell him that even if he were President of the United States, the answer would be no. Only the Congress could undo—or compensate for—the ancient injustice" (Patterson 1988:80). Patterson promised the White House would look at the demands and respond in accord with the law, but the Indian representatives thought that "the Sioux were challenging the entire framework of U.S. Indian relations" (Akwesasne Notes 1974:253).

Means insisted that the White House had promised to return for a second meeting on May 31, but "Instead Leonard Garment, the same Nixon henchman who had rejected the 'Twenty Points' from the Trail of Broken Treaties, sent an insulting note" (Means 1995:293). This insulting note was apparently a nine-page memorandum in which Leonard Garment responded to the expressed concerns point by point.[59] Like his response to the twenty points of the Trail of Broken Treaties, his commentary was largely concerned with showing the recourses available to the Sioux under existing law and the efforts the administration had underway to promote new legislation and procedures.

An example of the exchange was his comment on their request for a "treaty commission" to review the 1868 treaty. He reminded them of the 1871 legislation putting an end to the treaty process and suggested "the Congress is, in effect a Treaty Commission and you should make sure your spokesmen appear before the Senate Subcommittee and present their views, as to which treaties should be amended and in precisely what way." He also wrote, "the President himself has proposed additions to and revision of the old legislation affecting American Indians. Enclosed is a copy of the President's July 8,

1970 Special Message to the Congress in which these proposals were first made; they have been repeated in the years since 1970; they have not yet been enacted by the Congress; the President still stands by them as embodying the changes most needed today for the benefit and protection of Indian interests."[60]

On "Protecting Mineral and Water Rights," he reminded them of the administration's efforts to create a trust counsel and of their practice of split briefs. In their request for a "Referendum Vote," he pointed to the procedures that the Sioux and the Bureau had established for such votes. To their concerns about criminal and civil legal violations, he pointed out the ongoing investigations. At the end, in response to their suggestion of "Other Wounded Knees," he said, "Indians will lose much of the sympathy and support they now enjoy from this administration, from the Congress and from the public. The possible actions I have indicated in this letter will become much less possible, the passage of constructive legislation will become less likely."[61] There were suggestions of a second meeting after the chiefs responded in writing.

Vine Deloria acted as intermediary and delivered a response of sorts to Bradley Patterson in the form of a "Bill of Particulars" from the traditional chiefs, which consisted entirely of questions about the stance of the U.S. government toward the 1868 treaty.[62] Garment again replied in detail, summarizing by writing that "the 1868 Treaty is still a valid document, with its obligations still in force except insofar as any of them have been changed by the Congress, by the parties, satisfied by litigation or expired—and that has happened in several specified instances." He ended by saying, "It is not enough to curse history to undo or repair historic wrongs. What is essential is realistic and sustained action using the intelligence of all those persons and groups in and out of government who understand the legitimacy of Indian grievances and the compelling need to act on them."[63]

There were no subsequent meetings or official exchanges. The process of discussion promised at Wounded Knee was at an end.

For AIM itself the outcome of Wounded Knee was something of an organizational disaster. Its best-known leaders were dispersed into hiding or held under indictment. "The federal government prosecuted some one hundred and fifty persons for crimes arising from the seizure of Wounded Knee" (Kleindienst 1985:88). Means and Banks hoped to turn this to their advantage by making "the proceeding into a political trial" (Means 1995:299). Garment, too, thought that they intended "to turn the upcoming Wounded Knee criminal trials into a media circus."[64]

In fact, the trials attracted little media attention, and AIM's moment in the spotlight appeared to be coming to an end. Many Native American leaders thought it had already gone on too long. Zuni Pueblo governor Robert Lewis observed during Wounded Knee, "The general public, I am sure do not know that AIM is wrong. That they do not speak for all Indians. The treatment my fellow tribal leaders and I received from the press in Washington after the shameful BIA occupation last November, convinces me that the press and the public feel AIM is right."[65]

The theatrical tactics of AIM had only a limited shelf life. They were in the Yippie tradition of "monkey (as opposed to guerrilla) warfare—actions so outrageous and absurd that the news media would be conned into carrying their message free to the masses" (Matusow 1984:412). But such antics were not long-playing. *Harper's* editors, commenting on AIM's coverage, noted, "Who can still remember the revolutionary suitors of the past decade? They flickered like butterflies in the light of the network television cameras, holding up their signs and shouting their strident slogans. The press dallied with each of them in turn" (1973:45). By the time of the AIM trials, at least some elements of the press expressed a new skepticism and a sense of having been had (Hickey 1973; Schultz 1973; Smith 1973; *Time* 1973:67). *Time* reported under the caption, "Trap at Wounded Knee," that "Most newsmen watched helplessly as the thin line between covering and creating news wavered." They also quoted NBC correspondent Fred Briggs, who said, "The story has been managed all along" (1973:67). Desmond Smith, writing in the *Nation* said, "From start to finish it was a staged event different in degree but no different in kind from the group theater of the Black September men" (Smith 1973:807). *TV Guide* ran a series, "Was the Truth Buried at Wounded Knee?" and noted, "Means often displayed a jocular streak to the newsmen, 'Cameras over here' he would bellow, prior to a briefing, 'And be sure to shoot my good side'" (Hickey 1973:46). In "Bamboozle Me Not at Wounded Knee" for *Harper's*, Terri Schultz said, "We wrote good cowboy-and-Indian stories because we thought it was what the public wanted" (1973:56).

Whether out of a fit of media conscience or simply a mayfly-like shift of attention, AIM was now yesterday's news. Without media attention AIM began to fall apart. "Out of the spotlight, AIM's penchant for internal dissension and what Ramon Robideaux called its 'preference for publicity over policy' crippled the movement" (Lazarus 1991:329). The larger movement of social protest that had generated AIM had itself had the wind taken out of it by Nixon and Kissinger's success in drawing down U.S. troops in Vietnam to a handful and the January 1973 signing of the Paris Peace Accords (Anderson 1995:408).

Without the unifying focus of the Vietnam War, the movement began to fragment, ending the automatic support for causes like AIM. Anderson noted: "While Native Americans did win concessions from the Federal government later, including much more self determination on their reservations, it appeared in 1973 that Red power was on the wane. So was student activism. Even though surveys demonstrated that college students ranked Native Americans with homosexuals as the group most oppressed in the nation, there was no outpouring of support, no mass marches, no bus brigades heading for Wounded Knee" (1995:408).

As their domestic impact lessened after Wounded Knee, the activists turned increasingly to a more appreciative international audience. AIM often found support in the socialist world, which enjoyed their denunciations of the United States more than the home folks. For example, in a speech from Peking reported by the Peking News Agency:

> In face of the Nixon administration's crimes of expanding its aggressive war abroad and stepping up exploitation and oppression of the people, the American Indians are launching fiercer struggle against violent repression. Since the beginning of the year, the American Indians have unfolded struggles in various forms in more than ten U.S. states. They attacked the offices of the 'bureau of Indian affairs,' set up in various cities by the ruling circles to govern and deceive the American Indians.[66]

Now largely ignored for itself, AIM often attempted to gain coverage in a "me too" role of endorsing or condemning whatever issue was the focus of media attention at the moment. Russell Means, for example, found himself in hot water with the rest of AIM when he chose to endorse the Miskito Indian side of the struggle in Nicaragua, rather than the more politically fashionable Sandinistas (Dodge 1986; Means 1995:463). Tracing this later international development of AIM is outside the scope of this study, but some insight into the perceptions of the group outside the United States can be found in "Who is Afraid of AIM" (Peyer 1987).

What impact did all of this have in Indian country? One observer suggested that, "Wounded Knee catapulted the AIM into the center of public attention, and into leadership of a mass Indian nationalist movement" (Ortiz 1984:160). But was AIM a mass social movement of the Indian people? Was it even a Leninist-style "vanguard" elite cadre "making revolution by making revolution" as in the theories of Che Guevara, popular at the time? If that was the aim of AIM, it would seem that, like the response to Che in Bolivia and the SDS in the United States, the masses were not much interested in being revolutionized (Matusow 1984:326). "Many—perhaps the vast majority of indigenous peoples—remained far more concerned with issues affecting their local communities and their kin" (Perry 1996:119). Native Americans in general did not seem to know quite what to make of all the AIM furor beyond some gut-level sympathy for any Indians who pulled the tail of the Bureau.

Certainly AIM's publicity made it widely known to the people on the reservations, as well as to the general public. Their reception on the reservations was clearly mixed and, ironically, seemingly least positive among the traditional, whom they often claimed to represent. Deloria and Lytle observed: "Tribal Indians, particularly the religious leaders, cast a jaundiced eye on the first activist demonstrations in the Indian movement. They supported individual efforts by people of their own tribes but looked with contempt on the spectacular and largely symbolic invasions of federal lands and buildings" (1984:240).

No systematic survey has been made, but a few scholars have provided ethnographic glimpses of how AIM was seen on some reservations. For the Arapahoe, Fowler noted: "In their rebellion against the hierarchal authority structure dominated by the elders and implemented by the younger generation, the young AIM leaders demonstrated an assertive confidence and combative oratorical style. Their behavior worried and alienated the Arapahoe community" (Fowler 1982:283–84). She described the reaction of a ceremonial elder to the remarks of AIM youths at a council meeting: "He spoke of people who had forgotten the Arapahoe ways, who did not speak the Arapahoe language, who did not respect the tribal elders. He said, 'Why was I not consulted by my younger relative before he announced to the people that he stood for closing the reservation?'" (283). She cited another Arapahoe: "'These seventies superskins left here and were in urban areas. They learned about Indians from books. You can tell they weren't raised traditional.' . . . The term 'seventies superskins' embodies the notion that the militant Indians wanted to be Indian only when it became fashionable or profitable to be one in the 1970's" (Fowler 1987:192).

Fowler found Gros Ventre elders perceived AIM as having a dangerous and inappropriate approach to the sacred. Sweat lodges were seized upon by many young militants as a sort of pan-Indian ritual:

> One elder, a man sixty-three years old, observed, "They sweat every week. That was never an occurrence with Gros Ventres. They would sweat twice a year. Now it's any time somebody gets the urge. . . . The old men I remember did it for a reason." . . . To these men, youths are trivializing the ceremony. One eighty-eight year old elder perceived the sweats as showing off because she saw an American flag being flown upside down during a sweat ceremony being held by militant youths. The inverted flag suggested to her that the ceremony was an effort by the American Indian Movement (AIM) to intimidate opponents. And as AIM symbols suggest violence to many people, their association with rituals reinforces the notion that youths may be seeking "bad" power. (Fowler 1987:155)

Despite AIM's own rhetorical emphasis on the traditional, some have suggested AIM was "more attractive to urban Indians or landless rural Indians because these are groups where traditions and identities are weak, there are more severe identity problems" (Bonney 1977:220). Similarly, Richard White noted: "Its tough, flamboyant, and clever leaders exerted a strong appeal for young second-generation urban Indians but their urban ways made the organization appear un-Indian to many reservation residents" (White 1991:586). Even in urban areas its appeal was not universal. In Los Angeles, Weibel-Orlando said:

> AIM's early militancy and anti-American stance found only a small episodic audience of supporters within the Los Angeles Indian community. In 1973 Los Angeles Indians were generally sympathetic to the plight of the cadre of Indians who . . . had taken over a church in Wounded Knee.

. . . I formed the opinion that most Indians in Los Angeles were glad to make donations to their beleaguered "Bros" on the reservation "just as long as they didn't try any of that strong arm stuff in Bell Gardens." . . . However, subsequent killings, arrests, and imprisonment of AIM leaders, along with rumors of internecine dissension, indiscretions, disaffections and flirtations with Third World revolutionary forces, have weakened the movement's allure to the general Indian public. (Weibel-Orlando 1991:103)

Some Native American critics have been harsh in their characterizations of AIM. Gerald Vizenor, for example, has referred to them as "peripatetic mouth warriors" (1983:64). Feminist observers have deplored AIM's tendency toward sexism: "Within the Red Power movement, subtle and overt sexism affected the gender division of labor and authority" (K. Anderson 1996:82). Yet some benign views have been expressed by surprising sources. Richard Kleindienst, attorney general during the crisis, observed: "They made their political statement and paid the price. . . . But perhaps they have aroused other young Indians to seek by political means solutions to the near tragic conditions under which they live on their reservations" (Kleindienst 1985:88). Starita went so far as to attribute a general cultural renaissance at Pine Ridge to the events at Wounded Knee, saying, "a rich new cultural identity began to emerge among a new generation of Oglala." He portrayed a generally strong endorsement of AIM in his study of the Dull Knife family (Starita 1995:317). The reviews were mixed in Indian country.

In March 1973, in the midst of Wounded Knee, the same basic Nixon legislative package was reintroduced, unaltered to include any of AIM's dreams (Officer 1984:91). To the extent AIM had any policy impact at all, it was to slow down still further the already stalled efforts of the administration to get this legislation through Congress. Responding to an inquiry from Ehrlichman about the delay in Congress, John Whittaker, then Interior undersecretary, wrote, "Both Houses of Congress will apparently investigate Wounded Knee before moving to hearings on the Indian package."[67] Similarly, Patterson noted that "Then along came AIM, and they began to raise hell . . . ironically just as the Executive Branch, which they detested so, was completely 180 degrees turned around, and they come on the scene with their antics, which in the end made it more difficult."[68] Patterson also said of AIM's impact: "It was all unnecessary. . . . The needed changes were already taking place and at a faster pace and with the most high level sponsorship in the history of Indian affairs" (quoted in Taylor 1983:213). Oddly, even AIM seemed to agree that at least Patterson was doing a good job—at least in a note Dennis Banks sent Patterson. "For all of your assistance and quick response to our calls we at AIM wish to take this opportunity to express our appreciation for a job well done." At the bottom of the note, Garment wrote, "Brad. This is one for your memory book. Point to it with pride and astonishment."[69]

The president summed up the administration's view of it all in a message to the NCAI convention in October 1973.

I am confident that the few noisy spectacles in the past twelve months will not for a moment divert either your focus or mine from the real progress which is occurring in meeting these needs. . . . Here in Washington men and women of fresh commitment and new energy are at work for Indians. . . . They are all striving, as I am striving, for Indian self determination without termination and for close consultation with responsible Indian representatives on matters which affect the Indian future.[70]

Between Mandate and Watergate

As a student of history, I should have known that leaders who do big
things well must be on guard against stumbling on the little things.
—Richard M. Nixon, *In the Arena*

*O*utside the patch of artificial light focused glaringly but briefly
on a corner of Indian affairs by the media, the real business of Indian policy
went on. Indian problems remained unresolved, and new legislation was still
being proposed by the administration to address them. But with Congress
refusing to act on the legislative proposals, Nixon and his staff continued to
do what they could to administratively implement their programs. In this
chapter I want to return to the mainstream of these events, briefly overshadowed by the media chiefs.

The key problem remained the lack of movement on proposed legislation. Nixon observed in his March 1973 "State of the Union Message on Human Resources" that "In the two and one-half years that Indians have been
waiting for the Congress to enact the major legislation I have proposed, we
have moved ahead administratively whenever possible."[1] William Babby,
Aberdeen area director, pointed out that tribal contracting in his area had
more than tripled between 1970 and 1973, but he felt that while "The administration has articulated a progressive, passionate and acceptable Indian policy
. . . our problem is that we do not have the machinery needed to effectively
carry out the policies that have been mandated."[2]

The BIA Rises Again

The period of receivership of the Bureau ended with the nomination of a
new commissioner, Morris Thompson, who was sworn in on December 3,

1973. Thompson had served as special assistant to Hickel early in the first
Nixon term and had since become area director in Juneau (Smith 1979). In
his swearing-in statement he said optimistically, "We have just endured some
of the stormiest months ever in Indian affairs. One positive result of this
period, however, is that this country now has a new awareness of Indian needs.
With the positive actions being taken by this Administration and this Congress, and the emergence of strong Indian leadership both at the local and
national levels, the climate is right for meaningful progress."[3]

After the chaos that had gone before, much of Thompson's energy had
to be devoted to completing the BIA reorganization begun by Marvin L.
Franklin and to putting the Bureau's house in order. However, because he
carried forward the strong Indian-preference policy already set in motion,
internal turmoil continued among the non-Indian staff (Officer 1984:92). In
the area of Indian education, a new set of so-called "Red Regs" was put together to meet Indian concerns about misuse of Johnson O'Malley funds,
putting them under more direct tribal control (Szasz 1977:201).

Of Morris Thompson himself, Officer observed, "In many respects,
Thompson's administration turned out to be unusual. He took few initiatives of his own with respect to policy, yet his three years in office were marked
by some of the most important legislation, judicial decisions, and internal
administrative developments recorded by any commissioner" (Officer
1984:92). Smith had a similar appraisal: "Although he did not provide the
dynamic leadership many would have wished, he conveyed to all concerned
that the idea of Indian self determination was a viable policy" (1979:345).
Whatever the extent of his personal contribution, he was to be the commissioner in office when the initiatives begun in the Udall era and long pursued
by the Nixon staff at last came to legislative fruition in the form of the Indian
Self-Determination Act of 1975.

Menominee Restoration

The Nixon administration saw the beginnings of the undoing of some of the
damage caused by the termination policy, a process that came to be called
"restoration." This started in 1973 with the restoration of the Menominee,
who had been terminated in 1961, to federally recognized tribal status. Al-

most from the moment the tribe was first listed for termination in 1954, the Menominee situation had been much debated. After termination, some tribal members began to organize to lobby for restoration with the semi-covert support of Philleo Nash at the Bureau (Lurie 1972; Peroff 1982; Spindler and Spindler 1971, 1984).

The Menominee social movement, organized under the name DRUMS (Determination of Rights and Unity for Menominee Stockholders), has been chronicled in considerable detail by Peroff and stands in some useful contrast to AIM as an example of effective Native American activism (1982). The DRUMS movement took formal shape in 1969, initially aimed at capturing the new corporate governing structure of the Menominee tribe, Menominee Enterprises. Ada Deer, a social worker who had been brought into the BIA by Philleo Nash, was among the key organizers (Deer 1989, 1994). In the early days of the movement, strong legal support was given by Wisconsin Judicare, an OEO legal service agency, and later by the Native American Rights Fund, an OEO offshoot (Deer in Philp 1986:231–34; Peroff 1982:177).

Although created in the same era as AIM and employing some of the same fierce rhetoric, DRUMS was by contrast a model of effective practical political organization. Perhaps the main difference was that the Menominee had clear and realistic goals. What they wanted, restoration, could be accomplished by Congress without the complete restructuring of Indian affairs demanded by AIM. DRUMS put their case to the public through skillful publicity, and by 1972, "Strong support for restoration was voiced by Wisconsin's two senators, several representatives, the governor, most of the state newspapers, the academic community, and a large block of the general public" (Peroff 1982:211).

The Menominee were equally successful when they took their case to Washington. Gary Orfield noted: "One of the most remarkable lobbying campaigns I have seen was the campaign for Menominee restoration. Nobody was safe from Ada Deer and her supporters. Members of Congress just gave up" (quoted in Philp 1986:138). They also got strong support from the administration. Peroff noted that "They received it from two members of the President's staff, Bradley Patterson, a White House executive assistant in Indian affairs, and Melvin Laird, the counselor to the president for domestic affairs" (1982:216). Patterson recalled:

Ada Dear organized the Menominees, took an uphill fight for months and months, but finally through court action, through public action, through newspapers, media, making a big noise, organizing the Indians, finally got the bank turned around and then came to us and said, "We want to draft some legislation overturning the termination, restoring the Menominee as a tribe." And we said you can count on it. She drafted the legislation and she handled it beautifully with Congress, she put on cocktail parties, she knew how to do this to a fair-thee-well. She organized that whole thing. We supported her. . . . By that time Watergate was going down—Garment and I had separated, he was working on Watergate and I was up on the fourth floor. But the bill came in and we sent the memo in to the President and said, "Sign this," and he did.[4]

Watergate was churning the administration by this time, and Melvin Laird had been brought in to replace the departed Ehrlichman as a presidential counselor on domestic affairs. Gary Orfield quoted Laird as saying of Menominee restoration, "Nixon did not care about that kind of stuff. He was just trying to save his skin, so one day I just typed up a notice that said the administration supports restoration and I had the secretary send it out" (quoted in Philp 1986:138). If Laird did express this view, it was something of a distortion of reality.

As Laird correctly indicated in the administration statement released on the Menominee (presumably the "notice"), restoration was "In keeping with President Nixon's rejection of the termination policy," which had been in place since 1970.[5] Laird had requested and received information from Bradley Patterson on the Menominee which had spelled out for him the administration's prior support of restoration. It was Patterson, in fact, who suggested that in order to "get some credit for this position" that Laird release a statement on behalf of the administration.[6] Laird's ill-founded later claim of sole authorship of administration policy on Menominee restoration is perhaps more understandable if seen as an act of political atonement.

In the statement he declared, "As the member of Congress who represented the area in which the Menominee Reservation is located I had opposed termination. . . . Through my efforts . . . we were able to defeat the Menominee legislative conference report requiring termination on two occasions."[7] In fact, in 1954 Congressman Laird had supported termination.

Peroff quoted him in the hearings on Menominee termination as saying, "I believe the Menominee Indian tribe is ready for complete emancipation as set forth in the resolution of the tribe" (Peroff 1982:75).

Laird's memo was not the definitive administration statement, since Nixon himself sent a message to the NCAI, then holding a conference whose theme was "Restoration Now." Nixon wrote, "I support the restoration of reservation status for the Menominee tribe of Wisconsin. I hope that before 1973 ends Congress will send me a bill which accomplishes this restoration."[8] On December 22, 1973, he received and signed such a bill.

At the signing, he said in an oblique rebuke to AIM, "I especially salute the Menominee people and their leaders for their persuasiveness and perseverance in using the tools of the political process to bring about peaceful change." He also noted that the bill "incorporates one of the most important features of my legislative agenda for Indian people—authority to make grants to Indian tribal government, upon their request to carry out Indian programs administered by the Secretary of the Interior."[9] The Menominee had not only achieved restoration but had succeeded in building in a degree of self-administration not yet made available legislatively to other tribes.

At one point AIM offered to join in the Menominee struggle and make it a "second Wounded Knee," but the Menominee leadership was not interested in their participation (Ourada 1979:219). The DRUMS movement did face AIM-like theatrics on the part of an internal dissident faction of their own—the Menominee Warrior Society. Almost on the eve of the successful passage of restoration, this small group staged a Wounded Knee-style thirty-day occupation of a novitiate of the Alexian Brothers (221). One commentator noted that among their demands was the " 'restoration' of patriarchal control of Menominee politics" by the removal of women leaders like Ada Deer, who they had not been able to defeat in elections (Anderson 1996:81).

Patterson observed of the contrast between AIM and DRUMS:

AIM was never interested in—now this is a very cruel thing to say. I don't think AIM was interested in any of the issues as issues—in the law and legislation. They were interested in making waves. This was guerrilla theater. . . . If I'd dreamed up a wave-making operation I could not have done it more brilliantly than they did, but they were not interested in the issues, the hard business of legislation, and not interested in the hard, tough, day-to-day work of administrating Indian affairs. . . . I think it was jazzing up the scene rather than contributing to the hard work. AIM could no more have drafted the bill restoring Menominee sovereignty— it took Ada Deer to do that.[10]

In the very last summer of the Nixon administration, the White House, still understandably AIM-shy, kept a wary eye on the June 8, 1974, AIM convention on the Standing Rock reservation. AIM billed it as "The First International Treaty Conference" (Means 1995:324). Patterson and Morris Thompson met with a group from other agencies, including Justice and HEW, "to go over strategy and tactics with regard to existing and potential problems with respect to the upcoming AIM convention."[11] They discussed requests of the host tribe for support for the convention, granting some but reaching "unanimous and strong agreement that none of the other requests made by the Standing Rock Tribe to assist in meeting the expenses, to the tribe, of the AIM convention were to be met at all."[12]

After the unexpectedly peaceful convention, some of the militants went to the Aberdeen area offices, demanding meetings with the area director of the BIA and also Commissioner Thompson.[13] The AIM representatives then requested a meeting with Thompson in Washington, and Patterson felt it necessary to warn the State Department that "Washington, unlike Mobridge, South Dakota will give AIM a national if not a world PR stage."[14] Nothing came of the fears. The AIM conference had decided to take its treaty case beyond Washington directly to the world stage, to the United Nations (Means 1995:325).

This prompted Patterson to send a warning memo to the State Department saying, "You and the USIA [United States Information Agency] should be aware that this 'Council' is not regarded by either Commissioner Thompson's Bureau or this office nor by the majority of the elected Indian tribal leaders of America as a group representative of the American Indian people."[15] The treaty council eventually went on to receive Non-Governmental Organization status at the UN, and from here on, it and AIM were more often heard abroad than at home (Weyler 1982:214; Ortiz 1984:35). AIM had no further impact on the few remaining days of the Nixon administration.

In the Courts

Despite the failure to pass authority for an Indian trust counsel, under Garment's urging the administration continued to support Indian positions in the courts, including the long-standing fishing dispute in Washington state. In 1973 the Justice Department filed a suit on behalf of Indian fishing rights in *Washington Department of Game v Puyallup Tribe* and again in a more comprehensive case, *The United States v Washington,* later that same year (Josephy 1984:204). The result was the "Boldt decision" in *U.S. v Washington,* February 12, 1974, favoring the Indian cause. The administration's support had been a critical factor in the outcome (Cohen 1986:82).[16]

In the face of continued resistance by Washington state and a series of appeals to higher courts after the decision, the administration continued its active trust advocacy (Castile 1985). A meeting of representatives from concerned agencies was held at the White House, and "It was agreed that the defense and protection of Indian treaty fishing rights in the instant circumstances and as defined by Judge Boldt are a part of the trust responsibilities which the United States government bears."[17] This spirited defense was not well received in the Northwest and eventually led Washington state representatives, including Senator Henry Jackson, to ask the attorney general "to consider the possibility of ending the government's trustee obligation to defend Indian rights and property in the courts" (Josephy 1984:209).

Despite Jackson's request, the Department of Justice, with White House urging, supported the Paiute tribe in its suit against the Truckee-Carson Irrigation District over reserved water rights at Pyramid Lake in Nevada (Knack 1984:338; Josephy 1984:169; McCool 1994:181). Meanwhile, on Indian cases before the Indian Claims Commission, Garment said to the Justice Department, "my hope is that the general principle could be adhered to of not appealing Claims Commission judgments and decisions unless the Solicitor General considers that an egregious mistake has been made."[18]

Congressional Sitzkrieg

Most of the administration's proposed Indian legislation remained stalled in Congress, as it had been since first proposed in 1970. In his second term, the president was still pressing for his Indian legislative package, but Congress was by then fully engaged in its "war" with Nixon (Ambrose 1991:59). "Nixon's proposed New American Revolution provided for changes in the American system of government . . . changes the Democrats and their allies were determined to stop" (Ambrose 1991:61). The war was underway before Watergate still further complicated legislative matters. Ambrose observed: "Had there never been a Watergate, there still would have been a war between Nixon and Congress" (Ambrose 1991:61). Changes in Indian policy were among the walking wounded.

The war was not one-sided. Ironically, at the same time as Nixon so consistently pressed Congress for Indian self-determination, he also consistently denigrated Democratic social programs of the past, including the Community Action programs that had provided the model for his Indian policy in the first place. "In a memo to Ehrlichman, he asked for a list of '10 or 15 horrible examples of how money has been wasted in model cities, community action, etc.'" (Ambrose 1991:62). Ehrlichman did not forward horrible examples of the Indian Community Action programs, although there were undoubtedly a few.

Twice more in 1973 Nixon chided Congress for its delays in considering and passing Indian legislation. In his September message on "National Legislative Goals," he referred to "six pieces of legislation pending in the Congress. . . . This legislation would help to foster greater self determination for the Indians."[19] In his message on the occasion of Menominee restoration, he took the opportunity to suggest, "I continue to believe that the Congress should rescind the outmoded House Concurrent Resolution 108 of 1953 in which this ill advised termination policy was set forth," and chided again about the stalled "legislative agenda in the area of Indian affairs. . . . Many of the items on that agenda are recommendations which I made fully 3 1/2 years ago."[20]

In his 1974 State of the Union address, Nixon recited the administration's accomplishments in Indian affairs, giving Congress some credit for "a spirit of bipartisan accomplishment." He also anticipated the passage of two bills, one "to speed Indian economic development" and the other "to upgrade the position of the Commissioner of Indian affairs to the Assistant Secretary level."[21] The upgrade of the commissioner did not pass, but the Indian Financing Act did, and on the occasion of its signing he observed, "This bill is the second to be enacted of the seven measures which I proposed four years ago when I pledged to follow a new philosophy of self determination. The first, enacted in 1970, returned the Blue Lake lands to the Taos Pueblo Indians. It continues to be my hope that with the support and encouragement of the Federal Government, we can create a new era in which the future of Indian people is determined primarily by Indian acts and Indian decisions."[22]

The Indian Finance Act was very similar to the omnibus bill defeated in the Udall years, focusing on development and the provision of loans. In its new guise it was made more palatable by loan guarantees backed with federal funds, not tribal assets, and with no reference to the alienation of land. This bill was to be the last new Indian-oriented legislation passed during the Nixon administration. Nixon's last public word on Indian affairs was on May 3, 1974, when he supported legislation regarding the restoration of Grand Canyon lands to the Havasupai, saying yet again in rebuke of Congress's dilatoriness, "I have concluded that the Havasupai have waited long enough."[23]

Self-Determination Progress

In 1973, the Senate had again held hearings on the self-determination legislation to which, by now, it had added an educational component. s.3157 became s.1017, a bill "To promote maximum Indian participation in the government and education of the Indian people."[24] The new educational component was largely based on the administration's s.1349, concerned with giving tribes greater control over the expenditure of Johnson O'Malley funds by allowing them to contract for their administration. The differences between the Senate and administration versions were not great except for the degree of discretion allowed the secretary of the interior in approving tribal contracts.

Frank Carlucci, testifying for the administration, said, "While we prefer enactment of s.1342 and s.1343, we believe that enactment of certain provisions of s.1017 as cited would be substantially consistent with the administration's policy of self-determination for Indians."[25] The administration also approved of the educational provisions that gave tribes Johnson O'Malley contracting authority, Part A of Title II, but regarded the rest of the bill's provisions as "duplication of existing programs."[26]

The testimony of Native Americans on the bill was still generally supportive but cautious, as seen, for example, in the testimony of Charles E.

Trimble of the NCAI. He commented on the shift of some education responsibility to the states from the federal government and noted: "We do believe
that there could easily be a move toward administrative termination as well
as legislative termination. And administrative termination could come about
through things as this. But in this bill I believe we haven't seen direct threats."[27]
On February 7, 1974, the Senate reported favorably on the bill, now amended
to meet the administration's objections to secretarial discretion but not
amended to meet concerns about the "duplicate provisions of the education
programs."[28]

By April 1 the bill had passed the full Senate, and in May the House
finally held hearings on the bill.[29] Morris Thompson, speaking for the administration on Title I, offered a number of relatively minor proposals for
modification and made a "recommendation that Title I of s.1017 be enacted,
subject to the above comments and suggestions, because of its critical importance to achieving Indian Self-Determination, strengthening tribal governments, and improving the general welfare of Indian people."[30] Commenting for the administration on Title II, John Kyl, assistant secretary of the
interior, again recommended approval of the JOM-related part A but not the
later sections, still on the grounds that they were "duplications."[31]

Indian spokesmen were yet again supportive of the legislation but still
offered a wide range of cautions and suggestions. Charles Trimble again endorsed the bill but could not resist a little Bureau bashing: "Overall Mr. Chairman we heartily endorse Title I of the bill in its intent and extensive provisions to help tribes serve their people. But, is there nothing we can do with
the paternalistic tyrants who would subvert the best intent of Congress to
emancipate the tribes from their heavy hands?"[32] Despite the hearings, the
House took no further action during the Nixon administration.

The Fall

Obviously, part of the difficulty the administration faced in getting any legislation through Congress in this period was the increasing clamor of the
Watergate affair. By March 1973, the investigation of the June 17, 1972 break-in
at the Democratic headquarters was occupying a good deal of the time of the
president and his key men. Ehrlichman, head of the Domestic Council, the
clearinghouse for all domestic policy, had left when Nixon asked for his res-

ignation on April 29, 1973 (Ehrlichman 1982:390). Garment said, "One of the many sadnesses of Watergate is that it dissipated the Nixon administration's ability to pursue the Indian initiatives it had started; John Ehrlichman, an indispensable agent of Nixon's Indian initiative, was soon gone from the White House" (1997:243). Ehrlichman's deputy, Kenneth Cole, provided some continuity when he became the Domestic Council executive director (Turner 1982:51). At Interior, Morton and Thompson were largely spared a part in the Watergate investigations, and both stayed on to the end of the administration.

In the White House, the most active players in Indian matters were Garment and Patterson. Patterson was not directly involved in Watergate at any level and continued his work on Indian policy uninterrupted. Garment was drawn into Watergate when he became the acting White House counsel in April 1973 after the departure of John Dean (Ambrose 1991:118). Garment had no prior role in the affair, and he noted of his role that "The White House needed an acting defense counsel who was completely uninvolved" (1997:253).

Garment remained involved in the administration's Indian program. In a May 1974 speech to the American Indian Lawyers Association, he struck some of the mystical notes of John Collier in insisting that Native Americans had a strong sense of community that others had lost. Referring to the stalled policies of New Federalism and Indian self-determination, he said, "Sooner or later these policies will be implemented in Indian and non Indian areas and as this occurs, the focus of the debates about Indian resources and priorities will increasingly move from Washington and from the BIA Area offices to Tribal Council tables."[33] As late as July 1974, a month before the fall, he was taking an active role in correspondence with the Justice Department on Indian claims policy.[34]

The role of the NCIO in Indian affairs declined. Authorization for the NCIO was scheduled to expire in November 1974, and the office of vice president, to which the organization was attached, found itself in turmoil. Vice President Spiro Agnew resigned on October 10, 1973, not as a result of Watergate but because of his own legal troubles (Nixon 1978:923). Nixon then named House Minority Leader Gerald Ford to the vice presidency (Greene 1995:13).

Sworn into office in December, Ford was to succeed to the presidency on August 9, 1974. In the slightly more than eight months of his vice presidential term, there was little time for him to take an active role in Indian affairs. He was more or less continuously occupied in dealing with the collapse of the administration and representing it in lieu of the beleaguered Nixon (Greene 1995:13). None of the accounts of Ford's brief vice presidency so much as mention the NCIO or Indian affairs in general, and no trace can be found in his vice presidential papers (Cannon 1994; Ford 1979; Greene 1995; Hartmann 1980).

During the changeover from Agnew to Ford, C. D. Ward of Agnew's staff wrote to new White House chief of staff Alexander Haig that, "In view of the situation, it is my recommendation that the status of the National Council on Indian Opportunity be reviewed. . . . It would be my recommendation that without a clear renewed directive that it was the President's desire for the Council to carry out its responsibility, it should be abolished."[35] Melvin Laird also recommended it be abolished and replaced with a subcommittee of the Domestic Council.[36]

The NCAI held a "National Indian Policy Conference" in Washington from June 5 to 7, 1974. One of the issues presented to it by the administration was the plan for a shift from the NCIO to the Domestic Council committee structure. "We are taking steps to establish a Committee of the Domestic Council to deal with formulation of Indian policy."[37] The precise mechanism for Indian participation was to be held open until after discussion with NCAI and other Indian organizations. "The Administration does not wish to design Indian consultative mechanisms of which Indian leaders themselves do not approve."[38] With Nixon under siege and no interest shown by Ford, the NCIO expired.

As early as November 1973, the Watergate crisis had reached such a point that Garment was recommending that Nixon resign (Ambrose 1991:264). Though the situation did nothing but get worse, Nixon soldiered on. It was not until July 1974 that the crisis became all-consuming, when the Supreme Court ruled against Nixon's executive privilege to withhold evidence and the Judiciary Committee voted to recommend impeachment (Ambrose 1991: 394–96). The Nixon era in Indian affairs abruptly ended on August 8, 1974, when President Richard Nixon announced his resignation.

The Nixon administration has received little historical credit for its accomplishments in Indian affairs. Much of this is perhaps simply due to the fact that many writers are unable to get beyond Watergate. Hoff had a chapter titled "Nixon Is More than Watergate," in which she noted: "Nixon not only lived up to our worst expectations as President but he also achieved more than most of us would like to admit" (Hoff 1994:4).

The Nixon White House presided over the introduction of significant legislative change in Indian affairs, although not as much as it had hoped for. It took the policy trend toward self-administration generated in the LBJ years and tried to turn it into law; the White House did succeed in making self-administration Bureau policy. It similarly changed Justice Department policy on federal support of Indian cases in the courts. It restored considerable amounts of lands, sacred and otherwise, to the Indian people and sorted out the status of the Alaskan Native Claims. It continued restructuring Indian education in the direction of self-administration.

The AIM hoopla and mythology has in many accounts largely overshadowed the realities of the administration's efforts in Indian affairs. In contrast to the Indian activists, the White House, even its White Hats, were cast as the bad guys. For example, one account said, "the Nixon strategy was to stabilize and pacify Indian protests: that is, destroy militancy in order to pave the way for the exploitation of Indian resources" (Ortiz 1981:9). Even while noting that resources were in fact restored to Indians, another account claimed that "the government embarked on a selective program of land restoration, returning Blue Lake to Taos Pueblo, Mount Adams to the Yakimas, and some 60,000 acres to the Warm Springs tribes of Oregon, but the restorations were more in the form of political payoffs for support than an acknowledgement of the justice of the case for land reform" (Deloria 1974:38). On the restoration of Blue Lake, one writer said that "As commendable as that act was, it was for show" (Stern 1994:323).

Some, like Forbes, damned with faint praise. "Indian reservations are colonies whose resources and 'cheap labor' is available for profitable use. Today, thanks to the Nixon years, they are partially self administered colonies" (Forbes 1981:123). Some writers were much stronger in their condemnation. Patterson recounted AIM activist LaNada Means, "rebutting my enthusiastic description of Nixon's Message with the comment, 'Anything Nixon says is shit.'"[39]

The Nixon policies set forth in 1970 seem to have simply eluded the notice of many. Patterson wrote in some evident frustration: "As an officer on his staff, my personal hopes and aspirations are the same as the President's. I am pretty much convinced however, that many if not most of our non-Indian but sympathetic readers do not realize, first hand, just what was in that 1970 message, and tend to look upon the BIA and the administration as if that message never existed."[40] Vine Deloria for one, entirely ignored the 1970 presidential statement on Indian policy in his account of Indian militancy, *Behind the Trail of Broken Treaties* (1974).

In the end there is no getting around the record, and as Hoff observed, on Indian affairs "Nixon's record continues to compare favorably with that of all other occupants of the Oval Office since World War II, despite all the numerous confrontational incidents that he faced that they did not" (Hoff 1994:44). Despite his critical analysis of the Nixon era, Forbes ended by saying, "Nonetheless, the Nixon years of 1969–1972, when compared to all that had gone before (and with all that has happened since) stand out as probably the most exciting, innovative period in the BIA's entire history, perhaps even surpassing the 1933–1941 years under F. D. Roosevelt and Commissioner John Collier" (Forbes 1981:124).

After the Fall
Ford in for Nixon

I have signed into law s.1017, the Indian Self-Determination
and Education Assistance Act.
—President Gerald R. Ford, "Statement on Signing the Indian Self-
Determination and Education Assistance Act, January 4, 1975"

*G*erald R. Ford, like the other presidents we have considered,
had no record of a prior interest in Indian affairs and made no mention of
Indian affairs in his own writings on his presidency; nor do any of his biographers (Cannon 1994; Casserly 1977; Ford 1979; Greene 1995; Hartmann 1980).
The only glimmer of a personal interest in things Indian was, like Nixon's,
football related. Though Ford had been a star player and Nixon only a bench
warmer, they had the sport in common. Where Nixon remembered his coach,
Ford took the trouble to write in support of the return of the Olympic med-
als stripped from Native American athlete Jim Thorpe. "Throughout my life
and my active participation in sports, the name of Jim Thorpe has represented excellence, dedication, pride and competitive zeal. . . . To Americans
of Indian heritage, Mr. Thorpe has meant much more."[1]

While it was Ford's administration that finally saw the passage of the
Indian Self-Determination Act, it was obviously not a Ford initiative but a
direct policy carry-over from the Nixon administration. The bill (s.1017) had
initially passed in the Senate in the waning days of the Nixon presidency;
final passage by both houses was on December 19, less than three months
into the new administration—little time for the personal impact of a new
president to take effect (CIS 1975:1001). Although Ford sought to put some
distance between himself and Nixon, the policy of Indian self-determination
was one of the Nixon legacies that the Ford administration accepted and
adopted as its own.

AIM was another legacy that the new administration discussed early on. Kenneth Cole recorded that at a cabinet meeting in September the possibility of "another Wounded Knee-BIA take over" was raised. He recorded Ford's comment: "P-Guidance—'The law will be upheld—the decisions will not be made on a political basis.'"[2] When Ford pardoned Nixon, Dennis Banks was moved to wire the president saying, "We denounce your pardon of Richard Nixon. . . . While pardoning criminals like Richard Nixon, you are leaving a life long sentence of termination hanging over the lives of Indian people." Bradley Patterson recommended no response be made, and none was.[3]

Ford Domestic Policy

Indian policy in the Ford administration was not a reflection and exemplar of a larger domestic policy scheme, as it had been under New Federalism or the Great Society. Ford simply did not have any such overall scheme. "For the most part, Ford's domestic policy was less an articulated agenda and more an exercise in crisis management" (Greene 1995:85). His administration faced one crisis after another, beginning with the furor over the Nixon pardon. At home, the economy was in trouble with inflation and the OPEC energy crisis; in foreign affairs, the regime in Saigon fell; and in the midst of it all, Ford suffered two assassination attempts (Ford 1979:310).

Even some Native Americans contributed to the crisis atmosphere when, in the second month of the administration, the Kootenai of Idaho threatened to "declare a condition of war as existing between the Kootenai Nation and the United States of America" if their disputes with the government, mostly over the restoration of tribal lands, were not resolved.[4] The matter was referred to Commissioner Morris Thompson and war was averted, but Patterson, still antsy about AIM, worried, "The danger would be if the AIM people move in on this 'opportunity.'"[5]

To the extent that there was a consistent Ford domestic policy scheme, it was directed toward cutting the costs of government programs. Indian programs were sometimes among those threatened with cuts: "an administration bill that would have cut monies to federal programs such as the Right to Read program and Native American education was stopped by Congress"

(Greene 1995:85). Proposed increases in funding for Indian health touched off an internal White House debate on the cost issue. Staffers Bobbie Greene Kilberg and Ted Marrs argued for it and were influential in exempting it from Ford's parsimony program. Kilberg observed, "Health Care for Native Americans is not the place to oppose program expansion," and Marrs said, "Pragmatically, there will be a veto override. Politically we can be made to look bad."[6]

The Domestic Council, previously a source of coordination of Nixon domestic policy, lost much of its function in a general Ford reversal of Nixon's concentration of power in the White House. "The Cabinet departments and agencies had lost power and influence to such White House appendages as the Domestic Council.... A Watergate was made possible by a strong chief of staff and ambitious White House aides who were more powerful than members of the Cabinet.... I wanted to reverse the trend and restore authority to my Cabinet" (Ford 1979:132). The result was to shift a good deal of decision making back to the individual agencies.

At Interior, self-determination was the prevailing policy, and absent any new presidential directive, it continued to be pursued. Morton, who remained at Interior in the new administration, had Ford's confidence. "We shared the same philosophy and political beliefs" (Ford 1979:130). Late in the administration, Morton moved to Commerce and was replaced at Interior briefly by Stanley Hathaway on June 11, 1975, who was in turn replaced by Thomas S. Kleppe on October 9, 1975 (Ford 1979:260; Prucha 1984:1216). Morris Thompson stayed on as commissioner until the very last days of the administration.

The NCIO had expired, and with it the special role for the vice president in Indian Affairs. In the Ford administration, Vice President Nelson Rockefeller was originally intended to play a strong role in domestic policy (Cannon 1994:368). Rockefeller proposed that he head the Domestic Council, but he and it were caught up in the midst of a White House staff civil war. A conflict raged between the members of the Nixon staff that Ford retained and his own new aides, especially between Chief of Staff Alexander Haig and presidential counselor Robert T. Hartmann, whom Ford had brought from his congressional staff (Ford 1979:185; Hartmann 1980:203). Rockefeller's proposal to become the executive director of the Domestic Council created yet another divisive issue over the primary responsibility of council staff—to the president or vice president?—and was opposed by Donald Rumsfeld and other top Ford aides (Turner 1982:54).

A compromise was reached with the appointment of Rockefeller's personal choice for executive director of the Domestic Council, James Cannon. The mixed loyalties this imposed on Cannon and the council created further confusion and resulted in a weakening of the council. After this struggle, "Rockefeller was ignored for the rest of the administration as a domestic advisor. He was not replaced, and for all practical purposes, no one was in charge of Ford's domestic and social policies" (Greene 1995:84–85). Rockefeller made no contribution to Indian policy. He was not sworn in until December 19, 1974, the date of the passage of the self-determination legislation, on which he obviously had no impact (Greene 1995:31).

Ford Indian Policy

Lacking any new directions or initiatives in Indian affairs from on high, the White House staff continued to pursue the policies already in motion. Self-determination was now clearly the core policy. However, in the first month of the new administration, still lacking the umbrella legislation to implement it, Bradley Patterson was trying to coordinate the inclusion of Native American governments into new social service legislation:

> Beginning with the signing of the General Revenue Sharing Act and more recently with the new CETA [Comprehensive Employment and Training Act] measure, community development, surplus property and the Intergovernmental Personnel Act, we are making sure that such legislation has written into it at least the authority for the elected tribal governments of federally recognized tribes, as responsible governmental units in their own right, to step in and take over programs directly, rather than compete or stand hat in hand at State capitols. This revised position of ours is greatly strengthened by the practically unanimous position of Indian leaders themselves that they prefer this route.... Of course all of BIA, plus HEW's own ONAP [Office of Native American Programs] function according to this principle.[7]

The White House staff members involved in Indian policy were among those swept up in the internal struggles and changes in the new administration. Hartmann's book *Palace Politics* described the clash between the newcomers and the Nixon holdovers, whom Hartmann called the "Praetorians" (1980:1). Leonard Garment and Kenneth Cole were among those who left office in a January 1975 general purge of Nixon staff (Ford 1979:234). By this time Garment had little formal role in Indian affairs, but as a former Nixon aide, he had concentrated on and been one of those influential in convincing Ford to issue Nixon a pardon (Garment 1997:301; Greene 1995:45).[8]

Bradley Patterson, however, was kept on and continued to exercise an influence on Indian policy throughout the Ford administration. His role was changed when early in October 1974 he was asked by the president to serve the First Lady as "Staff Coordinator," and then to manage the White House personnel office's operations center, but from these positions he continued to consult with those more directly charged with Indian matters.[9] He returned to a formal role as special assistant for Native American programs on August 26, 1976.[10]

Meanwhile, Indian matters in the White House were largely handled by Norman Ross of the Domestic Council and Theodore Marrs, special assistant to the president for human resources. Marrs, a physician with a military background, primarily concerned himself with matters of Indian health; after his time at the White House, he joined the Indian Health Service.[11] Bobbie Greene Kilberg had left the White House in 1971 but returned in 1975 to serve Ford as an "Associate Council to the President."[12] Though not directly charged with Indian matters, because of her experience she, like Patterson, was consulted on Indian policy for the remainder of the administration.

Congress and Indian Policy

The 1974 elections returned the so-called "Watergate babies" to Congress, giving the Democrats an overwhelming majority. "Knowing that getting a legislative package of his own passed would be next to impossible, Ford undertook a deliberate veto strategy, sending legislation back to Congress at an unprecedented rate" (Greene 1992:20). Among the legislation vetoed was the

Indian Employment Act, which would have provided "special retirement benefits" for those "adversely affected by Indian preference requirement." It was vetoed as being "discriminatory and costly."[13] The act was an attempt to deal with the unhappiness of non-Indian Bureau employees suffering under the strong Indian-preference program now firmly in place. A version of the bill did finally pass in 1979, referred to by some at the Bureau as the "Honky Out Act" (Feraca 1990:178).

During the Ford administration, Congress had clearly taken possession of the domestic policy ball. "Nixon then bequeathed to Ford a new relationship between the executive and legislative branches of government, and Congress clearly had the upper hand" (Greene 1995:54). In the case of Indian policy, this turned out to be not entirely bad news.

Domestic policies associated with Nixon, including the Indian legislation, had not flourished in the Democratic Congress. However, once Nixon's resignation was imminent, the Indian self-determination policy became in a sense politically orphaned. The Democrats, specifically Henry Jackson, had an opportunity to adopt the waif and pass it off as their own—to show *their* heart. Minorities were, after all, a traditional Democratic constituency only temporarily hijacked by Nixon. Whatever the motivation, Congress, which had held back Indian initiatives all through the Nixon years, gradually ceased its opposition during the Ford administration.

James Officer attributed the principal burst of post-Nixon congressional legislative movement in Indian affairs to Senator James Abourezk and Representative Lloyd Meeds (Officer 1984:93). Abourezk certainly took an activist position in Native American matters. The self-determination bill, however, was sponsored by Henry Jackson before Abourezk's arrival on the Senate Interior Committee, and he continued to be its sponsor and moving force at the time of passage. Abourezk himself thought that Jackson was still in charge of the fate of Indian legislation at that time. "Scoop Jackson had assigned only one staff member—Forest Gerard—to the Indian subcommittee. Although I was the subcommittee's chairman, Gerard took his orders from Scoop" (Abourezk 1989:215).

Senator Henry Jackson was in firm control of the Interior committee and was by now also trying to be thoroughly presidential. On the beginning of Jackson's shift toward a positive role in moving Indian legislation, Gross quoted an unnamed Jackson aide, probably Forest Gerard, as saying, "We began modifying legislation that Congress had set forward and which had been around a long time. . . . We looked for omnibus legislation to handle" (1989:91). Despite this shift from champion of termination to sponsor of self-determination, Jackson was not an entirely reformed man.

By 1974 the controversy over Indian fishing rights in Washington state was coming to a climax in the courts. The Ford administration continued the Nixon policy of supporting the Indian position. Patterson advised Marrs, "If we should lose this case on appeal—by any shortcoming of ours, we will be in the soup with the entire Indian Community."[14] He later wrote when the case (*U.S. v Washington,* the so-called Boldt decision), was adjudged favorable to the Indian cause: "Of course State, local, commercial and sports fishermen are unhappy about the decision. Lloyd Meeds got a lot of pressure about it. The President will be pressured, I think, to disavow or criticize or express personal disagreement with the decision. This would be a mistake of the first order. Americans generally (not just Indians) are slowly beginning to recognize that the government is at last stepping up to defend Indian treaty and trust rights; the Head of our Executive Branch should not flinch in the area"[15] (Cohen 1986:11).

The administration continued its support, but Jackson flinched and temporarily abandoned his presidential stance on Indian affairs to dutifully denounce these events on his home turf. He announced his intention to introduce legislation with Senator Warren Magnuson "to assure effective and fair management of the fish runs . . . such legislation could include an effort to rescind the treaties or buy out the Indians" (Castile 1985:8). When George H. Boldt's decision was finally upheld by the Supreme Court in 1979, Jackson and Magnuson said to the secretary of the interior that "we must urge your very serious consideration of less than full implementation of the Boldt decision" (Cohen 1986:106).

Representative Lloyd Meeds, also from Washington state, was long a strong supporter of Indian legislation in the House Interior committee, but in the face of the fishing controversy, he too flinched. In his case, what had played well in Washington, D.C.—support of Indian rights—was eroding his electoral base back home. As a member of the American Indian Policy Review Commission (AIPRC), he expressed his reversal by writing a dissent from the findings of that commission. Abourezk noted: "He eventually—I'm certain much to his own dismay—became the chief opponent of pro-Indian activities on the commission" (1989:216). It was, however, politically too little too late, and apparently convinced of defeat, he did not run again in 1978.

The American Indian Policy Review Commission was established the same month the Self-Determination Act passed. The AIPRC promised a thorough review of Indian affairs, and it was at least partly a device planned to give Abourezk some staff and independence from Jackson (Abourezk 1989:215). Though a strong tide of pro-Indian sentiment was now present in Congress, the AIPRC report, when eventually delivered during the Carter administration, seemed to some to have gone too far. In his dissent Meeds observed, "the report is the result of one-sided advocacy in favor of American Indian tribes. The interests of the United States, the States and non-Indian citizens, if considered at all, were largely ignored" (Prucha 1990:282). Whatever its merits, Prucha observed that "in the end the commission's work was largely ineffective" (Prucha 1990:281). In any case, its impact, if any, falls more properly in the next era of Indian policy, outside the scope of this book.

The Indian Self-Determination and Education Assistance Act of 1975

Meed's and Jackson's pro-Indian stance lasted long enough to see the self-determination legislation through to passage. After hearings held by the House Indian Subcommittee in May, which included a strong positive endorsement by Jackson, the full House Interior and Insular Affairs Committee reported favorably on s.1017 on December 16, 1974.[16] The House committee had been a good deal more responsive to the administration's suggestions than the Senate. "The Committee adopted several major amendments to s.1017 as passed by the Senate. Most of such amendments were recommended by the Department of the Interior and the General Accounting Office."[17] Most of the points of disagreement between administration and Senate versions, never great, were reconciled. The bill was considered and passed the House on December 19, 1974, with the Senate concurring in the amendments.

Kenneth Cole, as one of his last acts of the administration, sent a memo to the president conveying endorsements of the bill by all executive agencies concerned and a signing statement prepared at Interior.[18] President Gerald R. Ford signed the bill into law on January 4, 1975, as Public Law 93–38 (88 Stat.2203).[19] "An Act, To provide maximum Indian participation in the Government and education of the Indian people; to provide for the full participation of the Indian tribes in programs and service conducted by the Federal Government for Indians and to encourage the development of human resources for the Indian people; to establish a program of assistance to upgrade Indian education; to support the right of Indian citizens to control their own educational activities; and for other purposes" (Prucha 1990:274). The self-administration policy, which had been evolving since the 1960s was now fixed in law. Neither Ford's signing statement nor the language of the bill itself mentioned the roles of Presidents Johnson and Nixon in the long effort to arrive at this point. A few days later, however, in a message to the NTCA convention Ford said, "My two predecessors set the stage for this national goal . . . by establishing self-determination without termination as the foundation for dealing with these issues. . . . At this time I am happy to assure you that my administration will continue to press ahead in these matters with all vigor and resolve necessary to bring about even greater progress in the years ahead."[20]

Ford's staff attempted to develop a coherent position for him on Indian affairs built around the theme of self-determination embodied in the act, but it never quite came together. In June 1975, Theodore Marrs was made the head of an "Interagency Task Force on Indian Affairs" to coordinate policy.[21] There is no indication anywhere in the Ford Library files that this task force ever formulated any significant policy guidelines or even met.

In a speech in October 1975, Marrs tried to set out the Ford policy, which was simply de facto to continue pursuing the Nixon initiatives. He indicated that they would seek passage of two remaining major pieces of Nixon-proposed legislation, the Indian Trust Counsel Authority and the creation of an assistant secretary for Indian affairs.[22] He also sought to reassure those who still saw termination under the self-determination bed, saying, "Congressional passage of the Indian Self-Determination Act both by express language and basic purpose indicates that the termination policy no longer exists."[23]

A section of the "Vice President's Briefing Book," titled "Indians and Territorial Affairs," similarly indicated that the administration would continue to pursue the basic Nixon legislative program.[24] Under "Administration Policies" it stated the plan was "To continue the policy of Indian self-determination without termination of the special relationships between the Federal Government and Indian people."[25] Marrs explored the possibility of a Ford presidential message on Indian affairs in the tradition started by Johnson, but it never got beyond preliminary discussions.[26] Kent Frizzell, as acting secretary, indicated Interior was going forward to implement self-determination. "The Interior Department is developing a thorough set of regulations designed to be fully responsive to the needs of the Indian community."[27]

Some further progress was made in the Ford years. The Sioux, actively supported by Patterson, had continued to press their claims for a Black Hills settlement (Lazarus 1991:331). Congress finally passed, and Ford signed, a bill authorizing appropriations for the Indian Claims Commission covering costs of the Black Hills settlement.[28] In 1975, the Court of Claims adjudicating the settlement made a finding that would have reduced the award to a very small amount, and Senator Abourezk began hearings on new legislation to override that decision (Lazarus 1991:347). At those hearings the traditional chiefs last heard from at Wounded Knee reappeared, denouncing all forms of settlement and demanding return of the Hills. Lazarus indicated that the Senate committee paid little heed since "they represented only themselves. Their absolutist views did not hold sway in the elected tribal councils" (351).

These same traditional chiefs and headmen who had met with Patterson and corresponded with Garment after Wounded Knee also attempted to influence President Ford's policies. They sent a letter seeking a meeting to once again discuss the 1868 treaty, written in a curious mixture of modern and antique style: "For many winters and many generations we have suffered under this alien system (1934 Reorganization Act, etc)."[29] Presumably referring to the earlier meetings with Patterson and other staff, they said: "And each time we call for a meeting with the U.S. Government you have always responded by sending people from different governmental agencies who have no knowledge, experience or power to execute an effective program for all."[30] They were able to arrange to meet with Theodore Marrs on November 9, on which occasion "the President dropped by."[31]

Marrs, still trying to create a Ford Indian posture, later urged that the president hold a formal meeting with a larger and more representative group of "Indian Chiefs and Leaders," saying, "This meeting will provide a better identification with the past and future Indian programs" for the president and that "There is a strong national interest in the welfare of the Indian which is becoming increasingly significant. As other groups develop their own interest in heritage they seem to be identifying with the Indian as well. There is also the natural relationship between the Indian and the Bicentennial."[32]

Staffer William Baroody arranged for the meeting "to allay fears of fluctuant policy."[33] It was duly held on July 16, 1976, along with a day of meetings between the Indian representatives and various administration officials, including new Secretary of the Interior Thomas S. Kleppe. Ford made brief remarks reaffirming the self-determination policy. "I am committed to furthering the self-determination of Indian communities but without terminating the special relationship between the Federal Government and the Indian people. I am strongly opposed to termination. Self-determination means that you can decide the nature of your tribe's relationship with the Federal Government within the framework of the Self-Determination Act, which I signed in January of 1975."[34] The meeting was otherwise purely ceremonial, and some Indian leaders reacted negatively to the occasion, calling it a "campaign publicity pitch." Mel Tonasket was quoted as saying "There's no doubt we've been used."[35]

Ford also used the meeting to announce the resignation of Marrs and the appointment of Bradley Patterson as special presidential assistant "to improve the coordination among the various Federal agencies with programs that serve the Indian people," and "to insure that when Federal actions are planned which affect Indian communities, the responsible Indian leaders are consulted in the planning process."[36]

One of Patterson's first tasks was to join in the final stages of the internal White House struggle over the Indian Health Care Improvement Act, which Paul O'Neil, acting director of the Office of Management and Budget, was urging Ford to veto as part of the cost-cutting process and which Interior and HEW were supporting.[37] Patterson weighed in with a number of detailed points of practical and political reasoning, including a warning: "Carter's political staff is keeping a close track on Indian matters."[38] He also accurately put the bill in historical context: "For seven years there has been an unbroken series of Presidential actions which have reversed and rectified the past decades of neglect for Native Americans. It has been a brilliant executive/legislative accomplishment in which you and a bi-partisan Congress fully share. A veto of this bill would be the first turnaround in that seven year record and, as such, would have symbolic impact greater than the merits of the bill considered by themselves."[39]

Marrs and Kilberg had long supported the bill, and Kilberg wrote at this point, "As a political matter, a veto of this bill will be portrayed as direct Presidential action against the improvement of health care for the Native American community, a group for which the majority of people in this country has substantial empathy."[40] Ford signed the Indian Health Care Improvement Act of 1976, but reluctantly, saying, "This bill is not without its faults. Some of the authorizations in this bill are duplicative of existing authorities, and there is an unfortunate proliferation of narrow categorical programs."[41]

Other than the health bill, not much happened in Indian affairs in the Ford administration after the passage of the Self-Determination Act, but toward the very end of the administration there were some minor crises in Indian affairs. Members of the Puyallup tribe raised some new problems for the administration when, led by tribal chair Ramona Bennett, they occupied the former federal Cushman Hospital building in Tacoma (Indian Voice 1976:1). The administration continued the policy begun by Garment of supporting Indian claims and proposed "to take appropriate legal and/or administrative action as required for the return of the facility and property to the trusteeship of the United States for the Puyallup tribe," but only if the occupation were ended.[42] Kilberg wrote in support, "The hospital is on land adjacent to the present Puyallup reservation of about 30 acres and at one time the hospital land was within the exterior boundaries of the reservation."[43] The crisis was averted, and the facility did eventually become part of the revived Puyallup reservation, much enlarged by its settlement with the state of Washington in 1989 (Gardner 1989).

Despite repeated administration statements renouncing termination, residual fears were not immediately calmed, perhaps because of the cost-cutting orientation of the administration. Fears briefly flared when an OMB in-house memo was leaked that seemed to suggest the possibility of a return to getting out of the Indian business. Harold Borgstrom of the OMB wrote the internal confidential memo in April 1976, on "Organization for Indian Affairs," about fundamental aims of policy. It had unsettling things to say: "Self determination (local goal setting, resource allocation, program design, and program management) will only lead to the eventual cessation of special Federal Indian programs as a very unintended effect of the execution of the Indian policy." It also said, "Issues of sovereignty and entitlement are viewed as reference points insofar as they are perceived to be valid concepts by some participants, but they are not viewed as 'basic' or unconditional principles."[44] OMB's main proponent of program elimination seemed here to be repudiating the guarantees that self-determination would be without termination. Leaked to Ernie Stevens, staffer with the AIPRC, and to Richard La Course of the American Indian Press Association, it caused a brief uproar in Indian country. The ideas expressed were never seriously considered as policy, but their mere utterance by a member of the White House staff was obviously alarming.

In November, after Ford had narrowly lost the election to Jimmy Carter, yet another new policy issue emerged, but one which the lame duck administration side-stepped. The federal appeals court held that "The land conveyance in the treaties of 1794 and 1818 between Maine (then Massachusetts) and the Passamaquoddy and Penobscot Indians . . . may well be void. . . . This in turn puts a cloud over the ownership and titles . . . which amounts to 60% of the State of Maine."[45] Patterson summed up the situation and said, "Mr. Carter, then as President, will have to make the final judgment about what kind of lawsuits or a legislative package to support."[46] This was the last act, or nonact, of the Ford administration in Indian affairs.

By this point Native Americans, as well as Congress and the administration, had adopted the policy of self-determination as their own. Writing to Garment in October 1976 after attending the NCAI convention, Patterson noted, "Remembering what we considered *our* far sighted efforts in June-July 1970, to set forth a turnaround and a new direction for Indian policy, what Indians are giving *now* as their priority desires is impressive. They have really picked up on self-determination and in the spirit of Gompers have done a good deal 'more' with it."[47]

The story I set out to tell in this book properly ends with the passage of the Self-Determination Act, which formalized the policy shift that began in the 1960s. Self-determination without termination was federal policy by the end of the Ford administration. President Gerald R. Ford declared, "When I signed the Indian Self Determination and Education Assistance Act in January, 1975, I described that legislation as a 'milestone for Indian people.'"[48] In my view he was correct.

Epilogue

*I*n the years between 1934 and 1975 federal Indian policy might be described as having boxed the compass. In 1934 it swung through 180 degrees, reversing direction from assimilation. It swung 180 degrees back to termination after only twenty years, and then back 180 yet again after another twenty years, to self-determination. This book has been an attempt to say what happened in that last shift, from termination to self-determination, between 1960 and 1975. I have elsewhere made more general theoretical attempts at explaining long-range trends in federal Indian policy which the reader might want to consult (1974, 1992, 1993). Here it might be worthwhile and manageable to sum up what we have considered.

Termination as policy simply ran out of political steam in the 1960s. During the termination era, "freeing" Indian land, the dynamic behind the earlier assimilation period, was reduced to a purely regional concern and was thus less compelling to Congress at large. Even for western congressmen, what little Indian land remained to be freed was not critically important, and its pursuit could be easily overshadowed by larger concerns. Indian committees continued to be dominated by western congressmen, but the apotheosis of Henry Jackson and the apostasy of Lloyd Meeds reflected the fact that national rather than regional resource-based concerns were driving congressional views on Indian policy—at least some of the time.

The national issue that finally outweighed western parochial interests was the civil rights struggle. Termination/assimilation was too visibly blatant an attempt to eliminate a people's community and, as such, an affront to the large national political constituency supporting the rights of minorities. Under Truman, civil rights in its "integration" phase had lent strength to termination, but by the 1960s the civil rights thrust was increasingly toward "com-

munal" rights as well as simple integration. The Johnson era brought with it
the passage of major civil rights legislation, the inauguration of the Community Action programs, and the vocal social protest of the movement. Termination was increasingly an unhappy canary in this new political atmosphere.

But if termination was becoming a political embarrassment, what was
to take its place? Collier's IRA system was, by default, still in force and not
very satisfactory. Indians were sort of self-governing, sort of not. Most funds
and authority remained in the hands of external administrators even though
tribal governments were becoming more effective. The tribes were not happy
with the status quo but liked the prospect of termination even less. Despite
much rhetoric of Camelot, not much was happening in general domestic
policy in the JFK years that might have pointed to a new direction. The early
'60s are perhaps best characterized as policy "ad hoccery," as Bee has suggested, with no very clear direction (1992:140).

Then the OEO arrived on the reservations and, much to everyone's surprise, offered a better idea, the local administration of federal funds through
bloc grants. The appeal to Indian leaders was immediate. An OEO-style grant
system would continue the flow of government funding that was essential
because the tribes had long since become impoverished by resource looting
and could not generate sufficient revenues of their own to serve their clienteles. It would, however, in vivid contrast to the hundred years of Bureau
administration, allow the Indian peoples to take over and manage their own
affairs, or at least some substantial part of them.

One of the problems that neither Collier nor the terminationists ever
solved was a practical means of going from no Indian self-government to
complete Indian self-government. The terminationist solution, to simply push
them out of the boat to sink or swim, was both unworkable and unacceptable. The Collier-IRA approach tended toward permanently suspending them
half in and half out of the boat, not a comfortable position. What the new
OEO grant system offered was a mechanism for the tribes to move forward a
step at a time, a way to gain competence and confidence. Given their not so
paranoiac fears of termination, those steps had to be coupled with guarantees of the permanence of the "special relationship." This caused the emergence of the litany "self-determination without termination," repeated so often in later policy utterances.

In addition to its embrace by the tribal governments, this oeo contract model began to look like a workable new direction to insightful people at Interior—Udall, King, Officer—and to national Indian leaders like Vine Deloria and LaDonna Harris. But good ideas don't become policy just because they *are* good ideas. There has to be some political force to overcome policy inertia, and Indians themselves lacked such force. Major changes in Indian policy are all linked to larger scale shifts in federal social policy: assimilation to abolition and reconstruction, reorganization to the depression, termination to the war, and so on.

The "Big Daddy from the Pedernales" supplied the needed political force almost single-handedly (Conklin 1986). The sweeping social programs launched by lbj in his quest for the Great Society were at least as large-scale as those mounted to combat the Depression (Heclo 1986). Why he set out to war on poverty is not easy to explain and beyond my brief but he did, and that war shifted Indian policy. The civil rights movement had created a climate in which visibly doing right (and avoiding doing wrong) by any minority group had political advantage. The Johnson-inspired Community Action agencies set out to do right for all in need and then quickly ran out of steam, but not before they had succeeded on the reservations.

The Indian Community Action programs were among the clear successes of the lbj administration. The Indians liked the whole idea and said so. Udall and the Bureau thought they had finally found an answer to their problems and said so. All in all, it was something that the administration could point to with pride in troubled times, as can be seen in Johnson's history-making presidential message, the "Forgotten Americans." However, the turn to self-determination outlined in that message came too late to be conjured into legislation, which, given lbj's legislative track record, it surely would have been in a second Johnson term.

When a Republican president replaced Johnson, it might well have been the end of the new Indian policy direction, leading back once again to ad hoccery. The Nixon administration was generally opposed to Johnson's social spending and dismantled much of his Great Society, including the oeo. But the rights of minorities were still a politically high-profile issue, and Nixon's standing in the minority community and among its friends was not strong. Doing something that one minority group wanted done and which

could easily be done made political sense—to show heart! By pure coincidence, he was also the only president in modern times who seems to have
had a personal interest in Indian matters, thanks to the Chief.

Though spawned by the social-spending Johnson, the system of local
administration of federal funds also fit in rather nicely with where the Nixon
administration was going in domestic policy—to New Federalism. It was less
federal government, devolution of power to the local community and, who
knows, it might have even saved money. To implement a small-scale version
of New Federalism on the reservations would not cost much in dollars or
political capital, since it would not take from any other constituency. The
precedent wasn't a dangerous encouragement to separatism on the part of
other minorities, since it was clearly restricted to Indians. In the end, the oeo
model turned out to be an answer that worked just as well for the Nixon
administration as it had for Johnson.

It took until 1975 and the presidency of Gerald Ford to persuade Congress to go along with the policy enunciated in 1970 by Nixon. The delay was
in part a product of the distractions created by the media chiefs and in part
the Democratic Congress's natural desire to let any Nixon policy twist in the
wind. In the end it made the same good political sense for Congress to embrace the new policy as it did for Nixon—to show heart—and they finally
recognized that sense. In the long run it was a bipartisan shift. From 1960 to
1975, four presidents presided over Indian policy, two Democrats and two
Republicans, with a Congress which retained a Democratic majority throughout. It was finally the Republican Richard Nixon (of all people) who had
made it happen, in uneasy cooperation with Democrat and born-again
terminationist Henry Jackson (of all people).

Life after Self-Determination

A great deal has happened in Indian affairs since 1975, which I will not attempt to address more than briefly here—it's a suitable topic for another
book. Self-determination has remained federal policy, albeit with some shifts
in emphasis, particularly during the Reagan years (Esber 1992, Morris 1992,
Jorgensen 1986). It was not until 1988 that Congress finally got around to
formally repudiating the termination resolution (hcr 108) in the Tribally
Controlled Schools Act (pl 100–297). There, they at last flatly said, "Congress

hereby repudiates and rejects House Concurrent Resolution 108" (Prucha 1990:315).

The legislative momentum in Native American policy established during the Nixon years has continued. The status of Indian affairs in Interior was upgraded in 1977 with the creation of the position of assistant secretary for Indian affairs (Prucha 1984:1123). Additional protections for traditional religion were endorsed by a Senate resolution in 1978; when these protections were threatened by court decisions, the Religious Freedom Restoration Act of 1993 was passed (Peregoy et al. 1995:16). 1978 was a landmark year, with legislation establishing the "Federal Acknowledgement" process—granting unrecognized tribes federal status—the Tribally Controlled College Assistance Act, and the Indian Child Welfare Act (Prucha 1990:288–94).

In general, the legislative trend has continued toward increased Indian sovereignty with many existing policies, such as Indian control of education and the Alaskan Native Claims settlement, being strengthened. Indian control over cultural resources was expanded in the Archaeological Resources Protection Act of 1979, and the Native American Graves Protection and Repatriation Act of 1990 (NARF 1990:1). A very complex and ongoing issue was created with the Indian Gaming Regulatory Act in 1988, which promised to put an economic base under self-determination (Prucha 1990:316). Overall, since 1975, the federal courts have been very actively favorable on decisions affecting Indian rights (see Getches et al. 1993).

It has not turned out to be easy to implement the self-determination policy. Some delays were to be expected simply to allow the time necessary for the tribal governments to gain experience and confidence. Progress has been predictably uneven as some have moved toward self-administration with greater success than others (Cornell and Kalt 1990; Stull 1990; Stull et al. 1986). The 1975 legislation was amended in 1988 and again in 1994, in both instances to speed up what appeared to be a considerable reluctance on the part of the Bureau to cooperate in its own withering away. A number of sources have examined some of the complexities and difficulties encountered by both the Bureau and the tribes (Bee 1992:148–49; Danzinger 1984; McClellan 1990; Stuart 1990).

In 1994 the renamed House Subcommittee on Native American Affairs (formerly Indian Affairs) held oversight hearings on the Self-Determination Act and the amendments made to it in 1988.[1] They observed that those amendments had been made because "The Committee found that the original goal of ensuring maximum tribal participation in the planning and administration of federal services, programs and activities intended for the benefit of Indians had been undermined by excessive bureaucracy and unnecessary contract requirements."[2] The 1994 hearings castigated the Bureau, which after six years had not come up with the new procedures called for and promised in 1988. Yet despite the Bureau's foot-dragging and some tribal reluctance, in 1993 the tribes were contractually administering over half a billion dollars of BIA funds (about a third of the total) and almost the same amount of Indian Health Service funding.[3]

The outcome of the 1994 hearings was the Indian Self-Determination Act Amendments of 1994 (PL 103–413) titled, "An Act to Specify the Terms of Contracts Entered into by the United States and Tribal Organizations."[4]

With this attempt at streamlining the process and trying to lash the Bureau into motion, the matter legislatively rests for the moment. The last presidential word on the subject was that of William J. Clinton, who was addressing a gathering of Native American leaders in April 1994 when he said, "Today I reaffirm our commitment to self-determination for tribal governments."[5]

I leave the very last word to a Native American, Alberta Joseph of Acoma Pueblo, who, after meeting with Clinton cabinet officials, said, "I just hope they meant what they said they would do" (quoted in Becenti 1994:45).

Notes

Abbreviations Used for Manuscript Collections

EHSP   Edward H. Spicer papers, Arizona State Museum Library, University of Arizona, Tucson, Arizona
FL   Gerald R. Ford Presidential Library, Grand Rapids, Michigan
GCP   Papers in the author's personal possession
GP-LOC   Papers of Leonard Garment in the Library of Congress
HJP   Henry Jackson Papers, University of Washington Library
HTL   Harry S. Truman Presidential Library, Independence, Missouri
JFKL   John F. Kennedy Presidential Library, Boston, Massachusetts
LBJL   Lyndon Baines Johnson Presidential Library, Austin, Texas
NP   Richard M. Nixon Presidential Papers, National Archives II, College Park, Maryland
OP   Personal papers of James Officer, University of Arizona, Tucson, Arizona
RNL&B   Richard Nixon Library and Birthplace, Yorba Linda, California
UP   Papers of Stewart Udall, Special Collections, University of Arizona Library, Tucson, Arizona
WNRC   Washington National Record Center

Introduction

1. "Statement by the President Upon Signing the Bill Creating the Indian Claims Commission, August 13, 1946," Public Papers of the Presidents, Harry S. Truman, 1946, 414.

2. Nash interview, January 26, 1966, JFKL.

3. Jackson to Ogee W. Noble, prosecuting attorney, Republic, Wash., September 6, 1946, HJP.

4. "Statement by the President Upon Signing Bill Concerning Termination of Federal Supervision Over the Menominee Indian Tribe," June 17, 1954, Public Papers of the Presidents, Dwight D. Eisenhower, 1954, 582.

5. "Statement by the President Upon Signing Bill Relating to State Jurisdiction Over Cases Arising on Indian Reservations," August 15, 1953, Public Papers of the Presidents, Dwight D. Eisenhower, 1953, 564–65.

Chapter 1. The New Frontier and the New Trail

1. Nixon to La Farge, Kennedy to La Farge. October 18, 1960, JFKL. Philleo Nash suggested Richard Shifter, counsel to the AIA, not only provided the Kennedy staff with the questions but wrote the draft of answers. Nash interview, February 26, 1971, 9, JFKL.

2. Nixon to La Farge, October 28, 1960, JFKL.

3. Kennedy to La Farge, October 28, 1960, JFKL.

4. Ibid.

5. Udall interview, July 29, 1969, LBJL.

6. Officer interview, April 18, 1990, 1–3, GCP.

7. Ibid., 3; Jim Officer and William King to Udall, December 1960, UP.

8. Ibid.

9. Officer and King to Udall, December 1960, 3, UP.

10. Ibid., 4.

11. Ibid., 13.

12. Senator Barry Goldwater to JFK, January 3, 1961, JFKL.

13. Officer interview, April 18, 1990, 3 (GCP); Udall interview, January 12, 1970, 42, JFKL.

14. Nash interview, January 28, 1966, JFKL.

15. Udall interview, January 12, 1970, 40, JFKL; Officer interview, April 18, 1990, 4, GCP.

16. Nash interview, February 26, 1971, 17–18, JFKL.

17. Ibid.

18. Nash interview, January 28, 1966, 44, JFKL; Nash's remarks to Democratic Party, March 17, 1958, HTL.

19. Udall interview, January 12, 1970, 127, JFKL.

20. Ibid.

21. Comptroller General to Speaker of the House, March 21, 1961, JFKL.

22. Crow to Carver, February 9, 1961, HTL.

23. U.S. Congress, Senate Committee on Interior and Insular Affairs Hearings, Nomination for Commissioner of Indian Affairs, 87th Congress, 1st Session, August 14, 17, 1961.

24. Jackson to Carver, March 3, 1965, HJP.

25. Udall interview, January 12, 1970, 40, JFKL.

26. U.S. Congress, Senate Committee on Interior and Insular Affairs Hearings, Heirship Land Problem, 88th Congress, 1st Session, April 29, 1963.

27. Udall interview, January 12, 1990, 127, JFKL.

28. Ibid., 41.

29. See his complete bibliography in Landsman and Halperin 1989.

30. Nash address to NCAI, September 21, 1961, HTL; Nash to Conference of Superintendents, October 16, 1961, HTL.

31. Ibid.

32. Nash address to Sunday Evening Forum, Tucson, Ariz., March 3, 1963, HTL.

33. Ibid.

34. Based on this stress on development, Senese came to the remarkable conclusion that "Nash saw Indian cultures and societies as they existed on the reservations as a threat to national industrial progress" (1991:71).

35. Officer interview, April 18, 1990, 22, GCP.

36. Salinger to Udall, March 9, 1961, UP.

37. Kennedy to La Farge, October 28, 1960, JFKL.

38. "The President's News Conference of March 8, 1961." Public Papers of the Presidents, John F. Kennedy, 1961, 157.

39. "Letter to the President of the Seneca Nation of Indians Concerning the Kinzua

Dam on the Allegheny River, August 11, 1961," Public Papers of the Presidents, John F. Kennedy, 1961, 563.

40. Carver interview, October 7, 1969, 17–18, JFKL.

41. "Remarks to Representatives of American Indian Tribes, August 15, 1962," Public Papers of the Presidents, John F. Kennedy, 1962, 619.

42. "Remarks to Representatives of the National Congress of American Indians, March 5, 1963," Public Papers of the Presidents, John F. Kennedy, 1963, 233–34.

43. Aide (initials indecipherable) to RFK, June 15, 1962, JFKL.

44. McGovern to RFK, June 14, 1962, JFKL.

45. RFK to Wetzel, May 7, 1962, JFKL.

46. Lee White interview, May 25, 1964, 52, 205, JFKL.

47. Officer interview, April 18, 1990, 18, GCP.

48. Inter Cabinet Briefing book, March 12, 1962, JFKL.

49. Ibid.

50. Department of Interior proposed legislation, 88th Congress, 1st Session, November 1962, UP.

51. Nash interview, February 26, 1971, JFKL.

52. White House Press Release, August 15, 1962, "Remarks at Reception of Delegates of American Indian Chicago Conference," JFKL.

53. Nash to Fred Dutton, November 13, 1961, JFKL.

54. Udall interview, January 27, 1970, 129, JFKL.

55. Ibid.

56. Beatty interview, October 10, 1964, 187, JFKL.

57. Ibid., 188.

58. "Letter to the President of the Association on American Indian Affairs, March 25, 1963," Public Papers of the Presidents, John F. Kennedy, 1963, 289–91.

59. Ibid., 290.

60. Josephy to Secretary Udall, December 18, 1964, UP.

Chapter 2. The Great Society

1. Alabama-Coushatta, Tigua, and the Texas band of the Kickapoo have all achieved degrees of state and federal recognition since the 1960s (Taylor 1983:122).

2. James Gaither Oral History Interview, December 15, 1969, 11, LBJL.

3. Philleo Nash Oral History Interview, February 26, 1971, 10, JFKL.

4. "Annual State of the Union Address, December 8, 1964," Public Papers of the Presidents, Lyndon Baines Johnson, 1963–64, 114.

5. In a less bowdlerized version, "crooks, communists, and cocksuckers" (J. Patterson 1994:279).

6. OEO Administrative History, "American Indians, Migrants and Farm Workers," 385–390, LBJL.

7. Nash, "Remarks" to American Indian Capitol Conference on Poverty, May 12, 1964, HTL.

8. Udall, "Remarks" to Indian Affairs Conference of Superintendents, Santa Fe, June

16, 1964, 7, UP; Udall "Report to the President," June 9, 1964, UP.

    9. Memo, Nash to Udall, November 20, 1964, UP.

    10. Speech by Nash, January 25, 1965, HTL.

    11. Congressional Record 88th Congress, 2d Session, 1964, Pt. 13, 16708.

    12. Shriver to NCAI, November 5, 1965, UP.

    13. Officer to Udall, December 16, 1965, UP.

    14. Carver to Udall, January 29, 1965, UP.

    15. Officer interview, April 18, 1990, 34, GCP.

    16. OEO Administrative History, V2 Documentary supplement, 2–17, LBJL.

    17. Edward H. Spicer to editor, *Arizona Star*, "Pascua Project Accomplishments," March 13, 1970, EHSP.

    18. Officer interview, April 18, 1990, 35, GCP.

    19. Castile to Kravitz, March 30, 1966, GCP.

    20. Bennett to Udall, Weekly Report, Navajo Area, May 13, 1966, UP.

    21. Officer interview, April 18, 1990, 35, GCP; Bennett to Udall, May 13, 1966, UP.

    22. Officer interview, April 18, 1990, 35, GCP.

    23. Deloria to Tax, January 20, 1967, LBJL.

Chapter 3. A New Goal

    1. Beatty to Udall, March 14, 1964, UP.

    2. Beatty to Udall, November 5, 1964, UP.

    3. Meeting of BIA Personnel with Secretary Udall, January 5, 1965, OP.

    4. Udall interview, July 29, 1969, 4, LBJL.

    5. Udall to LBJ, February 26, 1966, LBJL.

    6. Macy to LBJ, March 9, 1966; LBJ to Macy, March 10, 1966; Nash to LBJ, March 9, 1966, LBJL.

    7. LBJ to Nash, March 10, 1966, LBJL.

    8. Udall to LBJ, February 26, 1966, LBJL.

    9. Carver to Udall, March 23, 1967, UP.

    10. Robert Bennett Oral History Interview, November 13, 1968, LBJL.

    11. U.S. Congress, Senate Committee on Interior and Insular Affairs, "Nomination of Robert La Follette Bennett of Alaska to be Commissioner of Indian Affairs," 89th Congress, 2d Session, April 1, 1966.

    12. "Remarks of the President at Swearing in of Robert L. Bennett, April 27, 1966," Public Papers of the Presidents, Lyndon B. Johnson, 1966, 459.

    13. Udall to Macy, May 31, 1966, LBJL.

    14. Udall to LBJ, "Weekly Report to the President," April 20, 1965, UP.

    15. Udall to Califano, December 27, 1965, UP.

    16. Ibid.

    17. Officer to Udall, November 8, 1965, UP.

    18. Gardner to LBJ, March 22, 1967, UP.

    19. King to Udall, April 8, 1966, UP.

    20. Ibid.

    21. Ibid.

22. "Views of the Reservation System by a Reservation Superintendent," n.d., OP.

23. "Remarks of the Secretary, Santa Fe, April 14, 1966," OP; Informal Remarks, April 15, 1966, LBJL.

24. Udall, "Remarks," April 14, 1966, 14, UP.

25. Nash to Udall, November 20, 1964, UP.

26. "Nomination of Robert La Follette Bennett," Senate Executive Report #1, 89th Congress, 2d Session, April 8, 1966.

27. Shriver address to NCAI, November 5, 1965, UP.

28. Udall, "Weekly Report to the President," April 12, 1966, UP.

29. James Officer's Notes on Secretary's Conference, April 28, 1966, OP.

30. Udall, "Weekly Report to the President," May 10, 1966, UP.

31. Udall to LBJ, "New Ideas and New Programs," June 25, 1966, UP.

32. Officer interview, April 18, 1990, 7, GCP.

33. Deputy Commissioner Theodore Taylor to Under Secretary, September 22, 1966, OP.

34. Legislative Liaison Office to Office of Reservation Programs, June 2, 1967, OP.

35. "A Free Choice Program for the American Indians," Report of the President's Task Force on American Indians, December 1966, LBJL; "Report of the Interagency Task Force on American Indians," October 23, 1967, LBJL.

36. Not named in the text, the other task force members were Charles Abrams, Columbia University; Lewis Douglas, Mutual Insurance; Everett Hagen, MIT; R. Bruce Jessup, California Public Health; Richard Lasko, Battelle Institute; Milton Stern, Union Carbide; Herbert Striner, Upjohn Institute.

37. Udall to Califano, September 13, 1966, UP.

38. McDermott to LBJ, December 23, 1966, LBJL.

39. Ibid., 11.

40. Ibid., 1.

41. Ibid., 10–11.

42. Ibid., 50.

43. Ibid., 56–57.

44. Ibid., 57.

45. Ibid., 85.

46. Officer interview, April 18, 1990, 5, GCP.

47. Donald Proulz, chief, Branch of Property and Supply, to Officer et al., February 8, 1967, OP.

48. Commissioner to Area Directors, August 22, 1968, OP.

49. John E. Robson, Executive Office of the President, BOB, "Indian Program," January 27, 1967, UP.

50. Udall, Statement by Secretary of the Interior on Indian Resources Development Act, May 16, 1967, UP.

51. U.S. Congress, Senate s.1816, "To provide for the economic development and management of the resources of individual Indians and tribes, and for other purposes," 90th Congress, 1st Session, May 18, 1967 (copy in UP).

52. Norman Hollow to LBJ, February 7, 1967, LBJL.

53. Ibid.

54. Udall to Califano, May 12, 1967, UP.

55. Udall to Bennett et al., "Indian Legislation," October 11, 1967, UP.

56. Udall interview, July 29, 1969, 10, JFKL.

57. Jackson to Ruby Gubatayo, February 13, 1964, HJP.

58. Jackson to Tandy Wilbur, Swinomish Tribal Community, September 30, 1964, HJP.

59. Udall interview, January 12, 1970, 41, JFKL.

60. Beatty interview, October 10, 1969, JFKL.

61. U.S. Congress, Senate "National American Indian and Alaska Natives Policy Resolution," 90th Congress, 2d Session, September 12, 1968.

62. Sue Lallmang, "Indian Division Nixon/Agnew Campaign to Miss Agnes Waldren," September 26, 1968, RNL&B.

63. Udall interview, January 12, 1970, 129, JFKL.

64. Udall, Report to the President, December 12, 1967, UP.

65. Ibid.

66. Udall to Bennett, April 29, 1966, UP.

67. Robert Vaughn, deputy assistant secretary for public land management, to Udall, March 5, 1968, UP.

68. Paul Fannin wrote an article in which he confirms he called for the committee but makes no indication as to why the formation of the committee was not done under the auspices of the Interior Committee, of which he was a member (Fannin, 1968).

69. Opening Statement of Senator Robert F. Kennedy, December 13, 1967, Press Release, RFK papers, JFKL.

70. U.S. Congress, Senate Committee on Labor and Public Welfare, Subcommittee on Indian Education, "Hearings on the Study of Indian Education," 90th Congress, 1st and 2d Sessions.

71. Opening Statement of Senator Robert F. Kennedy, December 13, 1967, Press Release, RFK papers, JFKL.

72. Ibid.

73. Officer to Udall, April 30, 1968, UP.

74. Testimony of Senator Robert F. Kennedy, March 5, 1968, Press Release, RFK papers, JFKL.

75. U.S. Congress, Senate Committee on the Judiciary, Subcommittee on Constitutional Rights, "Constitutional Rights of the American Indian," 87th, 88th, 89th Congress.

76. Officer to Udall, March 27, 1968, UP.

77. Califano to White, August 19, 1967, LBJL.

78. "American Indian Program for FY 1969," White to Califano, October 23, 1967, LBJL.

79. Ibid.

80. Officer to Udall, 1967, UP.

81. Task Force on American Indians, October 23, 1967, 3, LBJL.

82. Ibid., 1.

83. Ibid., 35.

84. Ibid., 5.

85. Ibid., 2.

86. Ibid., 2–3.

87. Officer to Udall, October 5, 1967, UP.

88. Califano to Johnson, March 4, 1968, LBJL.

89. *Indian Record*, Special Issue, "President Johnson Presents Indian Message to Congress," March 1968, LBJL.

90. "Special Message to the Congress on the Problems of the American Indian: 'The Forgotten American,'" March 6, 1968," Public Papers of the Presidents, Lyndon B. Johnson, 1968, 336.

91. Ibid., 337.

92. Ibid., 338.

93. Ibid., 343.

94. *Indian Record*, Special Issue, "President Johnson Presents Indian Message to Congress," March 1968, 20, LBJL.

95. William J. Hopkins to Macy, April 29, 1968, LBJL.

96. Matthew Nimetz Oral History Interview, January 7, 1969, 42, LBJL.

97. In the second edition (1977), Szasz eliminated the sentence about Udall's supervision.

Chapter 4. New Federalism and a New Era

1. Nixon to the NCAI, September 27, 1968, RNL&B.

2. Nixon to La Farge, October 28, 1960, JFKL.

3. Nixon to the NCAI, September 27, 1968, RNL&B.

4. Ibid., 2.

5. Ibid., 3.

6. The La Jolla community is largely made up of peoples once called Diegueño, more recently Ipai. See Luomala, 1978.

7. The President's News Conference of May 8, 1970, Public Papers of the Presidents, Richard M. Nixon, 1970, 425.

8. Ehrlichman interview, December 1, 1994, GCP.

9. Haldeman to Keogh, January 13, 1969, from which, of course, this book's title was taken.

10. Garment to Nixon, January 10, 1971, GP-LOC.

11. Keogh to Haldeman, February 14, 1969, FL.

12. Ibid.

13. Keogh, Proposed Press Release on Indian Bureau Study, February 15, 1969, FL.

14. Stephen Bull to Ehrlichman, March 20, 1969, FL.

15. Ibid.

16. King to Udall, "Review of the Josephy Report," 1969 (no specific date), 1, UP.

17. Ibid., 11–12.

18. "Suggested Text for a paper on Bureau Reorganization," May 15, 1969, NP.

19. Bennett to Under Secretary of the Interior, "Legislative Activity and Problems," April 25, 1969, Bennett Desk Files, WNRC.

20. Senate Report 91–501. Subcommittee on Indian Education of the Committee on Labor and Public Welfare, U.S. Senate, 91st Congress; Opening Statement of RFK, December 13, 1967, JFKL.

21. Ibid., 2.

22. "Address to the Nation on Domestic Programs," August 8, 1969, Public Papers of the Presidents, Richard M. Nixon, 1969, 642.

23. Garment to Ehrlichman, "American Indians—A New Decade," December 24, 1969, NP.

24. Office of Native American Programs Issue Paper, April 22, 1974, FL.

25. "Address to the Nation on Domestic Programs," August 8, 1969, Public Papers of the Presidents, Richard M. Nixon, 1969, 237.

26. Agnew to Nixon, October 8, 1971, NP.

27. Patterson interview, December 18, 1993, GCP.

28. Patterson to Garment, October 26, 1976, FL.

29. Patterson Exit Interview, September 10, 1974, 2, 21, NP.

30. Ehrlichman interview, December 1, 1994, GCP.

31. Patterson interview, December 18, 1993, GCP.

32. Ibid.

33. Kilberg to Garment, March 19, 1970, NP.

34. Ibid.

35. Patterson interview, December 18, 1993, GCP.

36. Patterson to Cole, April 23, 1970, "Sketch of the Contents of an Indian Message/Statement," NP; Garment to the President, June 13, 1970, "Indian Policy and an Indian Message," NP.

37. James Schlesinger, BOB, to the President, November 20, 1969, NP.

38. Executive Order 11551, August 11, 1970, NP.

39. Ehrlichman interview, December 1, 1994, GCP.

40. Robert Robertson to C. D. Ward, March 23, 1971, "Summary: Kansas City Conference on Indian Self Determination," NP.

41. Ehrlichman interview, December 1, 1994, GCP.

42. According to Feraca (1990:23), Bruce later insisted on Sioux-Mohawk as the correct sequence, based on the matrilineality of the Mohawk, to whom his father belonged.

43. Hickel Press Release, November 25, 1970, "Secretary Hickel Unveils Dramatic Changes in BIA," GP-LOC.

44. Garment to Ehrlichman, November 27, 1970, "BIA Reorganization," GP-LOC.

45. Bruce to Secretary of the Interior, September 23, 1971. Bruce Desk Files, WNRC.

46. Special Message to the Congress on Executive Branch Reorganization, March 25, 1971, Public Papers of the Presidents, Richard M. Nixon, 1971, 481.

47. Patterson memo, February 10, 1971, "Future Location of the Bureau of Indian Affairs," NP.

48. Leo W. Vocu, executive director NCAI, to the President, March 15, 1971, NP.

49. "Remarks at a Question-and-Answer Session for the Northwest Editors, Publishers and Broadcast Executives Attending a Briefing on Domestic Policy in Portland, Oregon, September 25, 1971," Public Papers of the Presidents, Richard M. Nixon, 1971, 990.

50. To complete the "nicknames," Gross (1989:66) said they were "popularly known as the Katzenjammer Kids," while Nickerson (1976:66) called them "the insurgents."

51. "Special Message to the Congress on Indian Affairs, July 8, 1970," Public Papers of the Presidents, Richard M. Nixon, 1970, 565–76.

52. Ibid., 567.

53. Ibid., 567–69.

54. Ibid., 569.

55. Ibid., 569–70.

56. Ibid., 571.

57. Ibid., 572.

58. Ibid., 573.

59. Loesch to Bruce, January 16, 1970, "Adherence to our long standing policy of not providing special Bureau of Indian Affairs services to off-reservation Indians," Bruce Desk Files, WNRC.

60. "Special Message to the Congress on Indian Affairs, July 8, 1970," Public Papers of the Presidents, Richard M. Nixon, 1970, 574.

61. White House Press Release, July 8, 1970, "The White House Press Conference of Vice President Spiro T. Agnew and Leonard Garment, Special Counsel to the President," NP.

62. Arnold R. Weber (OMB), Memo to Leonard Garment and C. D. Ward, September 28, 1970, "Status of Legislative Proposals Arising from the President's Indian Message," NP.

63. Indian Record, August 1970, 12.

64. Special Message to the Congress on Indian Affairs, July 8, 1970, Public Papers of the Presidents, Richard M. Nixon, 1970, 569.

65. Commissioner to Area Directors, August 22, 1968, "Policy-Application of Buy Indian Act," OP.

66. King to Bruce, October 13, 1970, "Comparison of Salt River and Zuni Approaches to Increased Local Control," Bruce Desk Files, WNRC.

67. "Program Agreement between the Pueblo of Zuni and the Bureau of Indian Affairs," May 23, 1970, Bruce Desk files, WNRC.

68. Area Director to Branch Chief, Albuquerque Area Office, August 7, 1970, NP.

69. Charles Stoller, assistant solicitor, to Officer, September 16, 1970, OP.

70. Raymond C. Coulter, deputy solicitor to assistant secretary, Public Land Management, June 20, 1969, OP.

71. Louis Bruce to Zuni Tribal Chair, August 14, 1970, OP.

72. Commissioner to A1 Area directors and superintendents, August 14, 1970, 1, OP.

73. Ibid., 4.

74. Kilberg to Patterson, August 28, 1970, NP.

75. Garment to Ed Harper, June 24, 1971, NP.

76. Ken Belieu to Ehrlichman, April 22, 1970, "Blue Lake/New Mexico," NP.

77. Patterson interview, December 18, 1993, GCP.

78. Ehrlichman interview, December 1, 1994, GCP.

79. Ibid.

80. Hoff (1994:361) also questioned Wicker's version of this and the Alaskan Native Claims negotiations.

81. Patterson interview, December 18, 1993, GCP.

82. Belieu to Ehrlichman, April 22, 1970, NP.

83. Patterson interview, December 18, 1993, GCP.

84. "Remarks on Signing Bill Restoring the Blue Lake Land in New Mexico to the

Taos Pueblo Indians," December 15, 1970, Public Papers of the Presidents, Nixon, 1970, 1131–32.

85. Ibid., 1133.

86. Patterson interview, December 18, 1993, GCP.

87. Statement on Signing Executive Order Providing for Return of Certain Lands to the Yakima Indian Reservation, May 20, 1972, Public Papers of the Presidents, Richard M. Nixon, 1970, 609–610.

88. Wicker's version of this attributed the final package to Congress as being "considerably more generous" and understated the actual White House package, which was passed more or less as written, by half in money and one-fourth in land (1991:520). Patterson's version of the meeting was much the same in his exit interview, in his interview with me, and in his book. Garment to Ehrlichman, March 4, 1971, "Alaska Native Claims—The Administration's Position," NP.

89. Apparently the March 4, 1971, memo above sent to Ehrlichman.

90. Patterson interview, December 18, 1993, GCP.

91. Ehrlichman verified this version to me in our interview.

92. Patterson, March 12, 1971, "Memorandum for the Record—Alaska Native Claims," NP.

93. Special Message to the Congress on Indian Affairs, July 8, 1970, Public Papers of the Presidents, Richard M. Nixon, 1970, 573.

94. Jackson to Stan Morris, October 14, 1971, HJP.

95. Hearing Before the Committee on Interior and Insular Affairs, United States Senate, 92d Congress, 2d Session on s.3167, A Bill on the "Indian Self Determination Act of 1971," s.1573, s.1574, and s.2238, May 8, 1972.

96. "Statement of Honorable Harrison Loesch, Assistant Secretary of the Interior for Public Land Management," Hearings, 48.

97. "Statement of William Youpee, President, National Tribal Chairmen's Association," Hearings, 69.

98. Senate Report 92–1001, in Serial 12971–5.

99. Ibid., 6.

100. Senate Report 93–682 (Serial 13057-1) in its "legislative history" section gave the date as August 2, 1973—an error, since by June 1973 the Interior Committee was holding hearings on the alternative, s.1017.

101. Annual Message to the Congress on the State of the Union, January 20, 1972, Public Papers of the Presidents, Richard M. Nixon, 1972, 60–61.

102. Annual Budget Message to the Congress, Fiscal Year 1973, January 24, 1972, Public Papers of the Presidents, Richard M. Nixon, 1972, 89.

103. BIA news briefing, January 12, 1972, "Redirection of the Bureau of Indian Affairs," Bruce Desk Files, WNRC.

Chapter 5. The Media's Chiefs

1. Hoff counted forty-five in the same time period (Hoff 1994:30).

2. Norman Rambeau interview, n.d., NP.

3. Ramsey Clark to Senator Edward V. Long, May 6, 1964, NP.

4. Garment to Vice President, December 23, 1969, NP.

5. Some fifteen folders in the Leonard Garment papers indicated how closely he monitored the events on behalf of the administration (NP).

6. Garment to Ehrlichman, January 21, 1971, NP.

7. Bud Krogh to Ehrlichman, December 11, 1970, "Alcatraz," GP-LOC.

8. Robert Robertson to Indians of All Tribes, "A Proposal," March 31, 1970, Bruce Desk Files, WNRC.

9. "Statement by Tom Hannon, Regional Administrator, GSA," May 27, 1970, NP.

10. Garment to Vice President, February 7, 1970, NP.

11. Press Release, Governor Ronald Reagan, August 21, 1970, NP.

12. Garment to Ehrlichman, May 9, 1971, "Alcatraz Indians," NP; Krogh to Ehrlichman, May 10, 1971, bears a handwritten notation, "E. Agrees with you. GO!" NP.

13. Patterson Exit Interview, September 10, 1974, 32, NP.

14. Ibid., 31.

15. Although Alcatraz had little impact at the time, it has in later years taken on considerable symbolic importance. See, for example, Nagel and Johnson 1994.

16. FBI to Leonard Garment, January 30, 1974, FL.

17. Ibid.

18. The various accounts do not even agree on the time of arrival and occupation, Deloria putting it on November 3 (1974:530), and Burnette and Koster on November 1 (1974:203). Josephy had it best, "November 1 and 2—not everyone arrived at the same moment but the occupation took place on the 2d" (1984:239).

19. Banks to Nixon, October 4, 1972; Burnette to Nixon, October 18, 1972, both NP.

20. Ibid.

21. Garment to Banks, October 12, 1972, NP.

22. Burnette to Nixon, October 18, 1972, NP.

23. Garment to Burnette, October 27, 1972, NP.

24. Patterson to Dave Parker, November 11, 1972, "AIM Caravan of Broken Treaties," NP.

25. Activist Carter Camp made the rats the more traditional "size of cats," as in the old Quartermaster Corps song (*Akwesasne Notes* 1973:11).

26. "BIA Occupation: A Chronology of Events," n.d., NP.

27. Krogh, "Indian Situation, November 1972," NP.

28. Garment to Morton, "Arrangements Made with Trail of Broken Treaties Indians," November 8, 1972, NP.

29. Ibid.

30. Ibid.

31. Carlucci to Krogh, "Decision to Finance Travel Expenses for Return of Indians to their Homes," November 13, 1972, NP.

32. Ibid.

33. Morton, "Delegations of Authority," December 2, 4, 1972, NP.

34. Bruce to Nixon, November 8, 1972, NP.

35. Krogh, "Indian Situation," 3, NP.

36. Garment memo, "Definition and Objective of Current Assignment," December 1, 1972, GP-LOC.

37. "Steps Taken to Improve Operation of the Bureau of Indian Affairs," Interior Press Release, January 18, 1973, NP.

38. Interior Press Release, February 7, 1973, NP.

39. Patterson to John Whittaker, under secretary of the interior, "NTCA Press Release," June 29, 1973, NP.

40. Statement by Secretary Rogers Morton, November 6, 1972, NP.

41. NTCA "Position Paper," November 10, 1972, NP.

42. "TBT-Indian Reactions," NP.

43. Ehrlichman interview, December 1, 1994, GCP.

44. This was the only notice Hoff took of the Trail of Broken Treaties in what is otherwise the best treatment of Nixon Indian policy in a general work on his administration.

45. Garment to Adams, January 9, 1973, NP.

46. Sid Mills and Russell Means to Robert Robertson, n.d., NP.

47. Garment to Adams, January 9, 1973, NP.

48. Wilkinson to Garment, February 2, 1973, NP.

49. Garment to Nixon, "Memorandum for the President," August 3, 1973, NP.

50. Lewis to Nixon, March 15, 1973, NP.

51. Hank Adams to Vine Deloria, May 16, 1973, "Participation in Negotiations for the Wounded Knee Settlement," FL.

52. Garment to Cole, March 15, 1973, "Wounded Knee," NP.

53. Quoted in a draft of a letter, Garment to Dick Gregory, n.d., NP.

54. "Agreement" signed by both sides on April 5, 1973, NP. It was to this agreement that Garment referred to by date in later correspondence with the "traditional chiefs."

55. Garment to Fools Crow, January 8, 1974, 11, NP.

56. Warrior and Smith (1996:195) suggested there had been one prior instance of re-election.

57. Garment "To Headsmen [sic] and Chiefs of the Teton Sioux," May 15, 1973, NP.

58. Ibid.

59. Garment "To the Traditional Chiefs and Headmen of the Teton Sioux," May 29, 1973, NP.

60. Ibid., 2.

61. Ibid., 9.

62. Patterson to Garment, "'Bill of Particulars' from Messrs Fools Crow and King," November 19, 1973, NP; Fools Crow and King to Richard M. Nixon, "Bill of Particulars," November 19, 1973, NP.

63. Garment to Fools Crow and King, January 8, 1974, NP.

64. Garment to Attorney General Elliot L. Richardson, September 6, 1973, FL.

65. Governor Robert Lewis to Nixon, March 15, 1973, NP.

66. Patterson to Bruce, September 29, 1972, Bruce Desk files, WNRC.

67. Ehrlichman to Whittaker, February 12, 1973, GP-LOC; Whittaker to Ehrlichman, February 22, 1973, GP-LOC.

68. Patterson interview, December 18, 1993, GCP.

69. Banks to Patterson, December 17, 1973, NP.

70. Nixon to Charles Trimble, NCAI executive director, October 9, 1973, FL.

Chapter 6. Between Mandate and Watergate

1. "State of the Union Message to the Congress on Human Resources," March 1, 1973, Public Papers of the Presidents, Richard Nixon, 1973, 144.

2. Babby to John C. Whittaker, February 8, 1974, NP.

3. Statement of Morris Thompson, December 3, 1973, NP.

4. Patterson interview, December 18, 1993, GCP.

5. "A Statement by Melvin Laird," August 31, 1973, FL.

6. Patterson to Laird, June 26, 1973, NP.

7. "A Statement by Melvin Laird," August 31, 1973, FL.

8. Nixon to NCAI, October 9, 1973, NP.

9. "Statement on Signing the Menominee Restoration Act," Public Papers of the Presidents, Richard Nixon, 1973, 1023.

10. Patterson interview, December 18, 1993, GCP.

11. Patterson, "Memorandum of Conversation, AIM convention in South Dakota, June 8–16," June 1974, FL.

12. Ibid.

13. Patterson to Garment, June 18, 1974, NP.

14. Patterson to Garment, "AIM Coming to Washington," June 19, 1974, FL.

15. Patterson to William Buffam, assistant secretary international organizational affairs, Department of State, "Formation of a So Called International Indian Treaty Council," June 27, 1974, FL.

16. Garment speech to American Indian Lawyers Association, Albuquerque, March 14, 1974, NP.

17. Patterson to Garment, July 15, 1974, "Record of Action at the Meeting on Indian Fishing Rights, July 11, 1974," NP.

18. Garment to Larry Silberman, deputy attorney general, July 15, 1974, FL.

19. "Special Message to the Congress on National Legislative Goals," Public Papers of the Presidents, Richard Nixon, 1973, 776.

20. "Statement on Signing the Menominee Restoration Act," December 22, 1973, Public Papers of the Presidents, Richard Nixon, 1973, 1023.

21. "Annual Message to the Congress on the State of the Union," Public Papers of the Presidents, Richard Nixon, 1974, 76.

22. "Statement About Signing the Indian Financing Act of 1974," Public Papers of the Presidents, Richard Nixon, 1974, 355.

23. "Statement Supporting Legislation to Enlarge the Havasupai Indian Reservation," May 3, 1974, Public Papers of the Presidents, Richard Nixon, 1974, 410.

24. "Indian Self-Determination and Education Program." Hearings before the Subcommittee on Indian Affairs of the Committee on Interior and Insular Affairs, United States Senate, 93d Congress, 1st Session, On s.1017 and Related Bills, June 1 and 4, 1973.

25. "Statement of Honorable Frank Carlucci, Under Secretary, Department of Health, Education and Welfare," Hearings, 65.

26. Ibid., 66.

27. Ibid., 164.

28. Senate Report 93–682 (Serial 13057–1).

29. "Indian Self-Determination and Education Assistance Act." Hearings before the Subcommittee on Indian Affairs of the Committee on Interior and Insular Affairs, House of Representatives, 93d Congress, 2d Session, On s.1017 and Related Bills, May 20 and 21, 1974.

30. Ibid., 22.

31. Ibid., 26.

32. Ibid., 68.

33. Garment speech to AILA, Albuquerque, New Mexico, March 14, 1974, NP.

34. Garment to Silberman, July 15, 1974, FL.

35. C. D. Ward to Alexander Haig, October 25, 1973, FL.

36. Laird to Bruce Kehrli, October 29, 1973, NP.

37. "Proposed Domestic Council Committee on Indian Affairs," NP.

38. Ibid.

39. Patterson to Garment, October 26, 1976, FL.

40. Patterson to John A. Scruggs, staff director U.S. Commission on Civil Rights, November 16, 1973, NP.

Chapter 7. After the Fall

1. President Ford to Lord Michael Killanin, International Olympic Committee, August 8, 1975, FL.

2. Cole notes of cabinet meeting, September 1, 1974, "Comment re Indian Matters," FL.

3. Banks to Ford, September 20, 1974; Patterson to Morris Thompson, September 24, 1974, FL.

4. "Letter of Intent for the Kootenai Indians of Idaho to the Congress and the President of the United States of America," September 11, 1974, FL.

5. Patterson to Carlson, September 17, 1974, FL; Carlson to Jack Hushen, "Kootenai Indians to Declare War on U.S.," September 19, 1974, FL.

6. Kilberg to Paul O'Neil, April 29, 1976; Marrs to O'Neil, April 26, 1976, FL.

7. Patterson to Steve Kurzman, assistant secretary legislation (HEW), "Social Services Legislation and Federally Recognized Indian Tribes," September 6, 1974, FL.

8. Cannon, however, noted, "Ford never read the Garment memo. . . .[Ford] had learned not to rely on a Nixon lawyer for advice about anything concerning Nixon" (1994:371).

9. Biographical information, Bradley J. Patterson, Gerald R. Ford Library Finding Aid, FL.

10. Patterson to Mrs. Julia V. Taft, HEW, October 21, 1974, FL; Ford to Cabinet, August 26, 1976, FL; Biographical information, Bradley J. Patterson, Gerald R. Ford Library Finding Aid, FL.

11. Biographical information, Theodore C. Marrs, Gerald R. Ford Library Finding Aid, FL.

12. Biographical information, Barbara (Bobbie) Greene Kilberg, Gerald R. Ford Library Finding Aid, FL.

13. Public Papers of the Presidents, Gerald R. Ford, 1976, 2319.

14. Patterson to Marrs, February 19, 1975, FL.

15. Patterson to Baroody, "Important Note re the President's Trip to the State of Washington and Seattle," October 18, 1976, FL.

16. House Report 93–1600, Serial 13061–11.

17. Ibid., 21.

18. Cole to Ford, "Enrolled Bill s. 1017—Indian Self-Determination and Educational Assistance Act," January 2, 1975, FL.

19. "Statement on Signing the Indian Self-Determination and Education Assistance Act, January 4, 1975," Public Papers of the Presidents, Gerald R. Ford, 1975, 11.

20. Ford to NTCA, January 7, 1975, FL.

21. "Memorandum on the Establishment of an Interdepartmental Task Force on Indian Affairs," June 1, 1975, FL.

22. "Remarks by the Honorable Theodore C. Marrs, Special Assistant to the President, Before the Indian Pueblo Cultural Center in Albuquerque," October 29, 1975, FL.

23. Ibid. The speech may not have been well received. There was a hand-written notation, "Didn't clap for Bobbie," referring to Bobbie Greene Kilberg, who also spoke.

24. "Vice President's Briefing Book," n.d. (but late 1975—it contains references to 1976 budget proposals).

25. Ibid.

26. Commissioner of Indian Affairs Thompson to Marrs, "Presidential Indian Message," March 11, 1976, FL.

27. Frizzell to the President, "Major Indian Accomplishments in the Last Year," n.d. (late 1975), FL.

28. "Statement on Signing Indian Claims Commission Appropriations Legislation, October 29, 1975," Public Papers of the Presidents, Gerald R. Ford, 1975, 495.

29. Traditional Chiefs and Headmen, Oglala Nation of the Teton Sioux to Ford, July 24, 1975, FL.

30. Ibid.

31. Marrs to Baroody, June 10, 1976, FL.

32. Ibid.

33. Baroody memo, "Meeting with Indian Leaders," July 15, 1976, FL.

34. Press Release, "Remarks of the President to the American Indian Leaders," July 16, 1976, FL.

35. "Indians Meet with Ford, Charge Publicity Pitch," Washington Post, July 17, 1976, A-5.

36. Ford to the Cabinet, July 26, 1976, FL.

37. Cannon to the President, "Memo for the President, Enrolled Bill S 522—Indian Health Care Improvement Act," September 30, 1976, FL.

38. Patterson to the President, September 27, 1976, FL.

39. Ibid.

40. Kilberg to Cannon, September 28, 1976, FL.

41. Public Papers of the Presidents, Gerald R. Ford, 1976, 2384.

42. R. Dennis Ickes, deputy under secretary of the interior to Ramona Bennett, October 28, 1976, FL.

43. Kilberg to Ed Schmults, "Indian Occupation of Cushman Hospital in Tacoma, Washington," October 28, 1976, FL.

44. Harold Borgstrom to Mr. Mitchell, April 19, 1976, FL.

45. Patterson to the President, "Governor Longley's Inquiry re the Passamaquoddy/ Penobscot Case," November 15, 1976, FL.

46. Ibid.

47. Patterson to Garment, October 26, 1976, FL.

48. Press Release, "President Ford's Policies for American Indian People," September 17, 1976, FL.

Epilogue

1. Oversight Hearing before the Subcommittee on Native American Affairs of the Committee on Natural Resources, House of Representatives. 103d Congress, 2d Session on "The Implementation of the Indian Self Determination Act, and the Development of Regulations following Passage of the 1988 Amendments" (Serial 103–105).

2. Ibid., "Statement of Senator John McCain," 34.

3. Ibid.

4. 106 Stat. 4250–4278.

5. "Remarks to Native American and Native Alaskan Tribal Leaders, April 29, 1994." Public Papers of the Presidents, William J. Clinton, 1994, 801.

References Cited

Abourezk, James G.
  1989   *Advise and Dissent: Memoirs of South Dakota and the U.S. Senate*. Chicago: Lawrence Hill.
Adams, John P.
  1976   *At the Heart of the Whirlwind*. New York: Harper and Row.
Aitken, Jonathan
  1993   *Nixon: A Life*. Washington, D.C.: Regnery Publishers.
Akwesasne Notes
  1973   "Trail of Broken Treaties: BIA, I'm Not Your Indian Anymore." Rooseveltown: Akwesasne Notes.
  1974   "Voices from Wounded Knee, 1973: In the Words of the Participants." Rooseveltown: Akwesasne Notes.
Alinsky, Saul D.
  1971   *Rules for Radicals: A Programmatic Primer for Realistic Radicals*. New York: Random House.
Ambrose, Stephen E.
  1989   *Nixon*. Vol. 2: *The Triumph of a Politician, 1962–1972*. New York: Simon and Schuster.
  1991   *Nixon*. Vol. 3: *Ruin and Recovery, 1973–1990*. New York: Simon and Schuster.
American Friends Service Committee
  1970   *Uncommon Controversy: Fishing Rights of the Muckleshoot, Puyallup and Nisqually Indians*. Seattle: University of Washington Press.
Anders, Gary
  1994   "Social and Economic Consequences of Federal Indian Policy: A Case Study of the Alaska Natives." In *Native American Resurgence and Renewal: A Reader and Bibliography*, ed. Robert N. Wells. Metuchen, N.J.: Scarecrow Press.
Anderson, Karen
  1996   *Changing Woman: A History of Racial Ethnic Women in Modern America*. New York: Oxford University Press.
Anderson, Terry H.
  1995   *The Movement and the Sixties: Protest in America from Greensboro to Wounded Knee*. New York: Oxford University Press.
Arnold, Robert D.
  1978   *Alaskan Native Claims*. Anchorage: Alaska Native Foundation.

Baker, Richard Allan

    1985   *Conservation Politics: The Senate Career of Clinton P. Anderson.* Albuquerque: University of New Mexico Press.

Barsh, Russell Lawrence

    1991   "Progressive Era Bureaucrats and the Unity of Twentieth-Century Indian Policy." *American Indian Quarterly* 15(1):1–64.

Bauer, Carl M.

    1982   "Kennedy, Johnson and the War on Poverty." *Journal of American History* 69(1):98–119.

Becenti, Denise

    1994   "A Time to Listen." *Native Peoples* 7(4):42–45.

Bee, Robert

    1979   "To Get Something for the People: The Predicament of the Native American Leader." *Human Organization* 38(3):239–47.

    1981   *Crosscurrents along the Colorado: The Impact of Government Policy on the Quechan Indians.* Tucson: University of Arizona Press.

    1982   *The Politics of American Indian Policy.* Cambridge, Mass.: Schenkman.

    1990   "The Predicament of the Native American Leader: A Second Look." *Human Organization* 49(1):56–63.

    1992   "Riding the Paper Tiger." In *State and Reservation: New Perspectives on Federal Indian Policy,* ed. George Castile and Robert Bee. Tucson: University of Arizona Press.

Bennett, Robert L.

    1986   "The War on Poverty." In *Indian Self-Rule,* ed. Kenneth Philp. Salt Lake City: Howe Brothers.

Berger, Thomas R.

    1985   *Village Journey: The Report of the Alaska Native Claims Commission.* New York: Hill and Wang.

Bernstein, Alison

    1991   *American Indians and World War II: Toward a New Era in Indian Affairs.* Norman: University of Oklahoma Press.

Bernstein, Irving

    1991   *Promises Kept: John F. Kennedy's New Frontier.* New York: Oxford University Press.

Berry, Mary

    1975   *The Alaska Pipeline: The Politics of Oil and Native Land Claims.* Bloomington: Indiana University Press.

Biolsi, Thomas

    1992   *Organizing the Lakota: The Political Economy of the New Deal on the Pine Ridge and Rosebud Reservations.* Tucson: University of Arizona Press.

    1995   "The Birth of the Reservation: Making the Modern Individual among the Lakota." *American Ethnologist* 22(1):28–53.

Bluecloud, Peter, ed.

    1972   *Alcatraz Is Not an Island.* Berkeley: Wingbow Press.

Bodine, John J.

    1978   "The Taos Lake Controversy." *Journal of Ethnic Studies* 6(1):42–48.

Bonney, Rachel A.

    1977   "The Role of AIM Leaders in Indian Nationalism." *American Indian Quarterly* 3(3):209–24.

Brand, Stewart

    1988   "Indians and the Counterculture, 1960s–1970s." In *Handbook of North American Indians,* vol. 4: *History of Indian-White Relations,* ed. Wilcomb E. Washburn. Washington: Smithsonian Institution.

Brophy, William A., and Sophie D. Aberle

    1966   *The Indian: America's Unfinished Business.* Norman: University of Oklahoma Press.

Brown, Dee

    1971   *Bury My Heart at Wounded Knee: An Indian History of the American West.* New York: Holt, Rinehart.

Bruce, Louis

    1976   "The Bureau of Indian Affairs, 1972." In *Indian-White Relations: A Persistent Paradox,* ed. Jane F. Smith and Robert M. Kvasnicka. Washington, D.C.: Howard University Press.

Burke, Vincent J., and Vee Burke

    1974   *Nixon's Good Deed: Welfare Reform.* New York: Columbia University Press.

Burnett, Donald L.

    1972   "An Historical Analysis of the 1968 'Indian Civil Rights' Act." *Harvard Journal on Legislation* 9(4):557–626.

Burnette, R., and J. Koster

    1974   *The Road to Wounded Knee.* New York: Bantam.

Burt, Larry W.

    1982   *Tribalism in Crisis: Federal Indian Policy, 1953–1961.* Albuquerque: University of New Mexico Press.

    1992   "Western Tribes and Balance Sheets: Business Development Programs in the 1960's and 1970's." *Western Historical Quarterly* 23(4):475–495.

Butler, Raymond V.

    1978   "The Bureau of Indian Affairs: Activities since 1945." *Annals of the American Academy of Political and Social Science* 436:50–59.

Cahn, Edgar S., ed.

    1969   *Our Brother's Keeper: The Indian in White America.* Washington, D.C.: New Community Press.

Califano, Joseph A.

    1991   *The Triumph and Tragedy of Lyndon Johnson: The White House Years.* New York: Simon and Schuster.

Cannon, James
   1994   *Time and Chance: Gerald Ford's Appointment with History.* New York: Harper.
Caro, Robert A.
   1982   *The Years of Lyndon Johnson.* New York: Knopf.
Cash, John H.
   1979   "Louis Rook Bruce, 1969–73." In *The Commissioners of Indian Affairs, 1825–1977,* ed. Robert Kvasnicka and Herman Viola. Lincoln: University of Nebraska Press.
Casserly, John J.
   1977   *The Ford White House: The Diary of a Speech Writer.* Boulder: Colorado Associated University Press.
Castañeda, Carlos
   1968   *The Teachings of Don Juan: A Yaqui Way of Knowledge.* Berkeley: University of California Press.
Castile, George Pierre
   1968   The Community School at Rough Rock. Master's thesis, University of Arizona.
   1974   "Federal Indian Policy and the Sustained Enclave." *Human Organization* 33(3):219–228.
   1976   "Mau Mau in the Mechanism: Adaptations of Urban Hunters and Gatherers." *Human Organization* 35(4):394–397.
   1981   "Except Indians." Paper presented at NEH seminar Ethnic Groups and the State, University of Washington, Seattle.
   1985   "Indian Fighting for Fun and Profit: Sources of Indian Policy in the Pacific Northwest." Paper presented at the Society for Applied Anthropology, Washington, D.C.
   1992   "Indian Sign: Hegemony and Symbolism in Federal Indian Policy." In *State and Reservation: New Perspectives on Federal Indian Policy,* ed. George Castile and Robert Bee. Tucson: University of Arizona Press.
   1993   "Native North Americans and the National Question." In *The Political Economy of North American Indians,* ed. J. Moore. Norman: University of Oklahoma Press.
   1996   "The Commodification of Indian Identity." *American Anthropologist* 98(4):21–28.
Champagne, Duane
   1992   "Organization Change and Conflict: A Case Study of the Bureau of Indian Affairs." In *Native Americans and Public Policy,* ed. Fremount J. Lyden and Lyman H. Letgers. Pittsburgh: University of Pittsburgh Press.
Churchill, Ward
   1993   *Struggle for the Land: Indigenous Resistance to Genocide, Ecocide and Expropriation in Contemporary North America.* Monroe: Common Courage Press.
   1994   "American Indian Self-Governance: Fact, Fancy and Prospects for the

Future." In *American Indian Policy: Self-Governance and Economic Development,* ed. Lymon H. Letgers and Fremount J. Lyden. Westport, Conn.: Greenwood.

Churchill, Ward, and Jim Vander Wall
  1988   *Agents of Repression: The FBI's Secret War against the Black Panther Party and the American Indian Movement.* Boston: South End.
  1990   *The COINTELPRO Papers: Documents from the FBI's Secret Wars against Domestic Dissent.* Boston: South End.

CIS
  1975   "PL 93-638 Indian Self-Determination and Educational Assistance Act." *CIS Annual.* Washington, D.C.: Abstracts of Congressional Publications and Legislative Histories.

Claflin, Edward B.
  1991   *JFK Wants to Know: Memos from the President's Office.* New York: Morrow.

Clark, J. E., and M. E. Webb
  1989   "Susette and Susan La Flesche." In *Being and Becoming Indian,* ed. J. Clifton. Baldwinsville, N.Y.: Irwin.

Clarke, Blake
  1958   "Must We Buy America from the Indians All Over Again?" *Reader's Digest* 413 (March 1958):45–49.

Clarke, Jeanne Nienaber
  1996   *Roosevelt's Warrior: Harold L. Ickes and the New Deal.* Baltimore: John Hopkins University Press.

Clifton, James A.
  1970   "Factional Conflict and the Indian Community: The Prairie Potawatomi Case." In *The American Indian Today,* ed. Stuart Levine and Nancy Lurie. Baltimore: Pelican.

Cohen, Fay G.
  1986   *Treaties on Trial: The Continuing Controversy over Northwest Indian Fishing Rights.* Seattle: University of Washington Press.

Cohen, Felix
  1942   *Handbook of Federal Indian Law.* Washington, D.C.: Department of the Interior.
  1953   "The Erosion of Indian Rights, 1950–1953: A Case Study in Bureaucracy." *Yale Law Review* 62:348–90.
  1982   *Felix S. Cohen's Handbook of Indian Law.* Ed. Rennard Strickland et al. Charlottesville: Michie Company.

Collier, John
  1954   "The Genesis and Philosophy of Indian Reorganization Act Policies." In *Indian Affairs and the Indian Reorganization Act: The Twenty-Year Record,* ed. William H. Kelly. Tucson: University of Arizona Press.

Community Action Agency
  1965   *Community Action Agency Program Guide: Instructions for developing,*

conducting and administering a community action program as autho-
rized by Sections 204 and 205 of Title II-A, Economic Opportunity Act of
1964. Vol. 1: *Instructions for Applicants.* Washington, D.C.: OEO, October
1965.

Conkin, Paul Keith

    1986   *Big Daddy from the Pedernales: Lyndon Baines Johnson.* Boston: Twayne.

Conlan, Timothy

    1988   *New Federalism: Intergovernmental Reform from Nixon to Reagan.*
        Washington, D.C.: Brookings Institution.

Coombs, Madison

    1970   "The Indian Student is *Not* Low Man on the Totem Pole." *Journal of*
        American Indian Education 9(33):1–9.

    1972   "Rough Rock Revisited." *Arizona Teacher* 10 (March—April): 22–24.

Cornell, Stephen

    1988   *The Return of the Native: American Indian Political Resurgence.* New
        York: Oxford University Press.

Cornell, Stephen, and Joseph P. Kalt

    1990   "Pathways from Poverty: Economic Development and Institution Build-
        ing on American Indian Reservations." *American Indian Culture and*
        Research Journal 14(1):89–125.

Covington, James W.

    1993   *The Seminoles of Florida.* Gainesville: University Press of Florida.

Cowger, Thomas W.

    1996   "'The Crossroads of Destiny': The NCAI's Landmark Struggle to Thwart
        Coercive Termination." *American Indian Culture and Research Journal*
        20(4):121–144.

Cronin, Thomas E.

    1988   "John F. Kennedy: President and Politician." In *John F. Kennedy: The*
        Promise Revisited, ed. Paul Harper and Hoann P. Kreig. Westport, Conn.:
        Greenwood.

Crow Dog, Leonard, and Richard Erdoes

    1995   *Crow Dog: Four Generations of Sioux Medicine Men.* New York:
        HarperCollins.

Crow Dog, Mary, and Richard Erdoes

    1990   *Lakota Woman.* New York: Grove Widenfeld.

Dahl, Kathleen A.

    1994   "The Battle Over Termination on the Colville Indian Reservation."
        American Indian Culture and Research Journal 18(1):29–53.

Dallek, Robert

    1991   *Lone Star Rising: Lyndon Johnson and His Times, 1908–1964.* New York:
        Oxford University Press.

Danzinger, Edmund J., Jr.

    1984   "A New Beginning or the Last Hurrah: American Indian Response to

Reform Legislation of the 1970's." *American Indian Culture and Research Journal* 7(4):69–84.

Deer, Ada

1989   "Celebrating Philleo's Life." In *Applied Anthropologist and Public Servant. The Life and Work of Philleo Nash,* ed. Ruth H. Landsman and Katherine S. Halperin. *NAPA Bulletin* 7.

1994   "Ada Deer (Menominee) Explains How Her People Overturned Termination, 1974." In *Major Problems in American Indian History: Documents and Essays,* ed. Albert L. Hurtado and Peter Iverson. Lexington, Mass.: D. C. Heath.

Deloria, Vine, Jr.

1969   *Custer Died for Your Sins: An Indian Manifesto.* New York: Macmillan.

1971   "The Rise of Indian Activism." In Jennings C. Wise, *The Red Man in the New World Drama.* New York: Macmillan.

1974   *Behind the Trail of Broken Treaties: An Indian Declaration of Independence.* Austin: University of Texas Press.

1975   "The War Between the Redskins and the Feds." In *Solving the Indian Problem: The White Man's Burdensome Business,* ed. Murray Wax and Robert W. Buchanan. New York: New York Times Books.

Deloria, Vine Jr., and Clifford M. Lytle

1983   *American Indians, American Justice.* Austin: University of Texas Press.

1984   *The Nations Within: The Past and Future of American Indian Sovereignty.* New York: Pantheon Books.

Dial, Adolph, and David Eliades

1975   *The Only Land I Know: A History of the Lumbee Indians.* San Francisco: Indian Historian Press.

Divine, Robert A., et al.

1987   *The Johnson Years.* Vol 2. Lawrence: University Press of Kansas.

Dobyns, Henry F.

1965   "Therapeutic Experience of Responsible Democracy." In *The American Indian Today,* ed. Stuart Levine and Nancy Oestreich Lurie. Baltimore: Penguin.

1981   "Patterns of Indoamerican Chief Executive Tenure." *Human Organization* 40:78–80.

Dodge, Larry

1986   "Reason Interview: Russell Means." *Reason* 18(4):20–25.

Dollar, Clyde

1973   "The Second Tragedy at Wounded Knee: A 1970s Confrontation and Its Historical Roots." *American West* 10:4–61.

Drinnon, Richard

1987   *Keeper of Concentration Camps: Dillon S. Meyer and American Racism.* Berkeley: University of California Press.

Dugger, Ronnie

 1982 *The Politician: The Life and Times of Lyndon Johnson.* New York: Norton.

Eggan, Fred

 1989 "Philleo Nash: The Education of an Anthropologist." In *Applied Anthropologist and Public Servant: The Life and Work of Philleo Nash,* ed. Ruth H. Landsman and Katherine S. Halperin. *NAPA Bulletin 7.*

Ehrlichman, John

 1982 *Witness to Power: The Nixon Years.* New York: Simon and Schuster.

Ellis, Richard N.

 1979 "Robert L. Bennett (1966–1969)." In *The Commissioners of Indian Affairs, 1824–1977,* ed. Robert M. Kvasnicka and Herman J. Viola. Lincoln: University of Nebraska Press.

Erickson, Donald, Henrietta Schwartz, and Oswald Werner

 1969 *The Community School at Rough Rock.* OEO Contract B89–4534, Donald A. Erickson, Project Director. Washington, D.C.

Esber, George S., Jr.

 1992 "Shortcomings of the Indian Self-Determination Policy." In *State and Reservation: New Perspectives on Federal Indian Policy,* ed. George Castile and Robert Bee. Tucson: University of Arizona Press.

Evans, Rowland, and Robert Novack

 1966 *Lyndon B. Johnson: The Exercise of Power; A Political Biography.* New York: New American Library.

Fannin, Paul J.

 1968 "Indian Education: A Test Case for Democracy." *Arizona Law Review* 10:661–673.

Feraca, Stephen E.

 1990 *Why Don't They Give Them Guns? The Great American Indian Myth.* Lanham, Md.: University Press of America.

Ferrell, Robert H.

 1994 *Harry S. Truman: A Life.* Columbia: University of Missouri Press.

Fixico, Donald Lee

 1986 *Termination and Relocation: Federal Indian Policy, 1945–1960.* Albuquerque: University of New Mexico Press.

Forbes, Jack D.

 1981 *Native Americans and Nixon: Presidential Politics and Minority Self-Determination, 1969–1970.* Los Angeles: American Indian Studies Center, UCLA.

Ford, Gerald R.

 1979 *Time to Heal: The Autobiography of Gerald R. Ford.* New York: Harper.

Fowler, Loretta

 1982 *Arapahoe Politics, 1851–1978.* Lincoln: University of Nebraska Press.

 1987 *Shared Symbols, Contested Meanings: Gros Ventre Culture and History, 1778–1984.* Ithaca, N.Y.: Cornell University Press.

Fuchs, Estelle, and Robert Havighurst
  1972   *To Live on This Earth: American Indian Education.* Garden City, N.Y.:
          Doubleday.
Galambos, Louis
  1993   "Foreword." In *Reexamining the Eisenhower Presidency,* ed. Shirley Anne
          Warshaw. Westport, Conn.: Greenwood.
Gardner, Booth
  1989   *Puyallup Tribal Settlement, 1989.* Olympia: Office of the Governor, State
          of Washington.
Garment, Leonard
  1987   "Objectives and People." In *The Nixon Presidency: Twenty-Two Intimate
          Perspectives of Richard M. Nixon,* ed. Kenneth W. Thompson. Lanham,
          Md.: University Press of America.
  1997   *Crazy Rhythm: My Journey from Brooklyn, Jazz, and Wall Street to Nixon's
          White House, Watergate, and Beyond. . .* New York: Random House.
Geland, Mark
  1981   "The War on Poverty." In *Exploring the Johnson Years,* ed. Robert Di-
          vine. Austin: University of Texas Press.
Genovese, Michael A.
  1990   *The Nixon Presidency: Power and Politics in Turbulent Times.* Westport,
          Conn.: Greenwood.
Getches, David H., Charles Wilkinson, and Robert A. Williams Jr.
  1993   *Cases and Material on Federal Indian Law.* St. Paul: West.
Giglio, James N.
  1991   *The Presidency of John F. Kennedy.* Lawrence: University Press of Kan-
          sas.
Gitlin, Todd
  1980   *The Whole World Is Watching: Mass Media in the Making and Unmak-
          ing of the New Left.* Berkeley: University of California Press.
Goodwin, Richard N.
  1988   *Remembering America: A Voice from the Sixties.* Boston: Little, Brown.
Gordon-McCutchan, R. C.
  1995   *The Taos Indians and the Battle for Blue Lake.* Santa Fe: Red Crane Books.
Graham, Hugh Davis
  1987   "The Transformation of Federal Education Policy." In *The Johnson Years,*
          vol. 1, ed. Robert A. Devine. Lawrence: University Press of Kansas.
Green, D. E., and T. V. Tonnesen, eds.
  1991   *American Indians: Social Justice and Public Policy.* Madison: University
          of Wisconsin Press.
Greene, John Robert
  1992   *The Limits of Power: The Nixon and Ford Administrations.* Bloomington:
          Indiana University Press.

1995   *The Presidency of Gerald R. Ford.* Lawrence: University Press of Kansas.

Gross, Emma R.

1989   *Contemporary Federal Policy toward American Indians.* Westport, Conn.:
          Greenwood.

Haldeman, H. R.

1994   *The Haldeman Diaries: Inside the White House.* New York: Putnam.

Harrington, Michael

1964   *The Other America: Poverty in the United States.* Baltimore: Penguin.

Harris, LaDonna

1985   "The War on Poverty." In *Indian Self-Rule,* ed. Kenneth Philp. Salt Lake
          City: Howe Brothers.

Hartmann, Robert T.

1980   *Palace Politics: An Inside Account of the Ford Years.* New York: McGraw-
          Hill.

Hauptman, Lawrence L.

1981   *The Iroquois and the New Deal.* Syracuse, N.Y.: Syracuse University Press.

Haycox, Stephen

1994   "Felix S. Cohen and the Legacy of the Indian New Deal." *Yale University
          Library Gazette* 68(3–4):135–156.

Heath, Jim F.

1975   *Decade of Disillusionment: The Kennedy-Johnson Years.* Bloomington:
          University of Indiana Press.

Hecht, Robert A.

1991   *Oliver La Farge and the American Indian: A Biography.* Metuchen, N.J.:
          Scarecrow Press.

Heclo, Hugh

1986   "The Political Foundations of Antipoverty Policy." In *Fighting Poverty:
          What Works and What Doesn't,* ed. Sheldon H. Danzinger and Daniel
          H. Weinberg. Cambridge, Mass.: Harvard University Press.

Heller, Joseph

1961   *Catch-22: A Novel.* New York: Simon and Schuster.

Henggeler, Paul R.

1991   *In His Steps: Lyndon Johnson and the Kennedy Mystique.* Chicago: Dee.

Hertzberg, Hazel

1971   *The Search for an American Indian Identity: Modern Pan-Indian Move-
          ments.* Syracuse, N.Y.: Syracuse University Press.

1988   "Indian Rights Movement, 1887–1973." In *Handbook of North American
          Indians,* vol. 4: *History of Indian-White Relations.* Washington, D.C.:
          Smithsonian Institution.

Hickel, Walter J.

1971   *Who Owns America?* Engelwood Cliffs, N. J.:Prentice-Hall.

Hickey, Neil

1973   "Was the Truth Buried at Wounded Knee? Cameras Over Here! And be
          Sure to Shoot My Good Side." *TV Guide,* December 18, 1973, 43–49.

Hoff, Joan
    1994   *Nixon Reconsidered.* New York: Basic Books.

Hoikkala, Paivi H.
    1995   "Mothers and Community Builders: Salt River Pima and Maricopa Women in Community Action." In *Negotiators of Change: Historical Perspectives on Native American Women,* ed. Nancy Shoemaker. New York: Routledge.

Holm, Tom
    1985   "The Crisis in Tribal Government." In *American Indian Policy in the Twentieth Century,* ed. Vine Deloria. Norman: University of Oklahoma Press.

Hoxie, Frederick E.
    1989   *A Final Promise: The Campaign to Assimilate the Indians, 1880–1920.* Cambridge: Cambridge University Press.
    1992   "Crow Leadership amidst Reservation Oppression." In *State and Reservation: New Perspectives on Federal Indian Policy,* ed. George Castile and Robert Bee. Tucson: University of Arizona Press.
    1995   *Parading through History: The Making of the Crow Nation in America.* New York: Cambridge University Press.

Huffaker, Clair
    1967   *Nobody Loves a Drunken Indian.* New York: Paperback Library.

Indian Voice
    1976   "Puyallup Confront State, Feds." *Indian Voice* 7(11):1, 6.

Iverson, Peter
    1981   *The Navaho Nation.* Albuquerque: University of New Mexico Press.
    1982   *Carlos Moctezuma and the Changing World of Indians.* Albuquerque: University of New Mexico Press.
    1994   *When Indians Became Cowboys: Native Peoples and Cattle Ranching in the American West.* Norman: University of Oklahoma Press.

Jaimes, M. Annette
    1990   "The Hollow Icon: An American Indian Analysis of the Kennedy Myth and Federal Indian Policy." *Wicazo Sa Review* 6(1):34–44.

Jaimes, M. Annette, ed.
    1992   *The State of Native America: Genocide, Colonization and Resistance.* Boston: South End.

Johansen, Bruce E.
    1996   "Debating the Origins of Democracy: Overview of an Annotated Bibliography." *American Indian Culture and Research Journal* 20(2):155–172.

Johnson, Dorothy R.
    1992   *Singing an Indian Song: A Biography of D'Arcy McNickle.* Lincoln: University of Nebraska Press.

Johnson, Lyndon Baines
    1971   *The Vantage Point: Perspectives of the Presidency, 1963–1969.* New York: Holt.

Johnson, Troy R.

1996   *The Occupation of Alcatraz Island: Indian Self-Determination and the Rise of Indian Activism.* Urbana: University of Illinois Press.

Jorgensen, Joseph G.

1986   "Federal Policies, American Indian Polities and the 'New Federalism.'" *American Indian Culture and Research Journal* 10(2):1–13.

Josephy, Alvin M., Jr.

1971   "The American Indian and the Bureau of Indian Affairs: A Study with Recommendations, February 11, 1969." In *Red Power: The American Indians Fight for Freedom,* ed. Alvin Josephy. New York: McGraw Hill.

1984   *Now That the Buffalo's Gone: A Study of Today's Indians.* Norman: University of Oklahoma Press.

Keeler, William W., et al.

1961   "Report to the Secretary of the Interior by the Task Force on Indian Affairs, July 10, 1961." Washington, D.C.: Department of the Interior.

1962   "Report to the Secretary of the Interior by the Task Force on Alaska Native Affairs, December 28, 1962." Washington, D.C.: Department of the Interior.

Kehoe, Alice B.

1990   "Primal Gaia: Primitivists and Plastic Medicine Men." In *The Invented Indian,* ed. James A. Clifton. New Brunswick, N.J.: Transaction.

Kelly, Lawrence C.

1975   "The Indian Reorganization Act: The Dream and the Reality." *Pacific Historical Review* 44(3):291–312.

1983   *The Assault on Assimilation: John Collier and the Origins of Indian Policy Reform.* Albuquerque: University of New Mexico Press.

Kelly, William

1954   "Foreword." In *Indian Affairs and the Indian Reorganization Act: The Twenty Year Record,* ed. William Kelly. Tucson: University of Arizona Press.

Kennedy, John F.

1961   "Introduction." In *The American Heritage Book of Indians,* ed. Alvin M. Josephy Jr. New York: William Brandon.

Kennedy, Robert

1962   "Buying It Back from the Indians." *Life,* March 23, 1962, 17–18.

Kessel, John H.

1975   *The Domestic Presidency: Decision Making in the White House.* North Scituate, Mass.: Duxbury Press.

Kleindienst, Richard G.

1985   *Justice: The Memoirs of Attorney General Richard Kleindienst.* Ottawa, Ill.: Jameson Books.

Knack, Martha C., and Omer Stewart

1984   *As Long as the River Shall Run: An Ethnohistory of Pyramid Lake Indian Reservation.* Berkeley: University of California Press.

Knock, Thomas J.

1992   *To End All Wars: Woodrow Wilson and the Quest for a New World Order.*
New York: Oxford University Press.

Koppes, Clayton R.

1977   "From New Deal to Termination: Liberalism and Indian Policy, 1933–
1953." *Pacific Historical Review* 46(4):543–566.

Kravitz, Sanford

1969   "The Community Action Program—Past, Present and Its Future?" In
On Fighting Poverty, ed. James L. Sundquist. New York: Basic Books.

LaCourse, Richard

1973   "Indians and the Media: A Panel Discussion." *Civil Rights Digest* 6(1):41–
45.

Landsman, Gail

1987   "Indian Activism and the Press: Coverage of the Conflict at Ganienkeh."
Anthropological Quarterly 60:101–113.

Landsman, Ruth H., and Katherine Spencer Halperin, eds.

1989   *Applied Anthropologist and Public Servant: The Life and Work of Philleo
Nash. NAPA Bulletin 7.*

Lawson, Steven F.

1987   "Civil Rights." In *The Johnson Years,* vol. 1, ed. Robert A. Divine.
Lawrence: University Press of Kansas.

Lazarus, Arthur, and W. Richard West

1976   "The Alaska Native Claims Settlement Act: A Flawed Victory." *Law and
Contemporary Problems* 40(1):132–165.

Lazarus, Edward

1991   *Black Hills White Justice.* New York: Harper.

Lemann, Nicholas

1989   "Lesson from the Poverty Front: OEO Didn't Solve Our Urban Problems, But It Did Some Things Right. Things We Should Be Doing Now."
Washington Monthly 21(11):33–35.

Levine, Robert A.

1970   *The Poor Ye Need Not Have With You: Lessons from the War on Poverty.*
Cambridge: MIT Press.

Levitan, Sar A., and Barbara Hetrick

1971   *Big Brother's Indian Programs—With Reservations.* New York: McGraw-
Hill.

Levitan, Sar A., and William B. Johnston

1975   *Indian Giving: Federal Programs for Native Americans.* Baltimore: Johns
Hopkins University Press.

Luomala, Katharine

1978   "Tipai-Ipai." In *Handbook of North American Indians,* vol. 8: *California,*
ed. Robert P. Heizer. Washington, D.C.: Smithsonian Institution.

Lurie, Nancy O.

    1972   "Menominee Termination from Reservation to Colony." *Human Organization* 31 (Fall): 267–269.

Lyman, Stanley D.

    1991   *Wounded Knee 1973: A Personal Account.* Lincoln: University of Nebraska Press.

Mankiller, Wilma, and Michael Wallis.

    1993   *Mankiller: A Chief and Her People.* New York: St. Martins.

Mardock, Robert W.

    1971   *The Reformers and the American Indian.* Columbia: University of Missouri Press.

    1988   "Indian Rights Movement until 1887." In *Handbook of North American Indians,* vol. 4: *History of Indian-White Relations,* ed. Wilcomb E. Washburn. Washington, D.C.: Smithsonian Institution.

Matthiessen, Peter

    1983   *In the Spirit of Crazy Horse.* New York: Viking Press.

Matusow, Allen J.

    1984   *The Unraveling of America: A History of Liberalism in the 1960's.* New York: Harper and Row.

McCarty, T. L.

    1987   "The Rough Rock Demonstration School: A Case History with Implications for Educational Evaluation." *Human Organization* 46(2):103–112.

    1989   "School as Community: The Rough Rock Demonstration." *Harvard Educational Review* 59(4):484–503.

McClellan, E. Fletcher

    1990   "Implementation and Policy Reformulation of Title I of the Indian Self-Determination and Education Assistance Act of 1975–80." *Wicazo Sa Review* 6(1):45–55.

McCool, Daniel

    1994   *Command of the Waters: Iron Triangles, Federal Water Development and Indian Water.* Tucson: University of Arizona Press.

McDonnell, Janet

    1991   *The Dispossession of the American Indian, 1887–1934.* Bloomington: Indiana University Press.

McKee, Jesse O.

    1987   "The Choctaw: Self-Determination and Socioeconomic Development." In *A Cultural Geography of North American Indians,* ed. Thomas E. Ross and Tyrel G. Moore. Boulder, Colo: Westview.

McNickle, D'Arcy

    1973   *Native American Tribalism: Indian Survivals and Renewals.* New York: Oxford University Press.

    1980   "The Indian New Deal as Mirror of the Future." In *Political Organiza-*

tion of Native North Americans, ed. Ernest Schusky. Washington, D.C.: University Press of America.

Means, Russell, with Marvin J. Wolf
  1995   *Where White Men Fear to Tread: The Autobiography of Russell Means.* New York: St. Martins.

Mencken, H. L.
  1991   "Hymn to the Truth." In *The Impossible H. L. Mencken,* ed. Marion E. Rodgers. New York: Doubleday.

Morris, C. Patrick
  1992   "Termination by Accountants: The Reagan Indian Policy." In *Native Americans and Public Policy,* ed. Fremount J. Lyden and Lyman H. Letgers. Pittsburgh: University of Pittsburgh Press.

Morris, Roger
  1990   *Richard Milhous Nixon: The Rise of An American Politician.* New York: Holt.

Moynihan, Daniel P.
  1969   *Maximum Feasible Misunderstanding.* New York: Free Press.

Murray, Charles
  1984   *Losing Ground: American Social Policy, 1950–1980.* New York: Basic Books.

Nabokov, Peter
  1991   "Hopis and the Love Generation." In *Native American Testimony: A Chronicle of Indian-White Relations; From Prophecy to the Present, 1492–1992,* ed. Peter Nabokov. New York: Viking.

Nagel, Joanne
  1996   *American Indian Ethnic Renewal: Red Power and the Resurgence of Identity and Culture.* New York: Oxford University Press.

Nagel, Joanne, and Troy Johnson, eds.
  1994   "Special Edition: Alcatraz Revisited; The 25th Anniversary of the Occupation, 1969–71." *American Indian Culture and Research Journal* 18(4)1994.

Nash, Philleo
  1986   "Science, Politics and Human Values." *Human Organization* 45(3):189–201.
  1988   "Twentieth Century United States Government Agencies." In *Handbook of North American Indians,* vol. 4: *History of Indian-White Relations,* ed. Wilcomb Washburn. Washington, D.C.: Smithsonian Institution.

Nathan, Richard
  1975   *The Plot That Failed: Nixon and the Administrative Presidency.* New York: Wiley.
  1996   "NARF Celebrates its 25th Anniversary." *NARF Legal Review* 21(1):1–8.

National Congress of American Indians (NCAI)
  1966a   Editorial. *NCAI Sentinel* 11(1):1.

1966b   "Nash as Commissioner . . . Five Years of Progress and Understanding."
         NCAI Sentinel 11(1):12–13.

1966c   "Editorial." *NCAI Sentinel* 11(3):1.

1967   "The Ominous Interior Policy." *NCAI Sentinel* 12(2):8–9.

1968   "Where Were You When We Needed You?" *NCAI Sentinel* 13(2):9–10.

Native American Rights Fund (NARF)

1990   "Repatriation Act Protects Native Burial Remains and Artifacts." *NARF
         Legal Review* 16(1):1–4.

Nickerson, Steve

1976   "The Structure of the Bureau of Indian Affairs." *Law and Contempo-
         rary Problems* 40(1):61–76.

Nixon, Richard Milhous

1962   *Six Crises.* Garden City, N.Y.: Doubleday.

1969   "Statement of Richard Nixon, September 27, 1968." *Indian Record,* Janu-
         ary, 1–2.

1970   "President Nixon Presents a New Indian Doctrine, July 8, 1970." *Indian
         Record,* August, 1–11.

1978   *RN: The Memoirs of Richard Nixon.* New York: Grosset and Dunlap.

1990   *In the Arena: A Memoir of Victory, Defeat and Renewal.* New York: Simon
         and Schuster.

Novack, Steven J.

1990   "The Real Takeover of the BIA: The Preferential Hiring of Indians." *Jour-
         nal of Economic History* 50(3):639–654.

Officer, James

1956   *Indians in School: A Study of the Development of Educational Facilities
         for Arizona Indians.* American Indian Series Number One, Bureau of
         Ethnic Research. Tucson: University of Arizona Press.

1968   "National Congress of American Indians Convention Address." *NCAI
         Sentinel* 13(3):16–20.

1978   "The Bureau of Indian Affairs since 1945: An Assessment." *Annals of the
         American Academy of Political and Social Science* 436 (March): 61–72.

1984   "The Indian Service and Its Evolution." In *The Aggressions of Civiliza-
         tion: Federal Indian Policy since the 1880's,* ed. Vine Deloria and Sandra
         L. Cadwalader. Philadelphia: Temple University Press.

1986   "Termination as Federal Policy: An Overview." In *Indian Self-Rule,* ed.
         Kenneth R. Philp. Salt Lake City: Howe Brothers.

1988   "Philleo Nash, 1909–1987." *American Anthropologist* 90(4):952–956.

1989   "Philleo Nash: Anthropologist as Administrator." In *Applied Anthro-
         pologist and Public Servant: The Life and Work of Philleo Nash,* ed. Ruth
         H. Landsman and Katherine Spencer Halperin. *NAPA Bulletin* 7.

Ognibene, Peter J.

1975   *Scoop: The Life and Politics of Henry M. Jackson.* New York: Stein and
         Day.

O'Neill, Tip, with Gary Hymel

    1994   *All Politics Is Local and Other Rules of the Game.* New York: Random House.

Ortiz, Alfonso

    1986a   "The War on Poverty." In *Indian Self-Rule,* ed. Kenneth Philp. Salt Lake City: Howe Brothers.

    1986b   "Half a Century of Indian Administration: An Overview." In *American Indian Policy and Cultural Values: Conflict and Accommodation,* ed. Jennie R. Joe. Los Angeles: American Indian Studies Center, UCLA.

Ortiz, Roxanne Dunbar

    1981   "Foreword." In Jack Forbes, *Native Americans and Nixon.* Los Angeles: University of California Press.

    1984   *Indians of the Americas: Human Rights and Self-Determination.* New York: Praeger.

Ourada, Patricia K.

    1979   *The Menominee Indians: A History.* Norman: University of Oklahoma Press.

Parman, Donald L.

    1976   *The Navahos and the New Deal.* New Haven: Yale University Press.

Parmee, Edward A.

    1968   *Formal Education and Culture Change: A Modern Apache Indian Community and Government Education Programs.* Tucson: University of Arizona Press.

Patterson, Bradley H., Jr.

    1973   "The Federal Executive Branch and the First Americans: A Trustee's Report." *Civil Rights Digest* 6(1):51–54.

    1983   "Statement by Bradley J. Patterson." In Theodore W. Taylor, *American Indian Policy.* Mt. Airy, Md.: Lomond.

    1988   *The Ring of Power: The White House Staff and Its Expanding Role in Government.* New York: Basic Books

Patterson, James T.

    1994   *America's Struggle Against Poverty, 1900–1994.* Cambridge, Mass.: Harvard University Press.

Peregoy, Robert M., Walter R. Echo-Hawk, and James Bitsford

    1995   "Congress Overturns Supreme Court's Peyote Ruling." *NARF Legal Review* 2(1):1–25.

Peroff, Nicholas

    1982   *Menominee Drums: Tribal Termination and Restoration, 1954–1974.* Norman: Oklahoma University Press.

Perry, Richard J.

    1996   *From Time Immemorial: Indigenous Peoples and State Systems.* Austin: University of Texas Press.

Peterson, John H., Jr.

1992   "Choctaw Self-Determination in the 1980's." In *Indians of the South-eastern United States in the Late 20th Century,* ed. J. Anthony Paredes. Tuscaloosa: University of Alabama Press.

Pevar, Stephen L.

1992   *The Rights of Indians and Tribes: The Basic ACLU Guide to Indian and Tribal Rights.* Carbondale: Southern Illinois University Press.

Peyer, Bernd C.

1987   "Who is Afraid of AIM." In *Indians and Europe: An Interdisciplinary Collection of Essays,* ed. Christian Feest. Aachen: Rader Verlag.

Philp, Kenneth R.

1977   *John Collier's Crusade for Indian Reform, 1920–1954.* Tucson: University of Arizona Press.

1983   "Termination: A Legacy of the Indian New Deal." *Western Historical Quarterly* 14(2):168–180.

1986   *Indian Self-Rule: First-Hand Accounts of Indian-White Relations from Roosevelt to Reagan.* Salt Lake City: Howe Brothers.

1988   "Dillon S. Meyer and the Advent of Termination, 1950–1953." *Western Historical Quarterly* 19(1):37–59.

Piven, Frances Fox, and Richard A. Cloward

1971   *Regulating the Poor: The Functions of Public Welfare.* New York: Random House.

Porter, Frank W., III

1992   "Without Reservation: Federal Indian Policy and the Landless Tribes of Washington." In *State and Reservation: New Perspectives on Federal Indian Policy,* ed. George Castile and Robert Bee. Tucson: University of Arizona Press.

Prochnau, William A., and Richard W. Larsen

1972   *A Certain Democrat: Senator Henry M. Jackson, A Political Biography.* Englewood Cliffs, N. J.: Prentice-Hall.

Prucha, Francis P.

1962   *American Indian Policy in the Formative Years: The Indian Trade and Intercourse Acts, 1790–1834.* Cambridge, Mass.: Harvard University Press.

1976   *American Indian Policy in Crisis: Christian Reformers and the American Indian, 1865–1900.* Norman: University of Oklahoma Press.

1977   *A Bibliographical Guide to the History of Indian-White Relations in the United States.* Chicago: University of Chicago Press.

1982   *Indian-White Relations in the United States: A Bibliography of Works Published, 1975–1980.* Lincoln: University of Nebraska Press.

1984   *The Great Father: The United States Government and the American Indians.* 2 vols. Lincoln: University of Nebraska Press.

1990   *Documents of United States Indian Policy.* Lincoln: University of Nebraska Press.

1994   *American Indian Treaties: The History of a Political Anomaly.* Berkeley: University of California Press.

Redford, Emmette S.
1986   *White House Operations: The Johnson Presidency.* Austin: University of Texas Press.

Reichley, A. James
1981   *Conservatives in an Age of Change: The Nixon and Ford Administrations.* Washington, D.C.: Brookings Institution.

Robbins, Rebecca L.
1990   "The Forgotten American: A Foundation for Contemporary American Indian Self-Determination." *Wicazo Sa Review* 6(1):27–33.

Roell, Craig H., et al.
1988   *Lyndon B. Johnson, A Bibliography.* 2 vols. Austin: University of Texas Press.

Roessel, Robert A.
1960   *Handbook for Indian Education.* Los Angeles: American Indian Publishing Co.
1977   *Navaho Education in Action: The Rough Rock Demonstration School.* Chinle, Ariz.: Navaho Curriculum Center.
1979   *Navaho Education, 1948–1978: Its Progress and Problems.* Rough Rock, Ariz.: Navaho Curriculum Center.

Roos, Philp D., et al.
1980   "The Impact of the American Indian Movement on the Pine Ridge Indian Reservation." *Phylon* 41(1):89–99.

Safire, William
1975   *Before the Fall: An Inside View of the Pre-Watergate White House.* Garden City, N.Y.: Doubleday.

Salinger, Pierre
1966   *With Kennedy.* Garden City, N.Y.: Doubleday.

Satz, Ronald N.
1975   *American Indian Policy in the Jacksonian Era.* Lincoln: University of Nebraska Press.

Schlesinger, Arthur M., Jr.
1965   *A Thousand Days.* Boston: Houghton Mifflin.
1975   *The Imperial Presidency.* Boston: Houghton Mifflin.
1978   *Robert Kennedy and His Times.* Boston: Houghton Mifflin.

Schulte, Steven C.
1984   "Removing the Yoke of Government: E. Y. Berry and the Origins of Indian Termination Policy." *South Dakota History* 14(1):48–67.

Schultz, Terri
1973   "Bamboozle Me Not at Wounded Knee." *Harpers,* June, 46–48, 53–56.

Senese, Guy B.
1991   *Self-Determination and the Social Education of Native Americans.* New York: Praeger.

Sider, Gerald M.

    1993   *Lumbee Indian Histories: Race, Ethnicity and Indian Identity in the Southern United States*. New York: Cambridge University Press.

Smith, Desmond

    1973   "Wounded Knee: The Media Coup d'Etat." *Nation* 216:806–809.

Smith, Michael T.

    1979   "Morris Thompson, 1973–76." In *The Commissioners of Indian Affairs, 1825–1977*, ed. Robert Kvasnicka and Herman Viola. Lincoln: University of Nebraska Press.

Smith, Paul Chaat, and Robert Allen Warrior

    1996   *Like a Hurricane: The Indian Movement from Alcatraz to Wounded Knee*. New York: New Press.

Sorenson, Theodore C.

    1965   *Kennedy*. New York: Harper and Row.

Sorkin, Alan L.

    1971   *American Indians and Federal Aid*. Washington, D.C.: Brookings Institution.

Spicer, Edward H.

    1970   "Patrons of the Poor." *Human Organization* 29(1):12–19.

    1980   *The Yaquis: A Cultural History*. Tucson: University of Arizona Press.

Spindler, George, and Louise Spindler

    1971   *Dreamers without Power*. New York: Holt.

    1984   *Dreamers with Power: The Menominee Indians*. Prospect Heights, Ill.: Waveland Press.

Starita, Joe

    1995   *The Dull Knives of Pine Ridge: A Lakota Odyssey*. New York: Putnam.

Steiner, Stan

    1968   *The New Indians*. New York: Delta Books.

Stern, Kenneth S.

    1994   *Loud Hawk: The United States vs the American Indian Movement*. Norman: University of Oklahoma Press.

Stern, Mark

    1992   *Calculating Visions: Kennedy, Johnson and Civil Rights*. New Brunswick, N.J.: Rutgers University Press.

Strickland, Bernard, and Jack Gregory

    1970   "Nixon and the Indian: Is Dick another Buffalo Bill?" *Commonweal* September 4, 1970, 432–436.

Stuart, Paul H.

    1990   "Financing Self-Determination: Federal Indian Expenditures, 1975–1988." *American Indian Culture and Research Journal* 14(2):1–18.

Stull, Donald D.

    1990   "Reservation Economic Development in the Era of Self-Determination." *American Anthropologist* 92(1):206–210.

Stull, Donald D., Jerry A. Schultz, and Ken Cadue Sr.
    1986   "Rights Without Resources: The Rise and Fall of the Kansas Kickapoo."
            American Indian Culture and Research Journal 10(2):41–59.
Sundquist, James L., ed.
    1969   *On Fighting Poverty: Perspectives from Experience.* New York: Basic
            Books.
Szasz, Margaret C.
    1977   *Education and the American Indian: The Road to Self-Determination
            since 1928.* Albuquerque: University of New Mexico Press. Reprint of
            1974 edition.
    1979   "Philleo Nash, 1961–66." In *The Commissioners of Indian Affairs, 1824–
            1977,* ed. Robert M. Kvasnicka and Herman J. Viola. Lincoln: University
            of Nebraska Press.
Taylor, Graham D.
    1980   *The New Deal and American Indian Tribalism: The Administration of
            the Indian Reorganization Act, 1934–45.* Lincoln: University of Nebraska
            Press.
Taylor, Theodore W.
    1983   *American Indian Policy.* Mt. Airy, Md.: Lomond.
Thomas, Norman C., and Harold Wolman
    1969   "Policy Formulation in the Institutionalized Presidency: The Johnson
            Task Forces." In *The Presidential Advisory System,* ed. Thomas E. Cronin
            and Sanford D. Greenberg. New York: Harper.
Thompson, Hunter S.
    1979   *The Great Shark Hunt: Strange Tales from a Strange Time.* Gonzo Pa-
            pers, Vol. I. New York: Summit Books.
Time
    1973   "Trap at Wounded Knee." March 26, 67.
Tooker, Elizabeth
    1990   "The United States Constitution and the Iroquois League." In *The In-
            vented Indian: Cultural Fictions and Government Policies,* ed. James A.
            Clifton. New Brunswick, N.J.: Transaction.
Trennert, Robert A.
    1975   *Alternative to Extinction: Federal Indian Policy and the Beginnings of the
            Reservation System, 1846–51.* Philadelphia: Temple University Press.
Turner, Michael
    1982   *The Vice President as Policy Maker: Rockefeller in the Ford White House.*
            Westport, Conn.: Greenwood.
Tyler, S. Lyman
    1973   *A History of Indian Policy.* Washington, D.C.: U. S. Department of the
            Interior, Bureau of Indian Affairs.
Udall, Stewart
    1963   *The Quiet Crisis.* New York: Holt.

1968   "The State of the Indian Nation." *Arizona Law Review* 10 (Winter 1968): 554–557.

University of Utah, University of South Dakota, and Arizona State University

1966   *Indian Reservation Community Action and the Role of the Three University Consortium in Providing Technical Assistance and Training.* Report to oeo, Salt Lake City.

Utley, Robert M.

1984   *The Indian Frontier of the American West, 1846–1890.* Albuquerque: University of New Mexico Press.

Vizenor, Gerald

1983   "Dennis of Wounded Knee," *American Indian Quarterly* 7(2):51–65.

Walker, Deward E., Jr.

1967   "An Examination of American Indian Reaction to Proposals of the Commissioner of Indian Affairs for General Legislation, 1967." *Northwest Anthropological Research Notes* 1(1), Memoir #1.

Washburn, Wilcomb E.

1975   *The Assault on Tribalism: The General Allotment Law (Dawes Act) of 1887.* Philadelphia: Lippincott.

1984   "A Fifty-Year Perspective on the Indian Reorganization Act." *American Anthropology* 86(2):279–289.

Washburn, Wilcomb E., ed.

1973   *The American Indian and the United States: A Documentary History.* 4 vols. New York: Random House.

1988   *Handbook of North American Indians.* Vol 4: *History of Indian-White Relations.* Washington, D.C.: Smithsonian Institution.

Watkins, Arthur V.

1957   "Termination of Federal Supervision: The Removal of Restrictions over Indian Property and Person." *Annals of the American Academy of Political and Social Science* 311 (May): 47–55.

Wax, Murray

1970   "Gophers or Gadflies: Indian School Boards." *School Review* November, 62–71.

1973   "Indian Protest: Romance and Reality," *New Society* 19:135–137.

Wax, Murray, Rosalie H. Wax, and Robert V. Dumont

1968   "Formal Education in an American Indian Community." *Social Problems Supplement* 11(4).

Weibel-Orlando, Joan

1991   *Indian Country, L. A.: Maintaining Ethnic Community in Complex Society.* Urbana: University of Illinois Press.

Weisbrot, Robert

1990   *Freedom Bound: A History of the American Civil Rights Movement.* New York: Norton.

Weyler, Rex

1982   *Blood of the Land: The Government and Corporate War against the American Indian Movement.* New York: Random House.

White, Richard

1991   *"It's Your Misfortune and None of My Own": A New History of the American West.* Norman: University of Oklahoma Press.

Wicker, Tom

1995   *One of Us: Richard Nixon and the American Dream.* New York: Random House.

Wilkinson, Charles F.

1987   *American Indians, Time and the Law.* New Haven: Yale University Press.

Willard, William

1990   "The Comparative Political History of Two Tribal Governments." *Wicazo Sa Review* 6(1):56–62.

1994   "Self-Government for Native Americans: The Case of the Pascua Yaqui Tribe." In *American Indian Policy: Self-Governance and Economic Development,* ed. Lyman H. Legters and Fremont J. Lyden. Westport, Conn.: Greenwood.

Wilson, James J.

1969   "The Role of Indian Tribes in Economic Development and the Efforts of the Indian Division of the Community Action Program." In "Toward Economic Development for Native American Communities," 2. Papers submitted to Joint Economic Committee, U.S. Congress, Ninety-first Congress, First session. Washington, D.C.: Government Printing Office.

Wilson, Richard

1976   "Real Indian Leaders Condemn AIM." In *Contemporary Native American Address,* ed. John R. Maestas. Provo: Brigham Young University Press.

Wofford, Harris

1993   *Of Kennedys and Kings.* Pittsburgh: University of Pittsburgh Press.

Wolfe, Tom

1970   *Radical Chic and Mau-Mauing the Flak Catchers.* New York: Farrar, Straus.

Wood, Harlington, Jr.

1995   "Footnote to History: A Personal Account of a Segment of Wounded Knee Told for Lauren and Alex." *University of Illinois Law Review* 5(1):30–92.

Wood, Robert C.

1993   *Whatever Possessed the President? Academic Experts and Presidential Policy.* Amherst: University of Massachusetts Press.

Wunder, John R.

1994   *Retained by the People: A History of American Indians and the Bill of Rights.* New York: Oxford University Press.

Index

About the Author

George Pierre Castile received his Ph.D. in anthropology from the University of Arizona. He is a professor and chair of the Department of Anthropology at Whitman College. He has pursued an interest in federal Indian policy since the 1960s, when he first worked with Indian programs at the Office of Economic Opportunity. He is the author of numerous books and articles on Native American affairs, including the collection he edited with Robert Bee, *State and Reservation: New Perspectives on Federal Indian Policy* (University of Arizona Press, 1992).